*The New Testament
Interpretation of Scripture*

The New Testament
Interpretation of Scripture

ANTHONY TYRRELL HANSON

WIPF & STOCK · Eugene, Oregon

Wipf and Stock Publishers
199 W 8th Ave, Suite 3
Eugene, OR 97401

The New Testament Interpretation of Scripture
By Hanson, Anthony Tyrrell
Copyright©1980 SPCK
ISBN 13: 978-1-61097-351-9
Publication date 3/14/2011
Previously published by SPCK, 1980

*To Birger Gerhardsson
Professor of New Testament
at the University of Lund, Sweden
an old friend
and a source of scholarly
inspiration*

Contents

Acknowledgements		viii
Foreword		ix
Abbreviations		xi
1	The Significance of the Subject	1
2	A Quasi-Gnostic Pauline Midrash: 1 Corinthians 2.6–16	21
3	John 1.14–18 and Exodus 34	97
4	The Theme of Christ as the True Temple in the Fourth Gospel	110
5	The Scriptural Background to the Doctrine of the *Descensus ad Inferos* in the New Testament	122
6	John's Technique in Using Scripture	157
Notes		177
Bibliography		212
Index of Names		225
Index of Biblical References		229
Index of References to Non-Canonical Jewish and Christian Books		235

Acknowledgements

Translation by J. H. Charlesworth, *The Odes of Solomon*, © Oxford University Press 1973, by permission of Oxford University Press.

Professor R. McL. Wilson, *New Testament Studies*, Volume 23, pages 90-101, by permission of Cambridge University Press to reproduce as Chapter 3.

Foreword

I wish to acknowledge my indebtedness to Professor R. McL. Wilson of St Andrews University for a valuable criticism of an earlier draft of this work, and to Dr M. Knibb of King's College, London, for help in identifying an apocalyptic writing mentioned in note 71 at the end of Chapter 2. In Chapter 2 I have begun a new numeration of the footnotes at the beginning of each of the five sections, because I have a dislike of footnotes that run into three digits.

In transliterating Greek words I have followed the scheme advocated by H. Leclerque in his article 'A Note on the Transliteration of New Testament Greek', in *New Testament Studies* (January 1973), 187-9. In transliterating Hebrew words I have followed the system adopted by Professor J. Weingreen in his book *A Practical Grammar for Classical Hebrew*, 2nd edn, Oxford 1959.

I wish to express my gratitude to my colleague, Dr. E. J. Bickersteth, for her ready help with reading the proofs, given at short notice. I must also acknowledge the considerable labour and meticulous care which my wife expended on the task of compiling the indexes.

Abbreviations

BT	Babylonian Talmud, ed. I. Epstein, London 1938
ET	*Expository Times*
EVV	English Versions
HTR	*Harvard Theological Review*
JBL	*Journal of Biblical Literature*
JTS	*Journal of Theological Studies*
LXX	Septuagint
MT	Masoretic Text
NT	New Testament
NTS	*New Testament Studies*
Nov. Test.	*Novum Testamentum*
OT	Old Testament
Q	Qumran
1 QH	Thanksgiving Hymns from Qumran Cave 1
1 QS	Manual of Discipline from Qumran Cave 1
RB	*Révue Biblique*
RHPR	*Révue d'Histoire et de Philosophie Religieuses*
RSR	*Recherches de Science Religieuse*
RSV	Revised Standard Version
S-B	H. L. Strack and P. Billerbeck, *Kommentar zum Neuen Testament aus Talmud und Midrasch*, 2nd edn, Munich 1961
TWNT	*Theologisches Wörterbuch zum Neuen Testament*
ZNTW	*Zeitschrift für die Neutestamentliche Wissenschaft*

1

The Significance of the Subject

1

Since the New Testament is thickly studded with quotations from the Scriptures, scholars have always been interested in the subject of New Testament interpretation of Scripture, and valuable works have been written on this topic during the last hundred years.[1] However, it might be said that only during the last thirty years or so has the investigation of the New Testament use of Scripture emerged as a special subject of study. A milestone in the progress of the subject was the discovery in 1956 of the Neofiti manuscript containing the complete text of the Palestinian Targum on the Pentateuch. The appearance of the Qumran documents has also been of great importance in this area of study, since they reveal something like a new tradition of Scripture interpretation, or at least the elaboration of one which had hitherto been not fully understood.

One might distinguish in the course of the last century and a half three stages which appreciation of New Testament exegesis of Scripture has undergone as far as scholars and theologians are concerned. The first stage might be called the traditional; by and large scholars felt themselves bound to attempt to interpret Scripture as the NT writers interpreted it. If Paul said (or appeared to say) that something in Israel's history was a type of Christ, type it must be. If Matthew declared that Hosea 11.1 was a prophecy of the return of the holy family from Egypt, this must be accepted as the true meaning of Hosea's utterance. This attitude persisted longer among Roman Catholic scholars than among Protestants.[2] The second stage, corresponding roughly to the era of predominance of the liberal theology, witnessed a marked desire on the part of commentators to ignore, avoid, or explain away the NT interpretation of Scripture. Scholars and theologians had not abandoned the hope that NT writers could to some degree be represented as conforming, or at least conformable, to modern standards of biblical exposition. The more startling scriptural proofs were represented not as being proofs but illustrations; the word 'accommodation' was used to condone apparently bizarre interpretations of Scripture. It was even suggested that NT writers had a 'charismatic' approach to Scripture, a word which enabled the modern theologian to suggest at one and the same time that NT interpretation was to be sharply distinguished from rabbinic interpretation and that it need not be taken very seriously.[3]

The third stage is that at which I believe most of the scholars engaged in this study today have arrived. This is the stage at which we attempt first and foremost to discover what was the NT interpretation of Scripture, without necessarily trying to conform it to our aim (or vice versa) or passing moral judgements upon it. This does not mean that the question of the relation of NT interpretation of Scripture to our method of interpreting Scripture today can be ignored or treated as irrelevant to theology. On the contrary, it must be faced, and indeed we revert to it before the end of this essay. But the two questions must be kept distinct. In the past much confusion has been caused by mixing up the two questions: 'How does this NT writer interpret Scripture?' and 'Is his interpretation correct?'. Admittedly the second question can at times seem particularly urgent. When, for instance, we find the author of Hebrews quoting Psalm 102.25f, 'Of old thou didst lay the foundation of the earth', as an address by the Father to the Son, our first instinct is to protest: this cannot be the right interpretation, we say; it is perfectly obvious that these verses are addressed by the psalmist as a devout worshipper to God. To represent them as an address by the Father to the Son is to misinterpret them. This may well be true from our modern point of view. But if we want to understand the rationale of the author of Hebrews' interpretation of Scripture, we must accept that he did see Psalm 102 as an address by the Father to the Son. Perhaps when we have fully digested the implications of this we can find some common ground between him and us in this area of biblical exegesis. I shall be suggesting later on that it is rash to speak of a 'correct' or 'incorrect' interpretation of Scripture without reference to the purpose for which Scripture is being used.

The Significance of the Subject

As far as the theologian is concerned, the all-important conclusion which has emerged in stage three of the development of the study of our subject is this: the New Testament writers used an interpreted Bible, they did not expound the unadorned page of holy writ guided only by their knowledge of Jesus Christ. They approached Scripture, it is true, with strongly christocentric presuppositions, but they had all been brought up on Jewish traditions of exegesis, and except where their christocentric intentions interfered, they interpreted Scripture according to the technique which they had learned in Judaism. This does not imply that they had a monochromatic approach to Scripture, because the Jewish tradition of Scripture interpretation was not monochrome. But it does mean that they shared with their Jewish ancestors certain basic beliefs about Scripture and about the way in which one was justified in handling it. Thus they all agreed that Scripture was divinely inspired, inerrant, internally harmonious, and intended very often to give us information about events and persons many centuries later in time than the actual writers. They had no hesitation in describing both Moses and David as prophets. They shared the tendency in the Judaism of their day to an hagiographical approach to the characters of whom Scripture approved, the patriarchs, David himself, Elijah. They had no doubt about the complete historicity of many characters whom we would describe as mythical rather than even legendary: Adam, Cain, Abel, Noah. More than this, they often betray the fact that they take for granted some traditional interpretation of a verse or phrase in Scripture, or some piece of legendary embroidery of scriptural narrative.[4] In a word, the NT writers do not free themselves from Jewish methods of interpreting Scripture. The Scripture which they handled was not simply the Hebrew or Greek text of the Old Testament, untouched and virgin since Malachi or the author of Daniel penned the last page. It was a corpus of writings which had gone through a period of continuous interpretation during the centuries between its composition and the first century A.D. and had thereby been considerably altered from both the form and intention which it had when the original authors composed it. This does not mean that NT writers were incapable of ever recovering, or coming nearer to, the meaning of the original authors.⁵ But it does mean that there never was a time when the Bible (either the Old Testament alone or the Christian Bible) stood on its own, ready to be interpreted by fair-minded persons in such a way that they could gain the 'true' meaning. There never was a time when Scripture was not accompanied by interpretation.

This conclusion has profound significance for Christian theology. It has an important bearing on a debate which has been carried on between Catholics and Protestants ever since the Reformation. We give some consideration to it at the end of this chapter. But for the moment we must return to the proper subject of this book, the New Testament interpretation of Scripture. How is it related to other methods of New Testament criticism?

2

The Scriptures of Judaism were the main source from which NT writers drew their theological vocabulary and concepts. Hence a study in depth of how they used these Scriptures can tell us a great deal about their theology and thought-background. Such a study is in fact one way in to the pre-literary period in the formation of the New Testament. It follows that this study is in a sense an alternative to Form Criticism, or perhaps it would be more accurate to say that it is a special genus of Form Criticism. This is not to suggest of course that it is a rival to, or inconsistent with, Form Criticism as usually practised. Nevertheless the approach to the pre-literary period by means of the study of Scripture interpretation is bound to be different from Form Criticism as it has been employed hitherto, and even to some extent bound to appear as an alternative which is not wholly reconcilable with the Form Critical approach. This is because Scripture interpretation in the NT is, as we have seen, firmly fixed in the tradition of Judaism, whereas on the whole the tendency among Form Critics has been to approach the New Testament by means of parallels and analogies drawn from outside Judaism. This is no doubt because Form Criticism in Germany was born during the heyday of the *Religionsgeschichte* school[6] and the greatest Form Critic in the last generation, Rudolf Bultmann, was deeply influenced by that school. It would be grossly inaccurate to say that Bultmann did not make use of rabbinic parallels; but his extensive use of the concept of Gnosticism existing as a recognizable mode of thought during the first century A.D., and his readiness to attribute to both Paul and John direct access to non-Jewish sources of inspiration, imply that when he describes Christianity as a syncretistic religion, he does not merely mean that Christianity arose out of a Judaism that had absorbed many extraneous elements by the first century A.D. He means that Christianity is a syncretism between Judaism and various forms of paganism. But only Jews were interested in (or capable of using) the Jewish Scriptures. Hence the study of the interpretation of Scripture in the NT has on the whole produced results which are more reminiscent of the works of what we might call the rabbinic-orientated school in modern NT criticism than of the works of the *Religionsgeschichte* school. Those who engage in this field of study find themselves more naturally orientated to the works of such scholars as J. Jeremias, B. Gerhardsson, R. Leivestadt, and M. Hengel on the continent, and of W. D. Davies in the Anglo-Saxon world. They also find more light on their subject from modern Jewish scholars working on the origins of Christianity, men such as J. Klausner, H. J. Schoeps, and (latterly) G. Vermes. Though these scholars approach the NT from a critical-Jewish rather than a critical-Christian point of view, they often seem to have more appreciation of the NT interpretation of Scripture than has a scholar like Bultmann.

This emphasis on the Jewish background of NT thought to which workers in this field of study are by the very nature of the material committed does not imply that they must hold the unreal and utopian idea that somehow or other a pure tradition of Hebrew religion descended from the days of the classical prophets ready to be absorbed by the first Christians. Careful study of the Greek period of Israel's history has made it perfectly clear that when the *Hasidim* at the time of the Maccabaean revolt shut the door on Hellenism, erected a fence round the Torah, and intensified the separation even from Samaritans, they were in one very profound sense bolting the stable door after the pony had gone. Indeed, as M. Hengel makes clear in his great work,[7] in order to repel the formidable attack of Greek culture on Judaism, the champions of Judaism had to borrow the weapons which the Greeks had forged; they could not write their own history in the spirit which they believed it required till they had learned from the Greeks how to write history. They could not begin to demonstrate that Moses had anticipated Plato unless they went to school with Plato. They could not repel the cult of Isis in its Ptolemaic guise, or produce a rival to the *Logos spermatikos* of the Stoics by elaborating the concept of Wisdom, unless they were prepared to give the divine Wisdom many of the metaphysical features which the Greeks had already attributed to the divine Logos. The Qumran documents themselves have shown us the astonishing spectacle of an ultra-Jewish sect, located in the very heartland of Judaism, deliberately cutting itself off not only from contact with Gentiles but also with conventional Judaism, which nevertheless has plainly already been strongly influenced by currents of thoughts which had their origin outside Judaism. The talk about divine secrets, the remarkable interest in angelic mediators, the emphasis on knowledge, all those features which in the second century A.D. were to blossom in the form of overt Gnosticism must have entered the Qumran sect from outside well before the first century A.D. But they appear in a Jewish form inside a strongly biblicist sect. Modern study of the NT interpretation of Scripture will not take us outside Judaism; but the Judaism within which it took its origin already had a syncretistic element in it.

The actual technique of studying NT interpretation of Scripture is obvious enough. The beginning is to establish as accurately as possible what text and what form of that text the writer had in mind. This is not always easy, as NT writers do not always quote the LXX as we have it. The tendency on the part of scholars in the past to say that Paul or some other NT writer is quoting from memory when he seems to quote a variant version to that known to us now proves to be dangerous or misleading. Without very strong evidence (which is hardly ever available) we are not justified in saying that variants can be attributed to a faulty memory. They are much more likely to be due to a different version, either in Greek or Hebrew, or to the use of a traditional interpretation, perhaps allied to some Targumic tradition. I must also confess that I am unhappy when some scholar nowadays describes Paul as indulging in 'a free remoulding of the text', though this phrase has been used by very distinguished workers in this field. It is not that I believe all NT writers to have had a strict regard for the original text of Scripture, but rather that a phrase such as 'free remoulding' suggests that the NT writers felt themselves free to adapt Scripture to their own needs. I think this is to misunderstand them. Very often when they quote Scripture they do so in order to prove some doctrinal point. But if you have previously altered the text of Scripture in order to adapt it to your proof, it fails altogether as a proof. Even Justin in his dialogue with Trypho, much though he regretted Trypho's unwillingness to accept the LXX text as authoritative, had to abandon it if he wished to convince Trypho.[8]

But when we have fixed as far as we can the actual text cited by the NT writer, we are still only at the beginning. We must then look at the citation in its context in Scripture. And here again we meet a source of frequent misunderstanding. When we today speak of understanding a passage of Scripture in its context we mean studying the actual historical circumstances in which the passage was written. Because the NT writers had very little notion of doing this, they are often accused of an atomistic use of Scripture. They take isolated texts, it is said, from a wide variety of contexts and use them often as ammunition against their opponents, completely ignoring the context in which they occur. This, I believe, is unjust. It is always worth while to study the context in which a Scripture text cited in the NT occurs in its original format. It frequently transpires that the NT writer has made a careful study of the context and is fully alive to its significance, strange though his idea of its significance might seem to us.[9]

Having investigated the text quoted and the significance of its context, the next step is to find out if we can how the passage from which the quotation comes was understood in contemporary Judaism. For this there is now abundant material, though, as we shall be seeing, the assessment of the nature of that material is not always easy. For pre-Christian evidence we can very occasionally use some other part of the Scriptures themselves.[10] Failing that, we can turn to the inter-testamental literature, the *Wisdom of Jesus ben Sira*, the *Book of Wisdom*,[11] that very interesting midrash which goes under the name of the *Liber Antiquitatum Biblicarum* of Pseudo-Philo, the whole range of apocalyptic and midrashic literature from the pre-Christian period, such as the *Book of Enoch* and the *Book of Jubilees*, and Josephus's account of Israel's history in his *Antiquities*, a work which often shows a knowledge of traditional Jewish exegesis. Then there is Philo himself. Despite his determination to extract moral, philosophical, and psychological principles from the Pentateuch by means of allegory, he often betrays an acquaintance with rabbinic interpretation of Scripture. Today we can add to this the great treasure of the Qumran documents, all the more valuable because so relatively close in time and even situation to the NT.

But even all this does not provide anything like an exhaustive interpretation of the Scriptures for the period. We are dependent on what the various authors of these documents happened to be interested in, which was not by any means always identical with what NT writers are interested in. So, ever since the great pioneer work of Strack-Billerbeck, scholars have been increasingly turning for light to that huge volume of Jewish exegetic literature which is later in composition than the New Testament, the Mishna, the Talmud, the various Targums, and the other works of a midrashic nature such as the *Mekhilta de Rabbi Ishmael* and the *Pesiktas*. Here we have plenty of scriptural exegesis, much of it occasional and some of it influenced by anti-Christian polemic, but a great deal of it very relevant, and some of it consisting of material which can be convincingly shown to have been familiar to the writers of the NT. This is perhaps the area in which most rapid progress is being made at the moment. In particular, scholars are still engaged in digesting the evidence which recent research in the Targums is producing. The full impact of the Neofiti discovery has not yet been felt. Links between NT interpretation and the exegetical tradition which is enshrined in the Targums are being constantly discovered. In this respect the New Testament is, in a sense, being reconsidered against its indigenous Jewish background as contrasted with the Hellenistic background so often

The Significance of the Subject

supposed to exist by the disciples of the *Religionsgeschichte* school.

Here an objection to this technique of research is often made, sometimes by adherents of the *Religionsgeschichte* school themselves. 'In using the Mishna, the Talmud, and the Targums,' so the objection runs, 'are you not using material which is too late to be of any practical use? The Mishna was not completed till the end of the second century A.D. The Talmud is at least 200 years later. The dating of the Targums is more difficult, but the well-known Targums (Onkelos and Pseudo-Jonathan) were written down well on into the Christian centuries, and nobody really knows how to date the newly discovered Targum of Palestine. After all this Neofiti MS. which has caused such a sensation was actually copied only in the sixteenth century.' It is tempting to reply with a *tu quoque*. Disciples of the *Religionsgeschichte* school also rely for their evidence on documents which often date from centuries after the NT. The Mandaean literature, for whose influence on the NT such great claims have been made, was all written in the form we have it at least 400 years after the emergence of Christianity. If scholars of this tradition can argue for the influence of a tradition pre-existing their documents by several centuries, why should not students of NT Scripture interpretation do the same?

But *tu quoque* arguments and arguments *ad hominem* are unsatisfactory. A better answer to this objection is the observation that, despite the lapse of time, it sometimes happens that a piece of exegesis attested by a source contemporary with the NT occurs quite independently in a rabbinic document which was actually written centuries later. An interesting example of this turned up as I was working on the material for Chapter 4; Philo, commenting on Genesis 28.11,16: 'He came to a certain place . . . Surely the Lord is in this place', remarks that *topos* ('place') in this passage can be taken in three senses[12], (a) a place filled by a body; (b) the divine Logos; and (c) a name for God himself. All things are in him rather than he being in a place. Centuries later in the *Midrash on the Psalms* we have the following passage: 'R. Isaac taught . . . we did not know whether the Holy One, blessed be he, is the dwelling-place of the universe, or whether the universe is the dwelling-place of the Lord, until Moses came and gave us the answer by saying, *Lord*

The New Testament Interpretation of Scripture

thou hast been our dwelling-place ... R. José bar Halafta said, We did not know whether the Holy One, blessed be he, is contained in his world or whether his world is contained in him, until the Holy One, blessed be he, made the answer plain by saying, *Behold there is a place by me*, meaning that his world is placed in God. R. Huna said in the name of R. Ammi: Why is the name of the Holy One, blessed be he, called "place"? Because he is the place of the world ... Jacob called him "place" as is said, *How full of awe is this place.*'[13] If we did not have the evidence of the *Midrash*, we might naturally assume that Philo was merely applying Greek metaphysical notions to biblical interpretation. But the evidence from the impeccable rabbinic source shows us that this is not the case. Since it is not very likely that the interpretative tradition found there in the *Midrash on the Psalms* comes from Philo, we may legitimately conclude that both come from traditional Jewish exegesis of Genesis 28. The continuity of tradition through the centuries is most remarkable.

But, when we consider it more deeply, is it so remarkable after all? Very often New Testament exegetes of the Scripture and Jewish exegetes were facing very similar problems. Both groups wished to show that Scripture supported their particular theology and when that theology converges at any point scriptural exegesis tends to converge also. I have pointed out what I believe is an example of this, in Chapter 2.[14] Both Paul and rabbinic Judaism regarded Chapter 41 of the Book of Job as a likely repository for profound truths about how God created the world. Neither of them would have allowed that the author was merely writing an interesting poem about the crocodile of the Nile.[15] Both are therefore prepared to find here statements about some pre-existent entity, and sure enough both find what they are looking for. Paul finds the pre-existing Wisdom or Counsellor, or Son; the rabbis find the pre-existing Torah. What is significant from our point of view is that we have been led to an understanding of Paul's interpretation just because of the similarity of his situation to that of the rabbis.

I do not think this is a complete answer to the objection drawn from the lateness of the rabbinic evidence. Indeed, I do not think that a complete answer to this objection can yet be given. But it is relevant to put forward here another con-

The Significance of the Subject

sideration which at least blunts the force of the objection, and arises from the peculiar problem of the formation of the Targums. Till quite recently the view was generally held among experts in rabbinic literature that the Targums by their very nature must be late in date of composition. The earliest Targums must have been oral, and we know that the rabbis objected to the Targumist reading out a translation of the Hebrew. He must do it by rote. The aim was, of course, to avoid any appearance of producing a document which might rival the text of Scripture itself. Hence, the argument ran, any written Targum must come from a late period when (perhaps because the traditional halachic material had now been written down in the Mishna and subsequently in the Talmud) this objection did not hold. But there were always some scholars who maintained that some written Targumic traditions witnessed to a period before the polemic between Judaism and Christianity arose, and it now looks as if the full text of the *Palestinian Targum* goes some way to justifying that claim. There seem to be more elements which obviously date from a pre-polemic era in this Targum than in those Targums that have always been available. But what has given a fresh encouragement to those who claim that the Targums do contain early material, and that the writing down of Targums is not necessarily a phenomenon only of a late period, is the surprising fact that a Targum dating undoubtedly from the first century B.C. has now turned up in a fragmentary form among the Qumran documents. What is still more surprising is that it should not be a Targum on the Pentateuch, which we might well have imagined would have been among the first Targums to be written down, but on the Book of Job, a book which only belongs to the *Kethubim* and might seem to have very little claim to prior attention on the part of Targumists.[16] This should serve to remind us that a good deal of traditional exegetical material which has only reached us in written form dating from a late period may well have existed within the Jewish community (or *a* Jewish community) for centuries earlier. The argument that because any given tradition is only attested some centuries after the period of the NT it cannot be used as evidence for NT interpretation, no matter how relevant it might appear, is not one which can be convincingly sustained.

The New Testament Interpretation of Scripture

I have said that I do not think a complete answer to the objection from the lateness of the rabbinic material can yet be given. This is because the material itself is still very largely awaiting critical examination. Until we have some idea of how first the Mishna and then the Talmud came to assume the form which they have today, we cannot begin to date their contents with any approach to accuracy. This means in effect that both source criticism and form criticism have still to be applied to the Mishna and the Talmud with scholarly rigour. The process has indeed begun, as the two books edited by Jacob Neusner within the last few years witness.[17] But these two books also witness to the difficulties which this necessary enterprise faces. One obstacle is the sheer bulk of the material; another is the reluctance of orthodox Jewish scholars to accept a truly critical approach. Of course the parallel with the attitude of Christian scholars towards the critical approach to the New Testament is obvious. But we must remember that this task can in effect only be carried out by Jewish scholars, and in point of sheer numbers the cadre upon which they can draw for new recruits to this discipline is severely limited compared with the recruiting potential of Christian scholars. Again the period during which the Mishna and Talmud was being composed is distinctly longer than the composition period of the NT, at least twice as long in fact. Add to this the fact that Jewish critical students of the Mishna and Talmud are primarily and rightly interested in the development of their material from the point of view of Torah and Halaka. This is of course the proper scholarly approach. These documents were put together in order to serve the observance of the Torah by Israel; they were composed and preserved by rabbis whose main *raison d'être* was to enable Israel to obey the Torah. But this is not the primary concern of most of those who consult rabbinic literature in order to find light on the NT interpretation of Scripture. We are much more interested in the scriptural exegesis which the rabbis offer in the course of helping Israel to obey the Torah. Much of this will be Haggada: a great deal of it will be occasional, incidental, almost fortuitous. It is our good fortune that the rabbis did not always confine themselves strictly to Halaka, but indulged their profound love of Scripture by giving us plenty of midrash, haggada, and even biographical narrative in

The Significance of the Subject

the course of carrying out what they regarded as their main vocation. There is no doubt that progress is being made, and will continue to be made, in the task of dating and classifying the multifarious traditions embraced within the Mishna and the Babylonian Talmud alone. But it will be a slow process, not the work of one generation only.

3

During the Modernist controversy which raged inside the Roman Catholic Church in the early years of this century, one of the burning issues was the question of the interpretation of Scripture. A remarkable feature of the debate was that apparently both sides were agreed on one basic assumption: they agreed that in most questions of interpretation there was a 'correct' answer which could, in theory at least, be discovered. The traditionalist orthodox party believed that the answer could be found by consulting the divinely authorized and inspired *magisterium*. The critical 'Modernist' party believed that the correct interpretation of Scripture could be found by applying the methods of scientific criticism.[18] Some three quarters of a century later we can surely pronounce that in this belief both sides were mistaken. There is no objective 'correct' interpretation of Scripture which can be discovered if only the right methods are applied. This does not mean that we are thrown back into a condition of hopeless subjectivism, but it does mean that one cannot begin talking about a 'correct' or 'true' interpretation of Scripture until one has clarified the presuppositions with which one approaches Scripture. It is these presuppositions, and not anything inherent in Scripture itself, that determine whether any particular interpretation is correct. In fact, when one asks about the interpretation of any given passage, there are really two questions to be answered: 'What did the author mean when he wrote it in his peculiar situation?' This preliminary question can be answered with a certain degree of objectivity and does admit of the category 'correctness'. But the second question is the one that interests the theologian: 'How is this passage related to my belief, which (I hope) is based on the Scriptures?' This is the question which requires that we clarify our presuppositions.

The New Testament Interpretation of Scripture

We can illustrate this by looking at the four groups we have already mentioned: Pharisees, Qumran community, Philo (who probably represents more than himself), and the early Christians. To the question: 'What is the correct interpretation of this passage of Scripture?' each group would in most cases give a different answer, and each could be right according to their lights.[19] The Pharisees would in effect be asking: 'How can this passage help me to discover the right Halaka?' The Qumran sect would ask: 'What light does this passage throw on the history and destiny of the true Israel as inspired by the "teacher of righteousness"?' Philo might ask: 'What are the principles of moral or metaphysical philosophy which can be discovered from this passage?': and to the Christians the question would be: 'What light does this passage throw on the nature, career, and present significance of Jesus Christ?'

It must be confessed that when the issue is expressed in these terms, the modern scholar is inclined to protest. He is very much aware on the one hand of the demand for objectivity which the positivistic tendency of the last century has left as an inescapable legacy today. If his methods of biblical criticism can in any way be dignified with the epithet 'scientific', is he not entitled to expect a certain element of objectivity in his conclusions when they are applied in this field? And on the other hand he is, if he is either a Christian or a Jew, aware of a certain feeling of guilt because those who in the past have represented the tradition in which he stands have certainly been guilty of arbitrary interpretation of Scripture. If he is a Christian, he thinks of Origen's allegorical handling of Scripture and the immense influence which it had on both patristic and scholastic interpretation. If he is a Jew, he cannot but admit the rabbis could on occasion give the impression of making Scripture mean anything which they chose. At least he is entitled to ask: granted that each group approaches Scripture with its own presuppositions, are there any limits to the extent to which these presuppositions can be pushed?

Let us try to answer this very reasonable question as Christians. It takes this form: can *everything* in Scripture be legitimately interpreted in terms of Christ? I think that the NT writers implicitly answered this question with a negative. By concentrating their attention on certain parts of Scripture and

The Significance of the Subject

giving less attention to the rest, they admitted that some parts of Scripture were more amenable to a christocentric interpretation than others. They were more interested in the figure of Abraham in Genesis; in the concept of divinely instituted priesthood rather than in its institutionalization in Aaron and his line; in the Davidic promise; in the hopes and visions of the great prophets; in the religious and biographical utterances of the righteous sufferer in the Psalms; in the divine wisdom as described in Proverbs and hinted at in the Book of Job; in the figure of Jonah as a type of Christ. They were not much interested in Israel's history after the time of Solomon, and not at all interested in the detailed prescriptions of the Torah in the Pentateuch. They did not attempt to find types, foreshadowings, or allegories of Christ in these passages – as their successors too often did.[20]

This means that early Christianity was to some degree a 'back to the Bible' movement in Judaism. The early Christians brought into the limelight certain elements in the scriptural tradition and put other elements into the background. They certainly believed that they could legitimately cry 'back to the Bible', because we find them often disputing with Jews about the interpretation of Scripture, and we can be sure that a substantial element of Scripture interpretation which we encounter in the NT was originally worked out in a milieu of controversy with Jews. Perhaps this element of 'back to the Bible' was enhanced and emphasized just because the liveliest and (as it ultimately proved) predominant tradition in the Judaism which they opposed was claimed by its champions to be a teaching received from Moses and orally transmitted from him down to their own day. Orthodox Pharisees held that the Halaka was as sacred and as divinely authorized as Scripture itself; indeed it was regarded as in effect a continuation of Scripture. Thus when it came to be written down in the Mishna and the Talmud the same divine authority adhered to these works. Jewish scholars have noted in the two books edited by Neusner (referred to on page 12) the reluctance of orthodox Jewish scholars right up to our own day to admit criticism of the Talmud, because this was tantamount to criticizing Scripture itself.[21] This attitude of the Pharisees enabled Christians, who rejected the Halaka, to represent themselves as appealing from the traditions of men back to the word of God (cf. Mark 7.6-8).

In the course of its history the Christian Church proceeded to do exactly what Judaism did, build up a tradition of interpretation to which it attempted to give divine sanction. When Luther first challenged contemporary doctrine in the name of the Bible, he was told that he had no right to question the sacred tradition. Indeed, this way of dealing with an appeal from ecclesiastical tradition to Scripture is one which has been employed within the Roman Catholic Church up till quite recent times, and still appears to be the main answer which the authorities of the Eastern Orthodox Church give when similarly challenged. However, the very fact that there was a Reformation in Christianity, based on what its leaders believed to be a legitimate appeal to Scripture, is itself significant. It suggests that there is something in Christianity which prevents it from permanently becoming simply a self-justifying mode of religious experience. It suggests that the hope of finding something remotely approximating to a norm for the interpretation of Scripture may not be utterly vain.

Perhaps we may step aside for a moment to ask the not wholly irrelevant question: is Judaism a religion whose Scripture provides a norm to which appeal can be made? It is true that there has been nothing like the Reformation in the history of Judaism, but we can point to a number of movements which could be fairly described as being based on the principle of 'back to the Bible'. In the first place there was the Qumran movement.[22] The Qumran sectaries certainly did believe that they interpreted the Scriptures correctly, and that the rest of Judaism was wrong in its interpretation. Indeed they felt a great debt of gratitude towards the 'teacher of righteousness' just because he had shown them the right way to interpret Scripture. But they remained within the main framework of Judaism in that their aim, like that of the Pharisees, was to find the correct Halaka. They did not want to displace the Torah as the centre of their religion.

Some 800 years later, another 'back to the Bible' movement appeared within Judaism, what is known as the Qaraite movement. Its origins are obscure. It began in Babylonia. The essence of the movement seems to have been a protest against the

The Significance of the Subject

orthodox rabbinic Halaka. The Qaraites certainly rejected this. 'Back to the Torah,' they said, 'back to the word of God.' But, like the Qumran sect, they did not want to displace the Torah from the centre. What they disagreed about was how it should be interpreted and applied. This meant that, having repudiated the Orthodox tradition, they were faced with the question of how they were to apply the Torah to the predicaments of everyday life. At first, it appears, they thought they could manage by drawing precedents, examples, and analogies from Scripture itself. But this must break down in the end: Scripture is not inexhaustible and life is constantly producing new situations. They fell back on allegory. This method, properly applied, could be made to produce answers to all questions. But who is to know what is the proper way of applying it? A method that can be used to produce any answer that is required is a two-edged tool. It is not surprising that eventually the Qaraites were reduced to elaborating their own Halaka. Scripture without tradition is in the long run useless.[23]

In our own days, however, it could be said that another 'back to the Bible' movement has appeared within Judaism. This is Liberal Judaism. By this I mean that form of Judaism which accepts the critical approach to Scripture and is willing to adapt itself to the conclusions of that criticism.[24] This constitutes in fact a more radical challenge to traditional Judaism than that of either the Qumran or the Qaraite movement, because it qualifies and reduces the divine authority of the Torah, and does so to some extent in the name of Scripture itself. One of the most assured results of biblical criticism is that the Torah as a whole does not go back to Moses, was not all delivered at once on Sinai, and derives in part from primitive tabu and apotropaic ritual. Moreover the Torah as understood by the Judaism of the first century A.D. hardly existed in the time of the greatest prophets, and was certainly unknown in that form to David. Once accept these conclusions, and the centre of Judaism has drastically shifted. It can no longer be based as a religion on a divinely ordained Torah perfect in every detail. As a matter of fact the effect of this change may be to make Judaism a *more* scripturally orientated religion. It certainly did in the case of Claude Montefiore. If the detailed Torah as a guide to the details of daily living has lost some-

The New Testament Interpretation of Scripture

thing of its prescriptive authority, room may be found for a fresh appreciation of the faith of the great prophets. But it is too soon to say whether Liberal Judaism in this sense will ever become a significant force in Judaism. There are other ways of reacting to biblical criticism.

We cannot end this chapter without at least raising the question that must lie in the background for any Christian theologian who is working in this field. Is there any point in trying to find an area of reconciliation between the New Testament interpretation of Scripture and our modern understanding of Scripture?[25] I have in fact written on this subject at some length elsewhere,[26] so it may be sufficient to make three points here:

1. We must learn from the experience alike of Judaism and Christianity that Scripture without an interpretative tradition is dumb and useless. This does not mean that any old tradition will do, but that it is a delusion to imagine (as apparently some of the Reformers did) that Scripture is self-interpreting. Some element of tradition, some theological presuppositions are essential if we are to succeed in interpreting Scripture at all.

2. If we ask not just, 'How do the NT writers interpret Scripture?', but 'In interpreting Scripture as they did, what were the NT writers seeking to achieve?', we may find common ground more easily. I suppose we would say that they were intending to show how Scripture witnesses to the full significance of Jesus of Nazareth. If we are Christians, we today must share this aim. Our methods of doing so are very different from those of the writers of the NT, but we should be able to appreciate their methods better just because we share their aim. In one sense we are better off than they were: our Scripture includes their writings. This should mean that our task is easier than theirs was. They were dealing with material that (we would say) was not consciously Christ-orientated. What is for us the most important part of Scripture is just that. It puts us of course in a different position for ever to them, but it should make it much easier for us to find a norm by which to judge the relevance of Scripture. It is spelt out for us in the New Testament. Those who wrote the New Testament had no such objective norm.

The Significance of the Subject

3. We must therefore so adjust the relation of Scripture to tradition in our theological system that Scripture can act as a norm. I do not propose to attempt to say how this can be, for that is not the subject of this book. But I am quite sure that it must be accomplished somehow. There have not been lacking in the past voices both in Judaism and Christianity that have suggested that we can get on very well without a scriptural norm. How many modern Jews, for example, give one the impression that Judaism is simply Jewish practice? Judaism is what Jews do. I speak as an outsider, but this seems to me to be intellectual suicide on the part of Judaism, a suicide which I am sure the great body of devout, sensitive, learned, thinking Jews in the world will not allow to happen. Similarly, before the Second Vatican Council took place, it seemed to a good many thoughtful Christians outside the Roman Catholic Church that that Church was now proceeding on the disastrous principle that Christianity was what Roman Catholics believed at any given period. The task of the theologian had developed into the duty of trying to make it appear that this belief at any given time was not too monstrously inconsistent with what it had been at any other time in the past. The Council itself, and what has followed it, has shown that we were mistaken, and indeed is a striking demonstration that there is a norm of belief within Christianity, and that it makes itself felt in the long run. And this norm is certainly not independent of Scripture. But there is an analogous movement in Protestantism which would have exactly the same effect as the pre-Vatican II ultramontane independence of Scripture. This is a subjectivism about Scripture which is born of the very disintegrating effects of biblical criticism referred to above. The champions of this view conclude that, since Scripture is so very diverse, and since even the most positive theologians have used and interpreted it in so many mutually incompatible ways, it is no use trying to use it as a norm for belief or practice. Christianity is just what it happens to be at any time or place. There is no more to be said about it.[27] From the point of view of the Christian theologian, Protestant atomistic subjectivism seems to me to be no improvement on Roman Catholic triumphalist integralism.

In the chapters that follow I have tried to put to some use the

The New Testament Interpretation of Scripture

modern technique of examining the NT interpretation of Scripture. Chapter 2 is a close study of a very obscure passage in Paul, in which a great deal turns on his exegesis of Scripture. I think we can learn much about his Christology from this sort of study. Chapters 3 and 4 are examples of how the same technique can be used on the Fourth Gospel. Chapter 5 does the same thing from a different point of view; it takes one theme and attempts to see how it is integrated into the scriptural interpretation of a wide variety of traditions in the NT. Chapter 6 is an attempt on a modest scale to do for the Fourth Gospel what I tried to do for Paul in *Studies in Paul's Technique and Theology*.

2

A Quasi-Gnostic Pauline Midrash
1 Corinthians 2. 6–16

1

Few of those who are acquainted with Paul's writings are likely to deny that in the passage 1 Corinthians 2.6-16 we seem to encounter more overt traces of what later emerged as Gnosticism than in any other passage of similar length in his Epistles. Scholars such as Bultmann, who find many such traces in Paul, cite this passage as a leading example. It is not difficult to see why: we have in the first place the reference to a mystery (verse 7, 'God's wisdom in a mystery'); then we have the statement that the rulers of this age failed to recognize the Lord of glory, which looks very like an echo of the Gnostic myth of the descending redeemer; and thirdly we have the distinction between the mature (*teleioi*) and the rest, as well as that between the spiritual (*pneumatikoi*) and the merely natural (*psuchikoi*). Nowhere else in so small a space does Paul betray so many apparently Gnostic characteristics.

However, this feature in itself would not justify a separate treatment of this passage on the scale attempted here. It is perhaps appropriate, therefore, to suggest some other reasons why there is room for this study. In the first place, no one as far as I know, has yet brought to bear a study of Paul's use of Scripture on the question of his meaning here. On the whole those who are most convinced that Gnosticism lies behind this passage are least interested in Paul's use of Scripture. This is eminently true of Bultmann, who devotes very little detailed study to this latter subject. I would also include Schmithals in this category. It may be worth while attempting to see whether the modern technique of exploring Paul's use of Scripture may not have light to throw here. Some other most valuable works on Paul's use of Scripture, such as E. E. Ellis's *Paul's Use of the Old Testament* and B. Lindars's *New Testament*

Apologetics, have surprisingly little to say on this passage. Secondly, the fullest modern treatment of the mysterious citation in verse 9, that of A. Feuillet, was apparently written without the knowledge that the conflated citation actually occurs in a Jewish work which has no relation to Paul, the *Biblical Antiquities* of Pseudo-Philo. The significance of this needs examining.

Thirdly, one might refer to the astonishing failure of modern commentators on both 1 Corinthians and Romans to make any use of the fact that Paul quotes Isaiah 40.13 in both these Epistles. Even a commentator (Ernst Käsemann) who does use this fact in order to explore the meaning of Romans 11.34-5, and who thereby makes much better sense of it than most others, does not seem aware of the christological implications of the conflated citation there as expounded by a scholar such as W. L. Knox. I hope to show that Paul's second major citation in this passage (1 Corinthians 2.16) is no mere *obiter dictum*, but, like most of Paul's deliberate citations, plays an essential part in his argument. But in order to do this, I have to examine in detail the conflated citation in Romans 11.34-5.

We must begin by trying to establish what is the 'hidden wisdom of God in a mystery' to which Paul refers in 2.7, who are the 'rulers of this age', and why they failed to recognize 'the Lord of glory'. For convenience sake we take the second of these questions first, then the third, and only after that consider the first.

From ancient times there have been three distinct opinions as to the identity of the 'rulers of this age'. The first is the common sense one that Paul means the historical bearers of political power who were responsible for Jesus's death, Caiaphas and Pilate or the Sanhedrin and Caesar. The second opinion, which has much support in the Fathers, is that the rulers also include 'men of influence in the cultural realm, orators, poets, philosophers'.[1] The third opinion is that they are the elemental powers, identical with *ta stoicheia tou kosmou* of Galatians 4.3; and Colossians 2.20, superhuman astral forces. This view is now accepted by the majority of modern scholars and is the view adopted in this work. It is not inconsistent with the 'common sense' view, since Caiaphas and Pilate can be regarded as the unwitting tools of the powers. This third view is still rejected by

A Quasi-Gnostic Pauline Midrash: 1 Corinthians 2.6-16

some, but it certainly seems to make the best sense in this context. Bultmann claims that this belief in the world-rulers is essentially Gnostic: 'Both in name and meaning', he writes, 'the rulers of this age' who brought 'the Lord of glory' to the cross ... are figures of Gnostic mythology.[2] But belief in the astral world-rulers was spread far beyond the limits of Gnosticism and existed long before anything that could reasonably be described as Gnosticism had emerged. Arnold Ehrhardt has traced it back to Aristotle.[3] It was as common a belief in Paul's world as is the belief in evolution in our modern world.

Recently, however, A. W. Carr has taken up the cudgels on behalf of the first of the views outlined here.[4] Dr Carr maintains that *hoi archontes tou aiōnos toutou* in 2.6,8 must mean human rulers, in fact Caiaphas and Pilate, and not the superhuman powers. He claims that they must be associated with 'the wisdom of the world' in 1.20; in 1.17-24 Paul has nothing more in mind than human wisdom. The passage 2.6,8 is parallel to 1.17-24, and must refer to the same human wisdom, hence the rulers must be human. He also draws a parallel with the early speeches in Acts, where it is explicitly the human rulers of the Jews and the Romans who crucified Jesus. He believes that the use of *hoi archontes* for fallen angels is only found in Gnostic literature of a later period. He concedes that Ignatius uses *hoi archontes* for angels, but only for good angels.

This is a well-argued and learned statement of the case against understanding *hoi archontes tou aiōnos toutou* as referring to superhuman powers. But I am not convinced by it, and hold to my opinion that Paul is here referring to superhuman powers, for the following reasons:

a) Paul does use *archai* for the superhuman powers, and undoubtedly he does envisage them as hostile and as being quite capable of attempting to come between believers and Christ; see 1 Corinthians 15.24; Romans 8.38; and compare Colossians 1.16; 2.10,15; Ephesians 1.21; 3.10; 6.12. It is not a big step from calling them *archai* to calling them *archontes*.

b) The concept of *archontes* regulating the world by astral influence can be traced back to Aristotle. Though it was exploited by the Gnostics, it is not Gnostic in origin; see Ehrhardt, op. cit., pp. 133, 138-40, 169.

c) On Carr's assumptions, the nature of the 'wisdom of the world' of 1.20 is inconsistent with what Paul can possibly have meant. If the rulers are men such as Caiaphas and Pilate, their wisdom consisted in a form of *Realpolitik*: it was expedient that one man (however innocent) should die rather than all the nation perish: compare John 11.50. But this is not at all what Paul is fighting in 1 Corinthians, on any reasonable interpretation of the Epistle. The context is one of wisdom-disputers, purveyors of some philosophy or ideology. He was either opposing some form of what Carr calls 'halachic' wisdom, or Greek philosophic speculation. Either could well fit the theory that the rulers are evil powers, fallen angels who have gained control of men's minds. It seems likely that according to Paul the powers had used the Torah to enslave the Jews, and pagan religion (with which pagan philosophy was closely associated) to enslave the rest of the world. In either case we are led back to the concept of the rulers as superhuman powers.

d) Delling (art. cit., pp. 486ff; see note 22, p. 79) points out that *archon* is used of guardian angels of the nations in Theodotion's version of Daniel more than once and in the LXX once and he quotes a passage from *Pesikta de Rab Kahana* in which the fallen angels are called *śrym ʿmwt hʿwlm*. Since he wrote, the Qumran documents have shown that, in pre-Christian Judaism, angels could be described as *śrym*. The obvious translation for this is *archontes*.

e) Carr refers to Ignatius, but he does not mention the very significant fact that Ignatius in Ephesians XIX is in effect the earliest commentator on 1 Corinthians 2.6-8. Now Ignatius undoubtedly understood Paul to be referring to superhuman powers in this passage; and Ignatius's mention of the aeons also shows that he does not understand them in a merely temporal sense. Ignatius's evidence must weigh heavily in favour of interpreting *archontes* as referring to superhuman powers.

If my suggestion (outlined below) that behind this passage lies a reference to Psalm 24 is correct, this supplies an explanation of why Paul uses *archontes* here, but *archai* elsewhere. Here he is influenced by the language of Psalm 24.

A Quasi-Gnostic Pauline Midrash: 1 Corinthians 2.6-16

The rulers, says Paul, failed to recognize 'the wisdom of God in a mystery' (2.7-8). Some scholars have claimed that 'the wisdom of God' in verse 7 is simply another way of referring to Christ, like 'the Lord of glory' in verse 8 and that therefore in this passage Paul is explicitly identifying Christ with the divine wisdom mentioned in the Scriptures; see, for example, A. Feuillet's article already referred to on page 22, where he claims that in this passage Paul has for the first time identified Christ with the divine wisdom mentioned in the Scriptures.[5] Now it is quite true that Paul applies to Christ the attributes of the divine wisdom, and that this formed a bridge to his doctrine of pre-existence, as Feuillet says (art. cit., p. 74). But this is not the same thing as an explicit identification of Christ with wisdom. Wilckens seems to be nearer the truth when he says that Paul could not absolutely accept the thesis 'Christ is the wisdom of God', a thesis which Wilckens attributes to the gnosticizing party at Corinth.[6] After all, Paul has just said in 1.30 that Christ has become to us wisdom from God and righteousness and sanctification and redemption, which does not sound like a very specific identification of Christ with the divine wisdom alone. What the rulers failed to recognize was 'the wisdom of God in a mystery'. The wisdom is therefore better described here as God's plan carried out in the entire career of Jesus Christ rather than as Jesus Christ *tout court*. Bultmann and Wilckens both wish to introduce an element of eschatology into the concept of wisdom here. Wilckens varies between describing the wisdom as 'Heilsplan' and 'Heilsgut';[7] and Bultmann refers to 'the mysteries of the history of salvation or of the eschatological occurrence' in connection with this passage.[8] As long as the eschatology is understood as having been realized, Bultmann's description may well stand; but Wilckens's use of the word 'Heilsgut' seems to be influenced by an interpretation of the citation in verse 9 which makes it refer to future blessings. As far as verse 7 is concerned, 'the wisdom of God in a mystery' is best understood as God's design in Christ (see Weiss, op. cit., in loc.). Allo well describes this wisdom as 'a more profound understanding of Jesus Christ and his work';[9] and Bornkamm writes that the mystery of God 'is known in the sphere of God's history'.[10]

However, in 1967, R. Scroggs published an article in which

he argued for a distinction between the content of the kerygma in Paul and the wisdom.[11] He writes: 'The kerygma is the μαρτύριον τοῦ θεοῦ (ii.1). The σοφία is on the other hand the eschatological μυστήριον τοῦ θεοῦ (ii.7).' We may note *en passant* that acceptance of the very well attested reading μυστήριον τοῦ θεοῦ in 2.1 would destroy this theory at a blow. Böhlig actually prefers the reading *mustērion*, though he admits the other is the *difficilior lectio* (op. cit., p. 25, l.8). Scroggs goes on to claim that Paul has his own wisdom, consisting of several discrete mysteries, which he imparts to the mature and which has no necessary connection with God's mystery. He remarks that 'Paul does not disclose a single example of his wisdom', and he compares Hebrews 5.11: 'About this we have much to say which is hard to explain, since you have become dull of hearing', which he calls 'a tantalizingly similar passage'. However, he does point out that Paul uses *mustērion* for two other topics in his letters: in Romans 11.25 the *mustērion* is the blindness of the Jews and in 1 Corinthians 15.51 it is the fate of those who are alive at the parousia. Of the former passage Scroggs writes: 'In Rom. xi.25 Paul reveals a fragment of his wisdom teaching.'[12] We can sum up Scroggs's argument by saying that he defines 'the wisdom of God in a mystery' as 'the whole eschatological plan of glory – that glorious future far beyond the senses and man's imagination' (p. 47), thus heavily emphasizing the eschatological or futurist element; he denies that Christ is identified with the wisdom of God *tout court*; and he claims that Paul has a wisdom teaching of his own consisting of various mysteries having no necessary connection with each other.

We may well welcome Scroggs's insistence that Christ cannot be simply identified with the wisdom of God, but we must question both his distinction between the kerygma and the content of God's wisdom and also the distinction between God's wisdom and Paul's wisdom teaching. His claim that Paul does not disclose a single example of his wisdom may be answered by saying that this is because there was basically only one example of this wisdom, God's design in Christ. All the various mysteries of which Paul speaks fit into this; they are not discrete, contingent mysteries, but parts of one and the same mystery. Thus the blindness of the Jews, the mystery mentioned in Romans 11.25, is certainly part of God's design. We might say the same for the mystery in 1 Corinthians 15.51: the resurrection of the dead at the parousia was equally part of God's great design in Christ. First Corinthians 4.1 seems to be very much in favour of the view that *ta mustēria* is simply an alternative way of referring to the one great *mustērion*, God's revelation in Christ.

As for Scroggs's cross-reference to Hebrews 5.11, this certainly has relevance, since we can in fact make a fairly accurate conjecture as to what that teaching would have contained. It would have been an elaboration of the role of Melchisedech, and would probably have presented him as an appearance of the pre-existent Christ in Israel's history;[13] in other words, it would have consisted of speculation about salvation history. Indeed it is salvation history that provides the theme which links together all these mysteries; we can see the link operating in Romans 11, where Paul goes on from the particular mystery of the blindness of the Jews in verse 25 to a review of the whole mystery of God's wisdom in verses 33-6. As we hope to show later, Romans 11.34-5 is much more closely concerned with God's action in Christ than most commentators have realized. But there is a connection here with our passage, since Paul quotes the same text from Isaiah 40.13 in 1 Corinthians 2.16. If, therefore, we are right in claiming that salvation history (God's overall design in Christ, running all through Israel's history and culminating in the cross and resurrection, though still to be consummated at the parousia) is the basic content of all Paul's references to God's wisdom and to the divine mystery, this must at least reduce the strong eschatological emphasis in Scroggs's account of the matter. The centre of God's design is the life, death, and resurrection of Jesus, and this is precisely where the powers were both misled and undeceived.

Conzelmann has some helpful comments on our passage written in 1965.[14] He suggests that here Paul is concentrating on the 'disappearing wisdom' of the Jewish tradition, that came to earth, was rejected, and is now only available to the elect. He writes: 'Paul, despite his dependence on the motifs of wisdom speculation, does not treat σοφία as a christological hypostasis concept', and he describes 1 Corinthians 2.6f as 'a transformation of the motif of the hidden wisdom'. He adds that 'in itself it is neither apocalyptic nor Gnostic'. We ought, therefore, following Conzelmann here, to reject the claim made by

The New Testament Interpretation of Scripture

Ackermann in 1966. He writes: 'It is not surprising that some attempt was made in the early Church to identify Jesus with Wisdom. Paul does this', and he gives a reference to 1 Corinthians 2.6f.[15] Van Roon has more recently confirmed the view of the passage which we adopt here.[16] He rejects the thesis, which he ascribes to Windisch, that Paul explicitly identified Christ with the wisdom of God. He agrees that Christ is 'the subject of the mysterium', and says that when Paul writes of *mustēria* they are not discrete secrets but are all part of God's design. And he concludes: 'God's hidden wisdom is . . . entirely concerned with Christ, and Christ's death on the cross is at the very heart of the matter.' Finally we should quote W. L. Knox on the subject, since he has devoted so much attention to Paul's relation to wisdom-speculation. He thinks that Paul transferred 'the person of the historical Jesus from the category of the heavenly Messiah of Palestinian Judaism and Christianity into that of the divine Wisdom which was the centre of Hellenistic-Jewish speculation, where the term Logos had not yet ousted it under the influence of Philo'.[17] He describes Jesus as 'the wisdom of God which has been hidden even from the spiritual rulers of the universe, who in their ignorance had crucified the Lord of glory, but who [sic] was now made manifest by the revelation of the secret purposes of God: the word "mystery" here retained its proper Jewish sense of divine secret, hitherto concealed, but now revealed.' Later on, discussing Paul's use of 'mystery', he says: 'The other uses of the term in his writings (not including the Pastorals) all fall under the rabbinical usages of a divine revelation, usually of the revelation of God made in Christ.' We must bear in mind that these words were written before the discovery of the Qumran documents with their frequent use of *raz* for a divine secret revealed to the elect. This view of Knox's goes further towards identifying Christ with the wisdom of God than we would wish to go. But he does rightly hold that the 'wisdom of God in a mystery' is none other than the event of the life, death, and resurrection of Christ.[18]

Why then did the powers fail to recognize 'God's wisdom in a mystery', and what precisely was it that they failed to recognize? At this point we encounter a remarkable agreement between traditionalists and radicals. Both groups answer these questions thus: 'The powers failed to recognize the Lord of glory because his divinity was concealed by his humanity.' This is of course the apparent scriptural basis for the theory so popular among the Fathers which may be called 'the deception of the devil'. The devil eagerly grasped the opportunity of killing a sinless man, Jesus Christ, but was then frustrated by discovering that he was also the immortal Word who could not be destroyed. Thus, we find Weiss writing that Jesus's δόξα was 'hidden beneath the human guise'. E. Evans seems to find the beginning of the Chalcedonian doctrine of two natures here when he writes of the powers: 'They thought of Christ as a mere man, and so contrived what was intended to be his end but actually became the beginning of their own.'[19] In the same vein Allo gives quite a full account of the psychology of the supernatural powers; they recognized in Jesus, he says, a great prophet who fulfilled the messianic prophecies; but they did not see in him the Invincible himself. And Bultmann, entirely in line with this, writes: 'The Gnostic idea that Christ's earthly garment of flesh was the disguise in consequence of which the world-rulers failed to recognize him – for if they had recognized him they would not have brought about their own defeat by causing his crucifixion – lurks behind 1 Cor. 2.8.'[20]

But other commentators are more cautious: thus Wilckens, though he says of Christ 'he had hidden his true form', adds later 'in Christ God was acting'.[21] This is valuable as suggesting that what the powers missed was not just the god hidden under the human appearance, but the action of God carried out by means of the cross. Delling is aware of both interpretations, for he writes of the powers: 'In ignorance of God's plan of salvation they treated the Lord of glory as their prey', but adds in a footnote that it might have been in ignorance of Christ's divinity.[22] Best of all is C. K. Barrett, who writes: 'From the beginning it was God's purpose to redeem mankind through Christ, and paradoxical, self-giving wisdom was always the mark of his purpose.'[23] He adds that Paul means either that the powers did not understand God's design or that they failed to recognize Christ as the agent of God's salvation. But he rightly sees that the two come to much the same thing: 'Whether in outline or in the details of its operation, God's wisdom operates through sacrificial and self-giving love, and this was contradictory to the nature of the rulers.' Héring comes to the same conclusion when he says that the powers killed Christ because he was introducing into the world a new force, the love of God.[24]

This is no mere quibble. The question of why the powers failed to recognize Christ is important because it may throw light on the next problem we have to investigate, whether we have here the myth of the descending redeemer. It is relevant to point out that Paul, taking his cue from a strong tradition in Judaism, regarded the powers as fallen angels. They had fallen through disobedience, and this, as Barrett implies, explains why they failed to recognize the wisdom of God in Christ's career. It was a moral failure, not a mere case of mistaken identity, or a failure to penetrate the divine incognito. Indeed it is very questionable whether 'the divine incognito' adequately expresses what Paul means here. When we take into account the language he has used in the previous chapter about the 'weakness' and the 'foolishness' of God as manifested in the cross, we can understand that for those who have eyes of faith the cross was the revelation of God, not his veiling. Because they were disobedient the powers failed to realize that the humanity revealed the divinity. In other words, what the powers failed to recognize was God revealed in weakness. Here then is no disguise or incognito, but the peculiar wisdom of God which he has revealed to us (Christians) by means of the Spirit (2.10).

Several scholars have concluded that we have in this passage the myth of the descending redeemer. This belief is witnessed to in a number of sources all later than Paul's day; it describes the heavenly redeemer as having descended from the celestial sphere in order to gather together and bring back to heaven the elect (or even the scattered members of his body). In so doing he passed through the various intermediary spheres ruled by angels or superhuman powers, and disguised himself in various ways as he passed through, so that he was not recognized. Finally he reascended with the elect and triumphantly displayed his true form to the powers. Bousset, in an article published more than half a century ago, argued that the *descensus* theme can be found in Paul, notably in such passages as Romans 10.7f and 1 Corinthians 2.5-6.[25] In this version of the myth the redeemer descends to the underworld and overcomes the hostile powers there. Bousset is ready to concede that the Christian form of the myth may have transferred the struggle from Hades to the heavenly sphere; and he is uncertain whether Paul was the first to apply the myth to Christ or whether this had already been done in pre-Pauline Christianity. As an example of a version of the myth in which the redeemer passes through the spheres of the hostile powers unrecognized, he quotes *The Ascension of Isaiah*. Bultmann, on the other hand, argues against the view that in the Pauline literature we can find the concept of a descent into the underworld, on the grounds that Paul's mythology in this respect is Gnostic, and for Gnosticism the material world itself was the lowest and most degraded sphere.[26] He maintains therefore that the phrase in Ephesians 4.9, *ta katōtera merē tēs gēs*, means 'this degraded world' and not 'the underworld'. Similarly Schmithals, without mentioning our passage specifically, argues that behind Paul's 'Christ mysticism' lies the myth of the redeemer coming to collect his scattered members.[27] Wilckens also maintains that 1 Corinthians 2 betrays the existence in Paul's mind of the Gnostic concept of the *descensus* of the redeemer.[28]

We must here carefully define what we mean by 'descent'. It seems to me very likely indeed that Paul did hold a doctrine of a *descensus ad inferos* on the part of Christ. It appears to be implied in the midrash on Deuteronomy 30.11-14 which we find in Romans 10.6-8. The discovery of the full text of the Palestinian Targum has now made it clear that very early rabbinic exegesis connected these verses in Deuteronomy with Moses' ascent of Mount Sinai to receive the Torah and Jonah's descent into the abyss when engaged on God's service. It is a very probable conclusion that Paul saw both Moses and Jonah in this respect as types of Christ, in which case he certainly did believe that Christ had descended into the underworld.[29] It would naturally follow that Ephesians 4.9-10 does refer to Christ's *descensus ad inferos* and that Bultmann is mistaken in finding here a gnosticizing reference to the degraded material world. But what is in question in 1 Corinthians 2.6-10 is not a *descensus ad inferos*; it is the suggestion that behind this passage lies the myth of the redeemer who disguised himself in order to pass through the intermediary spheres and arrive at this inferior world. I confess that I cannot see any trace of such a *descensus* in this passage. The whole point, according to Paul, is that the powers failed to recognize what was happening in the earthly life of Christ. If the language of myth is to be used, it can only be called 'the myth of the descended redeemer'. There is no suggestion here of any disguise adopted during the descent from heaven, or indeed of any descent from heaven at all. One might here well refer to W. L. Knox's discussion of this question.³⁰ He writes 'but the Pauline explanation [sc. that the rulers failed to recognize Jesus] was obviously a natural way out of the difficulty involved in the crucifixion of Jesus by the "rulers" on earth. If they could crucify him on earth, where his death could effect the redemption of man, their prisoner, why had they not opposed him on his descent, and so prevented him from delivering mankind?' Thus Knox would seem to commit himself to the view that a disguised descent is implied in 1 Corinthians 2.6-8. However, on the next page he points out that what Paul is concerned to say is not that Jesus came down from heaven through the planetary spheres, but that the rulers 'did not understand God's purpose, which is known to every Christian'. The evidence therefore seems to point to the conclusion that Paul is here thinking of the non-recognition of Christ on earth because of his humility, and that the question of his descent does not arise.

The champions of the 'myth of the descending redeemer' draw their primary evidence from two sources, both at least a generation after Paul's death. The first consists of a passage from Ignatius's Epistles, Ephesians XIX, part of which we will reproduce here:

And the virginity of Mary and her child-bearing escaped the notice of the ruler of this age (*ton archonta tou aiōnos toutou*), likewise also the death of the Lord – three mysteries worthy of acclamation which were carried out in the silence of God ⟨τρία μυστήρια κραυγῆς ἅτινα ἐν ἡσυχίᾳ θεοῦ ἐπράχθη⟩.³¹ How therefore was it manifested to the aeons? ⟨πῶς οὖν ἐφανερώθη τοῖς αἰῶσιν;⟩ A star in heaven outshone all the other stars ... Consequently every form of magic and every bond was destroyed, the ignorance of malice disappeared, the old kingdom was torn down, since God was appearing as man ⟨θεοῦ ἀνθρωπίνως φανερουμένου⟩ for the purpose of newness of eternal life.³²

A Quasi-Gnostic Pauline Midrash: 1 Corinthians 2.6-16

Daniélou says of this passage: 'It is concerned with a *descensus* of the Word, hidden from the angels.'³³ As we shall be seeing, he connects it with a passage from *The Ascension of Isaiah* where there certainly is a *descensus* of the Word hidden from the angels. Now I cannot detect in this passage from Ignatius any suggestion of a descent in disguise such as Daniélou discovers here. What the devil failed to observe was three events: the virgin conception, the actual birth, and the death of Christ, all events taking place on this earth. Presumably what he failed to perceive about the conception was that it was a virginal conception taking place according to God's promise; and what he missed about both the birth and the death was that they were events of which God the Word was the subject. What we have here in fact is the traditional orthodox idea of Christ as God incognito, but not as far as I can judge a *descent* in disguise. The phrase θεοῦ ἀνθρωπίνως φανερουμένου would seem to point in this direction: it seems to indicate the beginnings of a two-nature Christology of which there are other traces in Ignatius.

It may be that Ignatius's emphasis on the divine silence in which these events took place has suggested a Gnostic type of *descensus*. Thus in Ephesians xv.1 he writes: 'There is therefore one teacher who spoke and it came to pass; and what he did in silence is worthy of the Father.' The reference is certainly to Psalm 33.9:

> For he spoke, and it came to be;
> he commanded, and it stood fast.

Camelot is no doubt right as against Lightfoot in seeing here a reference to the Word as the agent of creation.³⁴ Parallel to this is Ignatius's description of Christ in Magnesians vIII as 'the Word of the Father proceeding from silence', ⟨ὅς ἐστιν αὐτοῦ ⟨sc. τοῦ πατρός⟩ Λόγος ἀπὸ σιγῆς προελθών⟩. Since *sigē* was one of the aeons in later Gnosticism, some have seen a Gnostic element here. But it seems more likely that Ignatius is expressing an 'economic' doctrine of the godhead: the Word was 'quiescent' in the godhead before the creation of the world. At the creation he came forth from the Father (or the Father put him forth) for the purpose of creation. So the reference to the 'three mysteries that were carried out in the stillness of God' in Ephesians xIx is probably intended to link these events with the original creation, presenting them as a new creation.

The Gnostics tended to identify *sigē* with the primordial silence of the ineffable Father. Since any abstract noun in Gnosticism is liable to turn into an aeon, this did happen with *sigē*. Thus according to Irenaeus in the Valentinian system the pre-existent perfect aeon is called *Buthos*. He produced from himself a seed and deposited it in the womb of *Sigē*. She became pregnant and brought forth *Nous*. The *Nous* it was that produced the *Logos*. Here is the *Logos* coming forth from Silence at two removes (see Foerster, op. cit., vol. I, p.127). A similar lineage is found in the system of Marcus the Gnostic as related by Irenaeus: the aeon *Sigē* produced the first tetrad, which in its turn produced Jesus (ibid., p.208). Marcus, it is claimed, was addressed by his disciples thus: 'O thou that sittest beside God and the eternal, mystical silence . . .' (ibid., p.202). Epiphanius (op. cit., p.235) confirms that Valentinus called the thought (*Ennoia*) within the ineffable Father *Sigē*. Subsequently *Sigē* married a second Ogdoad and produced a litter of aeons. In the *Letter of Eugnostos* (Foerster, vol. II, p.34) we read 'the immortal man has a consort *Sophia*, who is also called *Sigē*'. It looks as if the original concept of an 'economic' Dyad, i.e. that the Father produced the Word from himself probably at the creation of the world, has been taken over by the Gnostics and worked into their elaborate systems. Ignatius is not being a Gnostic; he is merely using terms and concepts which were later taken over and assimilated by Gnostics.

One of Daniélou's reasons for claiming that there is in Ignatius a doctrine of a disguised descent is Ignatius's reference to the various hierarchies and dispositions of angels in Trallians V: 'I can perceive the heavenly things, and the dispositions of the angels, and the groupings of the archons, things visible and invisible.' If Ignatius believed he knew how the various angelic forces were placed in the celestial spheres it is not difficult to imagine that he thought of the redeemer as having passed through these spheres on his way to earth. But this does not necessarily follow. Ignatius does not make any use of the special knowledge which he asserts he possesses, and does not base any claim on it. In this respect he reminds us of Paul: Paul also says that he was snatched up to the third heaven and heard words that must not be uttered (see 2 Corinthians 12.1-4). But he is very careful not to integrate these experiences into his system of doctrine and not to base any claim on them. It seems likely that this sort of angelology was regarded in the early Church as a legitimate form of speculation, as long as it was not presented as part of the substance of the faith.

H. Schlier in *Religionsgeschichtliche Untersuchungen zu den Ignatiusbriefen* (Giessen 1929, in *ZNWT*, Beiheft 8) has argued the case for a markedly Gnostic background for Ignatius (pp. 28-30). Like Daniélou, he believes that *The Ascension of Isaiah* lies behind Ephesians XIX. All his parallels to Ignatius are drawn from later literature. But he presses strongly the view that the star to which Ignatius refers in this passage is not the star which the magi are described as following in Matthew's Gospel, but an independent star which, he claims, is actually identified with the descending redeemer, a view which is not actually repudiated by J. B. Lightfoot in his commentary on Ignatius's Epistles, and for which there is certainly evidence in later literature. If this is the case, however, we must point out that it entirely destroys the case for the view that in Ephesians XIX we have an example of the myth of the disguised descent of the redeemer. Far from being disguised, the star in its passage through the region of the air advertises its presence by its brightness and receives the homage of the other stars. I think myself that it is misleading to apply to Ignatius the categories of myths and concepts which only came to full fruition in later literature.

The second of the sources from which the primary evidence about the disguised descent of the redeemer is drawn is the work known as *The Ascension of Isaiah*. This is a composite work consisting of three parts, *The Martyrdom of Isaiah*, *The Testament of Hezekiah*, and *The Vision of Isaiah*. We are only concerned with the last of these, which comprises chapters vi.1-xi.40 in Charles's edition of the work.[35] *The Vision of Isaiah* is a Christian work which Charles dates at 'the close of the first century A.D.', though the three parts were probably only put together in the third century A.D. In this work we undoubtedly encounter the myth of the disguised descent of the redeemer. We will quote the relevant parts in Charles's translation: ix.13-15: 'And they will think that he is flesh and is a man. And the god of that world will stretch forth his hand against the Son and they will crucify him and slay him not knowing who he is.' Then in x.8 the Father commands the pre-existent Christ to go and descend to our world, being careful to adapt his appearance to that of each of the angels of the five heavens through which he must pass. In x.17f the Lord descends through the heavens and alters himself accordingly, giving the password at each heaven. Then in xi.16 occur the words:

> This [sc. the child's manner of birth] hath escaped all the heavens and all the princes and all the gods of this world.

In xi.23f the Lord reascends but not in his human form. As he passes through each heaven the angels there ask how it was that they did not perceive his descent. Charles claims that xi.16f is the source lying behind the passage we have quoted from Ignatius's Letter to the Ephesians xix. He writes: 'Throughout x.8-xi.19 the concealment of the real nature of Christ is the entire theme, and as a subordinate factor of this the concealment of Mary's virginity. In the Epistle of Ignatius, on the other hand, the subject is introduced abruptly and obviously forms part of a received doctrine, such as is presented in our text.'[36] He goes on to suggest that, though Ignatius took his 'concealment' doctrine from *The Vision of Isaiah*, he was anxious to repudiate the Docetic tendencies which one could detect in it. Charles adds that the source of the speculation to be found in this work is to be traced to 1 Corinthians 2.7-8. But he does not suggest either that Paul held a 'God incognito' Christology or that Ignatius necessarily held the doctrine of the disguised descent which he found in *The Vision of Isaiah*. By contrast Daniélou believes that the doctrine of the disguised descent of the Saviour lies behind all three works, 1 Corinthians 2, Ephesians xix, and *The Vision of Isaiah*.[37] He is confident that *The Vision of Isaiah* is earlier than Ignatius and that it has influenced him (p.13). Altaner in his *Patrologie* is content to place *The Ascension of Isaiah* in the second century without being more specific.[38]

It is difficult to decide on the question of priority between *The Vision of Isaiah* and Ignatius. Charles's argument is impressive, but Ignatius is not a writer whose thought flows evenly, and the fact that a subject is introduced suddenly does not

A Quasi-Gnostic Pauline Midrash: 1 Corinthians 2.6-16

necessarily imply that it is borrowed from a more closely woven narrative. The author of *The Vision of Isaiah* might have borrowed an idea from Ignatius and embroidered it. One could fairly put the relationship of these three passages to each other in the following way as far as Christology is concerned:

Paul: the powers fail to recognize God's design revealed in Christ.

Ignatius: the powers fail to recognize God rendered incognito in the humanity of Christ.

Vision of Isaiah: Christ deliberately disguises himself as he passes through the angelic spheres, and on earth deliberately hides his divinity by means of his humanity.[39]

As far as development of thought goes, one would naturally conclude that Paul was the original, that Ignatius modified Paul to the extent of turning his profound concept of the divinity revealed by means of the humanity into a 'God incognito' Christology, and that the author of *The Vision of Isaiah* gnosticized the entire schema by introducing for the first time the idea of a disguised descent and a humanity which was a mere veil cast over the divinity. But even if Charles and Daniélou are right about the priority of *The Vision of Isaiah* over Ignatius, this does not mean that Ignatius held a doctrine of a disguised descent. If he could reject the Docetism of *The Vision of Isaiah* he could also reject the notion of a disguised descent.[40]

The doctrine of the descent and ascent of the redeemer is found in later Gnosticism. Irenaeus claims that in the system which he attributes to Simon Magus *Ennoia* descended and was caught by the angels and entrapped in a series of physical bodies. Then Simon himself 'descended in transfigured form', looking like a man, though not in fact being a man (Foerster, vol. I, p.30). According to Irenaeus also the Ophites taught that Christ, in order to descend into the man Jesus, 'descended through the seven heavens, became like their sons, and gradually emptied them of power' (ibid., p.92). Hippolytus in his *Refutation* refers to Docetists who describe the descent of the only-begotten Son among the aeons: he disguised himself as a lightning-flash and entered this world of darkness (ibid., pp.

310-11). All this suggests that the doctrine of the descent of the redeemer developed a hundred years after Paul's day, based no doubt on the Pauline doctrine of the mystery of the cross and the ascent of Christ after his resurrection. It does not suggest that Paul himself was a Gnostic in this respect.

There is another feature of *The Vision of Isaiah* that must be briefly disposed of. In the Slavonic and the Second Latin versions of *The Ascension of Isaiah* there occurs at xi.34 the following addition. We quote it in Latin:

> Sufficit tibi Ysaia; vidisti enim quod nemo vidit carnis filius, quod nec oculus vidit, nec auris audivit, nec in cor hominis ascendit, quanta praeparavit deus omnibus diligentibus se.
>
> (The Slavonic has the equivalent of 'eum').[41]

Wilckens was misled by this passage so as to conclude that the conflated citation of 1 Corinthians 2.9 already existed in Gnostic circles and was borrowed by Paul from there. Unfortunately Wilckens only used Dillmann's edition of *The Ascension of Isaiah* (Leipzig 1877) and did not therefore realize that the conflated citation in *The Vision of Isaiah* is in fact an interpolation into the original text and cannot be certainly dated earlier than about the middle of the fourth century A.D. The passage quoted above only occurs in the Second Latin and the Slavonic versions and is not found in the Ethiopic or Greek versions. As Charles well remarks: 'There is no reason for the omission by E [sc. Ethiopic version] or G [the First Greek version] of such a striking statement, but rather every reason for its inclusion.'[42] Feuillet agrees that this addition in the Latin is a later interpolation.[43] Thus *The Ascension of Isaiah* provides no evidence that the conflated citation of 1 Corinthians 2.9 was known in Jewish or Christian circles before Paul, still less that it is of Gnostic origin. We shall have to revert to this interpolated passage later on in a different context.

We have perhaps shown sufficient evidence to suggest that there is no idea of a disguised descent behind 1 Corinthians 2.6-8. We must now bring forward evidence which indicates that Paul may have been thinking rather in terms of an ascension. In a book published in 1965 I maintained that behind these verses lies a Christian (very probably Pauline) Midrash on Psalm 24.[44] In Psalm 24.7a and 9a the MT has $ś,'w ś'ārym$

A Quasi-Gnostic Pauline Midrash: 1 Corinthians 2.6-16

rā'šēykem, which means 'Lift up, oh gates, your heads'. But the LXX has mistranslated this with ἄρατε πύλας, οἱ ἄρχοντες ὑμῶν 'Your rulers, lift up your gates' (LXX Psalm 23.7,9). The source of the mistranslation is obvious: the LXX translator has mistakenly rendered rā'šēykem as 'your leaders', a meaning which it could bear. But the consequence is that a group called *hoi archontes* is brought on the scene, exactly the phrase which Paul uses for the elemental powers. The rulers are urged to let the king of glory in. They ask who this king of glory is, and they are answered that he is *kurios tōn dunameōn*. Now *dunamis* is a word which Paul also uses for the elemental powers: see Romans 8.38; 1 Corinthians 15.24, and cf. Ephesians 1.21. If therefore he read this psalm in a Greek version which had the same rendering as our LXX, he would see in it a prophecy of what was to happen to the *ascended* Christ. The Lord of glory enters heaven and is now recognized by the powers who failed to recognize him on earth.

It is interesting to observe that Aquila has corrected the mistranslation of the LXX. He renders the verse with

ἄρατε, πύλαι, κεφαλὰς ὑμῶν,
καὶ ἐπάρθητε, ἀνοίγματα αἰώνια.

But the other two non-LXX versions, Symmachus and Theodotion, preserve the LXX mistranslation. Theodotion's translation is identical with that of the LXX, but Symmachus offers

μετάρατε πύλας, οἱ ἄρχοντες ὑμῶν,
ὑψωθήτησαν δὲ αἱ πύλαι αἱ αἰώνιοι.

This suggests that the tradition which found a reference to supernatural powers in this verse was a strong one. Only Aquila, anxious perhaps to remove a source of possible Christian interpretation, rejects it.

A hundred years after Paul's day we have evidence that Psalm 24 was interpreted in this way in Christian circles. Justin in his *Dialogue with Trypho* is challenged by Trypho to prove that Christ was declared in prophecy to be king and priest.[45] This is why Justin introduced Psalm 24. But Justin replies that he will first show that Christ is both *theos* and *kurios tōn dunameōn*; he will show that Jewish interpreters are wrong in claiming that this psalm belongs to the moment when Solomon was about to bring the ark of the covenant within the newly completed temple. He quotes the psalm in its LXX version, which of course favours his interpretation.[46] He argues that plainly Solomon cannot be called *kurios tōn dunameōn*. The truth is, says Justin, that when 'our Christ rose from the dead and ascended into heaven the rulers in the heavens appointed by God are commanded to open the gates of heaven, that he who is the king of glory may enter in and take his seat at the right hand of the Father'. He continues: 'For when the rulers in heaven saw that he had a disfigured and dishonoured appearance, not recognizing him they inquired, "Who is this king of glory?" And the Holy Spirit, either in the person of the Father or in his own person, replies, "The Lord of hosts, he is the king of glory." Now anyone must admit that none of those who had charge of the gates of the sanctuary in Jerusalem would have dared to say about Solomon, no matter how glorious a king he was, nor about the ark of the covenant, "Who is the king of glory?"' In §85, p.288 we have a reference to the same argument, only adding the fact that the *archontes* are *aggeloi kai dunameis*.[47]

We cannot claim that Justin's interpretation is identical with that which I have attributed to Paul. Justin's angels, for example, are not hostile, as Paul's are; they are appointed by God. It is interesting to note that in Justin's version the risen and ascended Christ retains his disfigured appearance, presumably disfigured by the cross. Thus in Justin as in Paul the difficulty which the powers have in recognizing the Lord of glory does not stem directly from his humanity but from his humility, consummated in the cross.

The *Dialogue with Trypho* is in fact the earliest evidence we possess for the traditional rabbinic exposition of Psalm 24. But it is amply confirmed by somewhat later evidence from the Talmud. Thus in *Tractate Shabbath* we read that when Solomon had built the temple he wanted to bring the ark into the holy of holies.[48] But the gates shut in front of him. He exclaimed, 'Lift up your heads, oh ye gates . . .' 'They rushed upon him to swallow him up, crying, Who is the king of glory? Solomon answered, "The Lord, strong and mighty".' This seems to have stopped their attack, but they would not open until he uttered the verse, 'Oh Lord, turn not away the face of thine anointed, remember the good deeds of David thy servant.' Apart from the confirmation which this provides for Trypho's interpretation of the psalm, this version is interesting because it endows the gates with life and purpose, almost as if they were viewed as the *archontes* of Justin's version. Also, the gates will only open for the anointed. Do we have here the vestige of an originally messianic interpretation of the psalm within Judaism itself?

The *Midrash on the Psalms* reflects this interpretation but it also provides a number of alternative interpretations.[49] 'Who shall ascend unto the hill of the Lord?' is applied to Moses, Abraham, and Jacob.[50] There is also a tendency to associate the phrase 'the king of glory' with the presence of God in the ark and in the pillar of cloud, an interpretation which would have been welcome to early Christians, since they liked to identify the pre-existent Christ with both these divine manifestations. Rabbi Hezekiah by means of an elaborate midrash which we need not reproduce, interpreted the words 'Who is the king of glory?' to mean 'Who is this king who gives a portion of his glory to them that fear him?' This is not so very far from what Paul is saying in 1 Corinthians 2.6-10.

We meet a very similar tradition in the Latin interpolation in *The Vision of Isaiah* to which we have referred above. It comes at xi.23 and runs as follows:

> Et vidi ascendentem in firmamentum qui non erat secundum formam transfigurans se. Et videntes omnes angeli, qui erant super firmamento, expaverunt et adorantes dicebant: Quomodo ascendisti in medio nostri, domine? et non cognovimus regem gloriae?

> And I saw rising up into the firmament one who was not according to their appearance, who was transfiguring himself. And all the angels who were above the firmament, when they saw him, were greatly afraid, and worshipping him they said: How hast thou ascended into our midst, Lord, and we did not recognize the king of glory?[51]

The Slavonic version, instead of 'How hast thou ascended?' has 'How did the Lord in our midst escape our notice?' Charles believes that the Latin is corrupt and that it should read

'Quomodo descendisti?' But in view of the parallel in Justin we need not necessarily adopt this conjecture. The Latin interpolator may have intended the scene to be an ascension, as Justin (and, I believe, Paul) does. This interpolation seems to come from the middle of the fourth century A.D. (it was known to Jerome). But it does witness to a traditional connection between a Christian interpretation of Psalm 24 and the ascension or else with a disguised appearance of Christ on earth.

A final witness to this tradition can be found in a work referred to by Daniélou called the *Physiologus*. It belongs apparently to the end of the fourth century A.D. and was wrongly attributed to Epiphanius.[52] In it the descent of the Saviour is described as taking place in such a way that the angels did not recognize him: 'They did not recognize him in his descent from on high, and said "Who is this king of glory?" Then the Holy Spirit answered: "The Lord of hosts, he is the king of glory".' This is set in the context of a descent, but in fact the words of the psalm would fit an ascension much better.

All that Paul says about the powers in the passage in 1 Corinthians 2 which we are studying is that they failed to recognize God in Christ on earth and most particularly on the cross. Presumably, however, Paul believes that they were undeceived at some point of time subsequent to the cross, since in 2.6 he describes the powers as 'doomed to pass away' ($\kappa\alpha\tau\alpha\rho\gamma\text{ου}\mu\acute{\epsilon}\nu\omega\nu$). The only point at which this undeceiving can have happened is at the Son's resurrection-ascension. If we are right in suggesting that behind this passage lies an interpretation of Psalm 24, this must be the case. At any rate it is more likely in the nature of things that Paul should come to the concept of the powers' failure to recognize Christ by means of a midrash on Scripture rather than by direct borrowing from Gnosticism (even if a system deserving that name existed in Paul's day). Naturally Paul's tradition of interpreting Psalm 24 may itself have been influenced by wisdom-speculation within Judaism itself.

If the resurrection was the moment of undeception, we can appreciate better why Ephesians 3.10 has 'that through the Church the manifold wisdom of God might now be made known to the principalities and powers in the heavenly places $\langle\tau\alpha\hat{\imath}\varsigma\ \dot{\alpha}\rho\chi\alpha\hat{\imath}\varsigma\ \kappa\alpha\grave{\imath}\ \tau\alpha\hat{\imath}\varsigma\ \dot{\epsilon}\xi\text{ου}\sigma\acute{\imath}\alpha\iota\varsigma\ \dot{\epsilon}\nu\ \tau\text{ο}\hat{\imath}\varsigma\ \dot{\epsilon}\pi\text{ου}\rho\alpha\nu\acute{\imath}\text{οι}\varsigma\rangle$'. The Church exists in the realm of the Spirit – the Spirit was the new dimen-

A Quasi-Gnostic Pauline Midrash: 1 Corinthians 2.6-16

sion into which Christ rose from the dead. This is where his triumph over the powers is to be made known. The author of Ephesians is completing the story which Paul began in 1 Corinthians 2.6-8, or bringing into clear expression what is implicit there.[53]

2

Before dealing directly with the mysterious citation in 1 Corinthians 2.9, we must examine a very popular solution of the problem posed by this citation, that is the theory that Paul is not quoting Scripture at all but has drawn his text from an unknown apocryphon which he regarded as scriptural. The remarkable divergence between the texts which Paul quotes and the nearest equivalent texts in canonical Scripture makes this seem at first sight an attractive suggestion. But, apart from the fact that good reasons can be produced to account for this divergence, a number of other weighty considerations can be brought forward which ought in future to relegate this theory to the lumber room.

The first person to have mentioned the possibility that Paul is quoting an apocryphal work seems to have been Origen, who suggested that Paul was quoting from the apocryphal writings of Elijah.

As this view has been accepted by many scholars, it is worth while referring to the context in Origen. In his homilies on Matthew, Origen, à propos Matthew 27.9, contends that either there has been a copyist's mistake whereby 'Jeremiah' was written for 'Zechariah', or that there exists some secret writing of Jeremiah which contains the passage about the thirty pieces of silver. To support this last conjecture he points to 1 Corinthians 2.9: 'Quoniam Apostolus scripturas quasdam secretorum profert, sicut dicit alicubi *Quod oculus non vidit, nec auris audivit*: in nullo enim regulari libro hoc positum invenitur, nisi in secretis Eliae prophetae' ('Now the Apostle refers to certain writings of apocryphal books, as he says in another place, *what eye has not seen nor ear heard*. This phrase is not found written in any canonical book, but only in apocryphal writings of the prophet Elijah').[1] We must observe that Origen's reference is vague. He does not name the book; it seems very unlikely that

43

he had read it. He goes on to refer to another apocryphal book which he thinks is mentioned in 2 Timothy 3.8; this he says is called 'The Book of Jannes and Mambres'. We cannot help contrasting his definiteness here with his vagueness in referring to Elijah's book. Also he can hardly have studied 1 Corinthians 2.9 very carefully, since the words he quotes *do* occur in canonical Scripture.

This suggestion has, however, been taken up by a succession of scholars, sometimes, one cannot help suspecting, because it is so much easier a solution than one which entails the labour of trying to trace what are the passages in canonical Scripture which Paul appears to be quoting. Thus Schmiedel accepts that it comes from *The Apocalypse of Elijah*.[2] Lietzmann takes for granted that a lost apocryphal work is the source of the quotation.[3] O. Michel adopts the same opinion,[4] and so do Héring[5] and Conzelmann.[6] This last scholar, however, seems to adopt it less for its intrinsic merit than because there does not seem to him to be any other solution. We have already observed that Wilckens believed the citation comes from a Gnostic source.[7]

A preliminary objection to this 'unknown apocryphon' theory is that Paul introduces the citation with *kathōs gegraptai*. This surely suggests that he believes he is quoting Scripture. But could he have regarded any apocryphal writing (let alone one which has received so little acclaim from anyone else that it either has not survived or cannot be identified) as Scripture? It seems most unlikely. This consideration alone is enough to convince Oepke that the 'unknown apocryphon' theory is wrong.[8] G. Schrenk seems to doubt the possibility of this theory on the same grounds.[9]

However, in 1974, E. von Nordheim claimed with some hesitation that he might have identified the unknown apocryphon in which the quotation originally occurred, and which Paul was therefore quoting.[10] He begins by pointing out that two short works survive in fragmentary form, *The Apocalypse of Elijah* and *The Book of Elijah*, in neither of which is there any trace of this quotation. But he then draws attention to a small work called *The Testament of Jacob*, preserved in Arabic, Coptic, and Ethiopic. A passage occurs in the account of Jacob's journey up to heaven in which the patriarch is shown the place of the righteous dead. I give my own translation of Nordheim's rendering into German of the Coptic version:

> And he showed me all the places of rest with all good things which are prepared for the righteous, and those things which no eye has seen, nor ear has heard, and which have not occurred to the hearts of men, those things which God has prepared for those who will love him, and for those who will perform his will on earth; that is to say, if they end well inasmuch as they do his will.

Nordheim admits that *The Testament of Jacob* as we have it is a Christian work of the middle of the fourth century, but he claims that it has a Jewish kernel: the Christian redactor has confined himself to altering the beginning and the ending. He concludes that we cannot be sure Paul is quoting from this work, but that it remains a possibility.

Alas for the ephemeral nature of scholarship! Only a year later there appeared in the same journal a refutation of this modest suggestion from von Otfried Hofius.[11] He says that he had himself already noted the citation as occurring in *The Testament of Jacob* in a work of his already in print. But he rejects von Nordheim's thesis on the grounds that *The Testament of Jacob* is a Christian work which makes use of Christian themes throughout. He claims to find echoes in it of 1 Corinthians 6.9; Romans 1.30; Revelation 21.8; 22.15. He also finds echoes of the Synoptic Gospels and Hebrews. He argues that the citation in *The Testament of Jacob* is taken from 1 Corinthians 2.9, and he concludes with the words: 'The question whence Paul himself has taken the utterance quoted from him remains still, as before, unanswered.' We may, I think, regard von Nordheim's tentative suggestion as having been decisively disproved.

One way in which the 'unknown apocryphon' theory has been supported has been by means of the quotations of 1 Corinthians 2.9 which occur in early Christian works. The argument is that, because these works do not reproduce the citation in exactly the same form as that in which it occurs in Paul, they must be quoting it not from 1 Corinthians, but from its original source, whatever that was. We must therefore devote some attention to these citations in order to decide whether this argument is well founded.

We may first refer to a citation in *The Gospel of Thomas*, logion 17:

Jesus said: I will give you what eye has not seen and what ear has not heard and what hand has not touched, and (what) has not arisen in the heart of man.[12]

Guillamont describes the codex of *The Gospel of Thomas* as dating from the second half of the fourth century A.D. He writes that the 'primitive text . . . must have been produced in Greek about A.D. 140 . . . and was based on much earlier sources' (p. vi). Here Jesus himself is represented as being the author of the citation; the same attribution occurs in *The Acts of Peter* 39. M. R. James claims that this work was written 'not later than 200 A.D. in Greek' (see his *The Apocryphal New Testament* (Oxford 1924), p. 300). On the basis of the last citation, Resch in 1889 suggested that the citation does actually go back to Jesus and is an *agraphon*. But this suggestion has received no acceptance from others. The text looks like a loose quotation of 1 Corinthians 2.9ab with the addition of the phrase 'what hand has not touched', an embroidery of the author. He certainly understands the quotation in a futuristic sense; for in logion 18 the disciples respond by saying, 'Tell us how our end will be.'

The citation also occurs in I and II Clement.[13] We may note at this point that the citation in 1 Corinthians 2.9, on any account of its origin, is a conflated one. The phrase καὶ ἐπὶ καρδίαν ἀνθρώπου οὐκ ἀνέβη can be traced in Scripture, whatever may be said of the rest of the quotation. This in itself goes some way to undermine the thesis that Paul is quoting from an apocryphal work. One of the attractions of this theory is that it seems to make short work of the labour of tracing Paul's question back to its scriptural source. If we have to do this anyway for 1 Corinthians 2.9b, is it likely that Paul has quoted half a verse from an unknown apocryphon, combining it with a piece of genuine Scripture? Or must we imagine that the author of the apocryphon effected the combination and that Paul, so to speak, threw the mantle of Scripture over the non-scriptural element provided by the apocryphal writer? Whatever such a theory does, it does not simplify matters.

The citation in I Clement occurs in 34.8: Clement is exhort-

A Quasi-Gnostic Pauline Midrash: 1 Corinthians 2.6-16

ing his readers to look forward to being found worthy of God's promise in the end time:

> We therefore, being gathered together harmoniously with one purpose, let us resolutely cry to him as with one mouth that we may become partakers of his great and glorious promises. For he says [or it says], λέγει γὰρ ὀφθαλμὸς οὐκ εἶδεν καὶ οὖς οὐκ ἤκουσεν, καὶ ἐπὶ καρδίαν ἀνθρώπου οὐκ ἀνέβη, ὅσα ἡτοίμασεν τοῖς ὑπομένουσιν αὐτόν.[14]

The only way in which Clement differs from Paul's version of the citation is that he writes *tois hupomenousin auton*, thus agreeing with the LXX version, rather than Paul's *tois agapōsin auton*. Clement sees the quotation as applying to the world to come; in 35.3 he explains that the Father has prepared these wonderful things for those who remain steadfast in the faith. Indeed he probably has the parousia in mind, for he writes in 35.4: 'Let us strive to be found in the number of those who await him.' The fact that Clement apparently corrects Paul's quotation by means of the LXX translation is evidence against the theory that Clement took the whole passage from an apocryphal work. Clement at least thought it came from Isaiah 64.3 and went to his Greek version in order to correct Paul.

D. A. Hagner has given considerable attention to Clement's quotation here.[15] He argues strongly that Clement is quoting directly from 1 Corinthians 2.9 and not from any other source: 'It can be seen that Clement's text is almost identical with that of 1 Corinthians.' He points out that Codex C of Clement's Letter actually reads *tois agapōsin auton*, but maintains, no doubt rightly, that this text has been corrected by Paul's. He rejects the suggestion that Paul uses the quotation in a sense quite different to Clement's (a point to which we must revert later). He concludes: 'Thus there is no reason why Clement's application of the quotation may not have been readily derived from 1 Corinthians 2.' He is a strong champion of the view that the quotations of 1 Corinthians 2.9 in the Apostolic Fathers and later patristic writings all derive from Paul. He says: 'Indeed, it is futile to argue that they do not trace back to 1 Cor. 2.9 when pre-Pauline evidence for the citation in its present form is totally lacking.' He argues that Paul can use

The New Testament Interpretation of Scripture

kathōs gegraptai elsewhere for loose quotations from the canonical Scriptures and refers to Romans 9.33; 10.6-8; 14.11. His final word is that Paul's departure from the LXX of Isaiah 64.3 'may possibly be due to a free handling of the text in accordance with his own immediate purposes' (p. 208). We may well welcome this forthright rejection of the theory that Clement is quoting from a source other than Paul, without accepting all Hagner's conclusions. There is in fact one rabbinic work in which the citation occurs independently of Paul. Whether it is actually earlier than Paul, we must discuss later. Anyone who has studied Paul's use of Scripture must treat with reserve a phrase such as 'Paul's free handling of the text'. We have no justification for assuming that Paul had our LXX text before him. If he was intending to adapt the text to his own immediate purpose, he would have been better advised to substitute τοῖς πιστεύουσιν εἰς αὐτόν for the LXX τοῖς ὑπομένουσιν αὐτόν. I hope to show later on that a case can be made for the theory that Paul had τοῖς ἀγαπῶσιν αὐτόν in his Greek text of Isaiah 64.3.

The citation also occurs in II Clement; we find it in fact in two separate passages of this work. In 11.7 we read:

τὰς ἐπαγγελίας, ἃς οὖς οὐκ ἤκουσεν
οὐδὲ ὀφθαλμὸς εἶδεν, οὐδὲ ἐπὶ
καρδίαν ἀνθρώπου ἀνέβη.

If therefore we do righteousness before God, we will enter into his kingdom and receive the promises which ear has not heard nor eye seen nor has it occurred to the heart of man.

And 14.5 runs:

οὔτε ἐξειπεῖν τις δύναται οὔτε λαλῆσαι
ἃ ἡτοίμασεν ὁ κύριος τοῖς ἐκλεκτοῖς αὐτοῦ.

Such wonderful life and immortality can this flesh share if the Holy Spirit is joined to it. No one is able to declare or speak of the things which the Lord has prepared for his elect.[16]

The context is markedly eschatological; 12.1 has the exhortation: 'Let us therefore hourly expect the kingdom of God in love and righteousness, since we do not know the day of the appearance (*epiphaneias*) of God.' We should note Donfried's recent interesting suggestion that II Clement contains the

A Quasi-Gnostic Pauline Midrash: 1 Corinthians 2.6-16

answer which the Corinthian presbyters gave to Clement's letter.[17] If this is correct, II Clement is as early a witness as Clement is himself to Paul's quotation. It looks very much as if II Clement is not quoting independently but merely echoing I Clement. I do not think that his variant *tois eklektois autou* for LXX *tois hupomenousin auton* is to be taken as indicating a variant reading in whatever text of whatever work II Clement is supposed to be quoting. It is much more likely to be a paraphrase of I Clement's quotation. The whole sentence in XIV.5 looks like a loose paraphrase anyway. I cannot therefore agree with Donfried when he writes: 'It is likely that II Clement, 1 Cor. 2.9, and I Clement 34.8 are independently citing the same Greek version of the Old Testament.' He suggests that I Clement 34.8 stands closest to the original version; Paul, he suggests, altered *tois hupomenousin auton* to *tois agapōsin autou*, whereas II Clement altered it to *tois eklektois autou*. He even toys with the notion that the citation was originally put together in a lost apocalypse, but does not commit himself to it.[18] We must insist that Paul does not arbitrarily alter scriptural citations in order to suit the need of the moment, least of all when his particular (alleged) alteration does not exactly suit the need of the moment. A closer study of the MT version of Isaiah 64.3 would, I am sure, have convinced Donfried that Paul's reading is founded on something more solid than arbitrary preference.

Perhaps one should refer briefly to the citation in *The Martyrdom of Polycarp*.[19] The martyrs are described as 'seeing with the eyes of the heart the good things stored up for those who wait, which ear has not heard nor eye seen nor has it occurred to the heart of man':

> τὰ τηρούμενα τοῖς ὑπομένουσιν ἀγαθά,
> ἃ οὔτε οὖς ἤκουσεν οὔτε ὀφθαλμὸς εἶδεν
> οὔτε ἐπὶ καρδίαν ἀνθρώπου ἀνέβη.

We should note that this does not represent an alternative reading; the author echoes the LXX, and obviously believed that Isaiah 64.3 was the source of the citation: *ta tēroumena* is a paraphrase of Paul's *ha hētoimasen*. This reference is therefore quite close to that of I Clement in that he quotes Paul but corrects him by the LXX. This concurrence of I Clement and

The New Testament Interpretation of Scripture

The *Martyrdom of Polycarp* actually convinces Vollmer that the citation cannot have been taken from an unknown apocryphon.[20] Here then is no solid evidence for this will-o'-the-wisp of an unknown apocryphal work. It should be allowed to lapse into oblivion.

3

We have now cleared the way so that we can proceed to examine Paul's citation in 1 Corinthians 2.9:

a) ἃ ὀφθαλμὸς οὐκ εἶδεν καὶ οὖς οὐκ ἤκουσεν
b) καὶ ἐπὶ καρδίαν ἀνθρώπου οὐκ ἀνέβη,
c) ἃ ἡτοίμασεν ὁ θεὸς τοῖς ἀγαπῶσιν αὐτόν.

We will begin by confining ourselves to a study of (a) and (c). The middle line (b) comes from a different context in Scripture and must be reserved for separate treatment. I assume without further argument that (a) and (c), however we account for the differences which they exhibit from our texts of Scripture, are in fact a citation of Isaiah 64.3. The claims of any other Scripture passages to be the original are very feeble indeed (e.g. Isaiah 52.15cd). The MT of Isaiah 64.3 is as follows (EVV 64.4):

*wmēʿwlām loʾ šāmʿw
loʾ heʾᵉzynw ʿayn loʾ rāʾātāh
ʾᵉlohym zwlātʾkā yaʿᵃśeh limʾhakēh lw*

Rudolph Kittel in his edition of the MT suggests *loʾ heʾᵉzynah ʾozen*[1] and transposes this phrase to follow *ʿayn loʾ rāʾātāh* simply on the basis of Paul's citation. He also suggests reading *ywśyʿa* for *yaʿᵃśeh*.[2] He points out that the versions seem to have read *limʾhakēy*. For example the Vulgate translates with: 'A saeculo non audierunt, neque auribus perceperunt: oculus non vidit, deus, absque te, quae praeparasti expectantibus te' (64.4). The rendering 'praeparasti' may have been influenced by Paul's *hētoimasen*. The LXX offers:

ἀπὸ τοῦ αἰῶνος οὐκ ἠκούσαμεν
οὐδὲ οἱ ὀφθαλμοὶ ἡμῶν εἶδον
θεὸν πλήν σου καὶ τὰ ἔργα σου,
ἃ ποιήσεις τοῖς ὑπομένουσιν ἔλεον.

A Quasi-Gnostic Pauline Midrash: 1 Corinthians 2.6-16

Field cites *alia exempla* as reading:

καὶ τὰ ἔργα σου ἀληθινὰ καὶ ποιήσεις τοῖς ὑπομένουσίν σε ἔλεον.[3]

The Targum paraphrases this:

Yea, from of old ear hath not heard the voice of might, nor hearkened to the speech of trembling [or *terror*]; eye hath not seen what thy people have seen, *even* the Shekinah of thy glory, O Lord; for there is none beside thee, who art about to work for thy people, even the righteous who wait for thy salvation.[4]

Naturally, editors have commented on the divergences between Paul's text and the LXX, not to mention the MT. Héring notes that *tois agapōsin auton* is 'an expression which is hardly Pauline but one which forms part of the citation'. Ellis's discussion of the citation is rather inconclusive.[5] He writes: 'If Paul had a variant text closer to his quotations, a textual solution is not improbable for 1 Cor. 2.9.' Later he conjectures that Paul is quoting a combination of Isaiah 64.3 and 65.16, but puts a question mark against the passage. Bauer, in an article written in the same year as Ellis's book was published, claims that the whole phrase which Paul quotes already existed either in a collection of passages or in an apocryphon (he does not seem to be aware of the reference in *Biblical Antiquities*).[6] He points out that the Targum renders 'those who wait for thy redemption'. (But in fact this can hardly be used to support Kittel's conjectural substitution of *ywšyʿa* for *yaʿaśeh* since the Targum also translates *yaʿaśeh*.) Bauer believes that Paul has deliberately altered the rabbinic thought of waiting for God's redemption to make it apply to those who follow Jesus's law of love. He concludes in fact that in writing *tois agapōsin auton* Paul was paraphrasing, but in no arbitrary sense, since waiting on God and loving God are closely akin. C. K. Barrett thinks that Paul believes he is quoting the Old Testament; he is either quoting inaccurately from memory or he had a text different to ours.

As can be seen at a glance, the MT is by no means straightforward. It can hardly stand exactly as pointed. Literally translated it would run: 'From of old they have not heard, we have not hearkened, eye has not seen a God besides thee; he does for him who waits for him.' The LXX with *poiēseis* seems to imply a reading *t'śh* and the Targum seems to point in the same direction with *l'mk*. The LXX and the Targum and the Vulgate seem to assume a plural *lmhkym*, and they have supplied a direct object to this verb, the LXX *eleos* (which almost certainly represents *ḥesed*), the Targum *pwrqnk* 'thy salvation', and the Vulgate simply 'thee'. The introduction of the phrase *ta erga sou* before *ha poiēseis* in the LXX may reflect embarrassment at *y'śh* being left without a direct object. The reading of the *alia exempla* quoted by Field, τοῖς ὑπομένουσίν σε ἔλεον does suggest that the object of *lmhkh* was not identical in all Hebrew manuscripts. One cannot help speculating about a possible relation between the Greek versions' *eleon* and Paul's τοῖς ἀγαπῶσιν αὐτόν. Presumably the LXX as it stands reads *t'śh lmhky ḥsd*. Paul's text presupposes *y'śh l'hbyw*. Now a very familiar description of God, based on the decalogue in Exodus 20.6, is *'śh ḥsd l'hby* (LXX ποιῶν ἔλεον τοῖς ἀγαπῶσίν με).[8] If the original reading were *y'śh ḥsd l'hbyw*, it would account for both the MT and the LXX, and would explain how Paul's version of the Greek came to have τοῖς ἀγαπῶσιν αὐτόν.

On the other hand, when we compare 1 Corinthians 2.9 with Romans 8.27-9, we cannot help being struck by the parallel.[9] Here also the activity of the Spirit is brought into connection with Christians loving God. Verse 28 could be understood so as to mean that God works for good for those who love him, which is very close to the sentiment of 1 Corinthians 2.9c. Another link is provided by the word *eraunan*, 'search': in 1 Corinthians 2.10 the Spirit searches all things, even the deep things of God; in Romans 8.27 God, who searches the heart, knows what is the Spirit's intention. Thus the suggestion that the phrase τοῖς ἀγαπῶσιν αὐτόν is not really Pauline, and therefore must have been in Paul's text of Isaiah 64.3, can hardly stand. But it still remains true that, as far as the exact argument in 1 Corinthians 2 is concerned, τοῖς πιστεύουσιν εἰς αὐτόν would have fitted in better with Paul's line of thought, if he was freely composing or freely 'rehandling the text'. One could equally argue that Paul, having τοῖς ἀγαπῶσιν αὐτόν in his Greek text, was attracted by this scriptural passage and therefore reproduced the thought of it in Romans 8 also.

A Quasi-Gnostic Pauline Midrash: 1 Corinthians 2.6-16

What may be said with a fair measure of confidence is that the MT is corrupt in Isaiah 64.3. It is very unlikely that what we have in the MT is what the original author wrote. In particular, *y'śh* used absolutely, is suspect. Presumably it would mean 'he acts (or works) for those who wait for him'. Torrey comments: 'The verb is used absolutely here, as occasionally elsewhere with this preposition, with the meaning "do well by (someone)".'[10] Koehler-Baumgartner cite three examples none of which exactly fits the context.[11] In 1 Samuel 14.6, Jonathan, speaking to the boy who fetches his arrows, says: *'wlay ya'ªśeh YHWH lānw*, 'It may be that the Lord will work for us.' The LXX offers εἴ τι ποιήσει ἡμῖν κύριος: 'Perhaps the Lord will do something for us.'[12] The second passage is Genesis 41.34: Joseph, offering advice to Pharaoh as to how to cope with the coming famine, says *ya'ªśeh par'oh*: 'Let Pharaoh act.'[13] This is further from the usage in Isaiah 64.3 than is the first passage. The third passage is Psalm 119.126: '*et la'ªśwt lYHWH hēpērw twrāt'kā*. The LXX is καιρὸς τοῦ ποιῆσαι τῷ κυρίῳ. The RSV translates 'It is time for the Lord to act, for thy law has been broken.' This is closer to the second passage. Symmachus here offers καιρὸς πρᾶξαι τῷ κυρίῳ,[14] and ἄλλος reads καιρὸς κατορθώσεως, κύριε. All these alternatives suggest that *l'śwt* without an object could be ambiguous. In general one may say that these three examples are too specific to offer an exact parallel to the usage in Isaiah 64.3.

The context of Isaiah 64.3 in the Book of Isaiah is the plea of God's people in adversity, reminding God of his mighty acts of old and hoping for similar manifestations in the present. It is worth quoting Delitzsch's comment: 'The justification of the wish, wrung out by the misery of the present, is founded on the incomparable acts of Jehovah, seen in a long series of historical facts ... to hear and see God is to learn his existence by observing and considering his works.'[15] Westermann significantly adds that behind these verses lies a very ancient Epiphany tradition.[16] Thus the original text dealt with God's appearances, his historical revelation of himself to Israel. This is important for understanding Paul's use of it. Duhm comments: 'A sure restoration of the original wording is hardly possible', but this does not prevent him, with that supreme confidence typical of nineteenth-century scholars, from an attempted restoration, very much along the lines of Paul's text: *'el rwaḥ lo' 'āl'tāh yiś'eh m'hobeb*: 'It has not occurred to (man's) mind (Spirit); he saves him who loves him' – thus explaining all Paul's divergences at one fell swoop!¹⁷ Strack-Billerbeck quote Rabbi Johanan (A.D. 279) as having interpreted the text in such a way as to suggest that he read *y'śh* as Niph'al *yē'āśeh*: 'what has been done'.¹⁸ This would bring the text closer to Paul's. This is not to suggest that the original text was meant to read as *yē'āśeh* but that this reading suited the markedly futuristic interpretation of the rabbis better and therefore may have been standardized (and translated into Greek in this sense) by the time the composite quotation reached Paul.

We may therefore reasonably conclude that the original Hebrew of Isaiah 64.3 is sufficiently imprecise to allow some liberty of conjecture in restoring it and to suggest that there was a variety of Greek translations. In my opinion, Paul's version differs from both the MT and the LXX neither because he was quoting from memory nor because he has arbitrarily altered the text before him. It is more likely that the two citations actually reached him in the form in which he presents them.

We now have to trace the source of 1 Corinthians 2.9b, καὶ ἐπὶ καρδίαν ἀνθρώπου οὐκ ἀνέβη, and to ask how it became conflated with Isaiah 64.4. We may assume without argument that the phrase is translation Greek.¹⁹ In the LXX the phrase, or a very close parallel, occurs six times (and there is one other related passage we must note). They are as follows:

4 Kingdoms 12.5:
πᾶν ἀργύριον ὃ δ' ἐὰν ἀναβῇ ἐπὶ καρδίαν
ἀνδρὸς ἐνεγκεῖν ἐν οἴκῳ κυρίου (al. mss.
λάβῃ for ἀναβῇ).

MT: *kol kesep 'ᵃšer ya'ᵃleh 'al lēb 'ys l'haby' bēyt YHWH*
'All the silver which any man decides to bring into the house of the Lord'.

Isaiah 65.16:
ἐπιλήσονται γὰρ τὴν θλῖψιν αὐτῶν τὴν πρώτην,
καὶ οὐκ ἀναβήσεται ἐπὶ τὴν καρδίαν.

There is nothing exactly corresponding to the last clause in the MT of Isaiah 65.16; we shall be discussing this presently.

A Quasi-Gnostic Pauline Midrash: 1 Corinthians 2.6-16

Jeremiah 3.16:

οὐκ ἀναβήσεται ἐπὶ τὴν καρδίαν

MT: *lo' ya'ªleh 'al lēb*

The passage refers to the ark of the covenant in the end time. 'It will not occur to anyone's mind.'

Jeremiah 39.35:

καὶ οὐκ ἀνέβη ἐπὶ τὴν καρδίαν μου, τὸ ποιῆσαι τὸ βδέλυγμα τοῦτο

MT (32.35): *w'lo' 'āl'tāh 'al liby la'ªśwt hatw'ābāh hazōt*

God speaks and tells Israel that such an atrocity as child-sacrifice never entered his mind.

Jeremiah 51.21:

ἐμνήσθη ὁ κύριος καὶ ἀνέβη ἐπὶ τὴν καρδίαν αὐτοῦ

MT (44.21): *'otām zāhar YHWH wata'ªleh 'al libw*

Yahweh remembered the incense Judah had offered and it recurred to his mind.

Jeremiah 28.50:

οἱ μάκροθεν μνήσθητε τοῦ κυρίου καὶ Ἱερουσαλὴμ ἀναβήτω ἐπὶ τὴν καρδίαν ὑμῶν

MT (51.50): *zik'rw mērāhwq 'et YHWH wyrwsalaym ta'ªleh 'al l'bāb'kem*

The exiles are urged to remember Yahweh and to recall Jerusalem to mind. We may also add this passage from

Ezekiel 20.32:

καὶ εἰ ἀναβήσεται ἐπὶ τὸ πνεῦμα ὑμῶν τοῦτο

MT: *w'hā'ōlāh 'al rwḥªkem hāyw lo' tih'yeh*

'The thought you cherished in your mind will never come to pass.' The LXX has misunderstood the passage and gives the misleading sense: 'This will never occur to your mind.'

Before we try to decide which among these passages Paul is quoting, we should first consider the possibility that the phrase may simply be a tag; after all we can produce six parallels. But this may safely be rejected: the exact words are not reproduced anywhere. The passage which comes nearest to the exact words of 1 Corinthians 2.9b is 4 Kingdoms 12.5 and it is furthest away in sense. In fact when we look at them there are only two passages which seriously compete for the honour of being Paul's source, Isaiah 65.16 and Jeremiah 3.16, since only these two are eschatological. Jeremiah 3.16 is considered a little later. Isaiah 65.16 presents certain complications and must be considered now.[20]

But when we do so, we encounter a difficulty already mentioned: the LXX translation of Isaiah 65.16ef is completely different from the Hebrew. Perhaps the simplest way is to quote the whole of Isaiah 65.16-17 in English and then to indicate the Hebrew and Greek that lie behind the relevant lines:

  v. 16*a* So that he who blesses himself in the land
     b shall bless himself by the God of truth,
     c and he who takes an oath in the land
     d shall swear by the God of truth;
     e because the former troubles are forgotten
     f and are hid from my eyes.
  v. 17*a* For behold, I create new heavens and a new earth;
     b and the former things shall not be remembered
     c or come to mind.

The MT of verse 16ef is as follows:

ky niŠk'ḥw haṣārwt hari'šōnwt
wky nist'rw me'eynay

and the MT of verse 17bc is as follows:

wlo' tizokarnāh hari'šōnwt
wlo' ta"ᵃleynah 'al lēb

But the LXX renders verse 16ef thus:

ἐπιλήσονται γὰρ τὴν θλῦψιν αὐτῶν τὴν πρώτην,
καὶ οὐκ ἀναβήσεται αὐτῶν ἐπὶ τὴν καρδίαν.

And verse 17bc it renders thus:

καὶ οὐ μὴ μνησθῶσιν τῶν προτέρων
καὶ οὐ μὴ ἐπέλθῃ αὐτῶν ἐπὶ τὴν καρδίαν.

It is not difficult to see what has caused this divergence between the MT and the LXX: at some stage dittography has taken place. We can even make a reasonable guess as to when that stage was; in all probability it was a dittography at the Hebrew stage and not the Greek. Let us suppose the opposite, i.e. that the dittography took place when a copy was being made of the Greek: we must imagine that the scribe reached verse 16f and his eye slipped down to 17c. He copies 17c (LXX) instead of the (presumably correct) translation of 16f. He then proceeds with the next verse and finds exactly the same phrase as the one he has just copied. His attention must be drawn to the mistake – surely he must correct it. But imagine now that he is translating from the Hebrew and has a Hebrew text before him in which 17c appears instead of 16f. He translates this duly with *ouk anabēsetai ktl.*, and then continues until he encounters the same phrase again in Hebrew. He is embarrassed by this and shows his embarrassment by using a different word to translate *t'lynh*, the verb *eperchomai*. This is the only place in the entire LXX where *'lh* is translated with *eperchesthai*. At verse 17c Aquila, Symmachus, and Theodotion all offer οὐδὲ οὐ μὴ ἀναβήσεται ἀπὸ καρδίας, which Field believes to be a mistake for ἐπὶ καρδίαν.[21] Presumably they were translating from a Hebrew text which did not contain the dittography (though we cannot be absolutely sure, as verse 16d is not extant in these versions).

The Targum of Isaiah 65.16cf runs: 'Because the former afflictions shall be forgotten and because they shall be hidden from before me'; and at 65.17bc it offers: 'And the former ones shall not be remembered, nor brought to mind.' If anything, therefore, the Targum has emphasized the eschatological element, for it represents not only the former troubles as forgotten, but also the old heaven and the old earth. We have still to ask how the future *anabēsetai* came to be changed into the aorist *anebē*; but this must have taken place after Isaiah 65.17c got conflated with Isaiah 64.3 (if Isaiah 65.17e is in fact the source of 1 Corinthians 2.9b), and to the question of how and why that conflation took place we must now turn.

So far we have not considered the question whether the conflation of the two texts may not have taken place before Paul used them. Quite apart from those who have espoused the theory of an unknown apocryphal source, a number of scholars have argued that the conflated text was known to the early Fathers who quote it independently of 1 Corinthians 2.9.

The New Testament Interpretation of Scripture

Notable among these is Prigent, who claims that those who quote it in the early centuries after Paul knew a form of the citation in which only the third line occurred (1 Corinthians 2.9c, to use our division set out above).[22] Unfortunately, however, Prigent relies on the evidence of *The Testament of Jacob* to establish the conclusion that the citation existed before Paul used it, and we have already seen that this cannot now be maintained. He believes that the two texts were linked in Jewish liturgical tradition before Paul used them. His only evidence for this is that they are often used in the early Fathers in a quasi-liturgical context. But we have followed Hagner's conclusion that the two earliest citations among the Fathers are simply reproducing Paul, so Prigent's evidence can hardly be called compelling.

There is, however, one citation of the two conflated texts which merits our attention, that which occurs in the *Biblical Antiquities* of Pseudo-Philo. This fact was actually noted seventy-six years ago by Thackeray;[23] it then fell into relative oblivion, until Philonenko published it in 1959 as if it had been his own discovery.[24] In the interval, however, M. R. James commented on this reference in his edition of the *Biblical Antiquities* in 1917;[25] and in his book already mentioned, published in 1959, Ellis shows himself to be aware that the citation occurs in Pseudo-Philo.[26] The *Biblical Antiquities* seem to be a midrash on the books of Judges and 1 Samuel, of a purely Jewish provenance. It is extant only in Latin. The context of our citation is a narrative concerning certain precious stones which had been taken from idols worshipped by unfaithful Israelites. God commands that the precious stones are to be put in the ark of the covenant; when the temple is destroyed, God will look after the stones. The text of the citation runs as follows:

> Et erunt ibi quousque memor sum seculi, et visitabo habitantes terram. Et hinc accipiam et istos et alios plures valde meliores, ex eo quod oculus non vidit nec auris audivit, et in cor hominis non ascendit, quousque fieret tale aliquid in seculo ... et surrexit Cenez et dixit: Ecce quantum bonum fecit Deus hominibus, et propter peccata eorum omnibus his defraudati sunt ...[27]

A Quasi-Gnostic Pauline Midrash: 1 Corinthians 2.6-16

M. R. James translates the sentence containing the quotation thus: 'And then will I take them and many others from that place which eye hath not seen nor ear heard neither hath it come up into the heart of man.' Philonenko points out that Cenez's remark which follows the citation is analogous to 1 Corinthians 2.9c, and he suggests that Paul's third line may already have formed part of the citation; but this seems a remote speculation.

Unfortunately there is great uncertainty as to both the date and the original language of the *Biblical Antiquities*. L. H. Feldman in his introduction to the republication of M. R. James's edition discusses all the issues very thoroughly but is almost entirely non-committal as to definite conclusions. The author, he says, certainly could read the Scriptures in the original Hebrew; the work might have been originally written in Greek.[28] The Latin version may even have been translated direct from the Hebrew.[29] Feldman suggests that the author had access to the Hebrew text of the Scriptures, to the Greek text, and to a Targum. He is on the whole inclined to date the work as pre-Pauline, though other scholars would put it at the end of the first century A.D. Harrington concludes that the Latin was translated from a Greek version, and that the Greek was translated from an original Hebrew text; but it looks as if the Greek translator had on occasion, when using citations from Scripture, translated direct from the Hebrew and not used the LXX.[30] What seems to be agreed by everyone, and what is most important from the point of view of our present study, is that the work was written quite independently of Paul. Thackeray[31] and Philonenko believe that the conflated citation was in circulation before Paul's day. Feuillet, in his article already referred to on page 22, also holds this view, though he is apparently unaware of the citation in *Biblical Antiquities*.[32] He agrees with Prigent that the citation originally occurred in a liturgical context.

In the light of the rather conflicting evidence, it is not easy to come to a decision. Perhaps it will be clearest if we draw up our conclusions under four heads.

1. The *Biblical Antiquities* are independent of Paul, whatever their date. The only doubt that might arise about this conclusion would be based on the fact that the work is extant in

Latin. Presumably the Latin translator was a Christian: a Latin translation would be used by Christians, not Jews. His version of the citation as far as it goes is almost identical with that of the Vulgate of 1 Corinthians 2.9ab.[33] But, if it was the Christian translator who inserted this citation from 1 Corinthians 2.9, it is surprising that he did not insert more of a more pronouncedly Christian nature. On the other side we must put the fact that in *Biblical Antiquities* this citation comes in the context of instructions being given to the apocryphal character Cenez as to what he is to do with certain jewels. He is to place them in the ark of the covenant, and God promises that when in Solomon's time the ark is placed in the temple, and when later the temple is destroyed, he will himself look after them. Then follows the excerpt given above. Afterwards we are told that in the end time these jewels will give light to the righteous in accordance with Isaiah 60.19-20. This affords an interesting comparison with 2 Maccabees 2.1-8, where Jeremiah is described as hiding the ark and the altar of incense in a cave on Mount Horeb. He instructs his followers: 'And the place will be unknown until God gathers the assembly of his people and becomes gracious; and then the Lord will show these things, and the glory of the Lord shall be seen and the cloud' (my translation). Now we have noted above that the only other passage in the Scriptures containing the phrase 'Come up upon the heart of man' which is a likely competitor with Isaiah 65.17 for the honour of being the source of Paul's citation is Jeremiah 3.16. But this is the very passage where Jeremiah declares emphatically that the ark of the covenant is to go into complete and permanent oblivion. Is the author of the *Biblical Antiquities* trying perhaps to modify this radical prophecy? Is he using this very phrase about the oblivion that will overtake the ark in the future specifically in order to put it in a different context and thus, so to speak, divert its power? Certainly the author of 2 Maccabees, if he knew of the prophecy in Jeremiah 3.16, is seeking to modify it.[34] The weight of probability lies heavily on the side of the conclusion that the *Biblical Antiquities* is independent of Christian influence.

2. The conflation of the two texts must have been already made when Paul used them. He was not the first to make it.

A Quasi-Gnostic Pauline Midrash: 1 Corinthians 2.6-16

Quite apart from the evidence of the *Biblical Antiquities*, we could guess this from the use of *anebē*. Whichever scriptural passage we regard as the original of 1 Corinthians 2.9b, Isaiah 65.17, or Jeremiah 3.16, the verb used in 1 Corinthians 2.9 was in that source in the future tense: the phrase referred either to past miseries which will be forgotten or to a cult object now outmoded. In the three quotations from early Christian literature which we have examined, and (as we shall be seeing) in rabbinic references extant, the context of the whole citation is futuristic; what eye has not seen, etc. is the joy of the end time or of eternity. Although, as we hope to show in the next chapter, Paul does not use the conflated citation in this futurist sense, the Fathers do, and the rabbis use Isaiah 64.3 in this sense also. Some time must be allowed for this change of tense to take place, from the meaning of the second line of the quotation to be altered from looking back at the past (or forgetting the past) to looking forward to the future. In the same way, we could argue that some time must be allowed for the original *y'sh* of Isaiah 64.3 (if it was original) to be read as Niph'al and thus to produce the translation *hētoimasen*. The same transference of meaning has taken place here. Stauffer (see P. Bachmann, op. cit., in loc.) argues that the two citations must have been conflated before Paul used them because they occur in such varied forms in the Fathers. But Stauffer was not aware of the citation in Pseudo-Philo and takes no account of the possibility that 2.9b may come from Jeremiah 3.16.

3. Was the conflation made at the Greek or at the Hebrew stage? If the *Biblical Antiquities* was translated direct from Hebrew into Latin (a possibility not dismissed by Feldmann at least), the question is answered at once: the conflation already existed in the Hebrew. But if the *Biblical Antiquities* was originally written in Greek, or if the Latin version was translated from the Greek (both possible theories), the likelihood is that the two citations were joined at the Greek stage and not the Hebrew. In favour of this is also the fact that Paul's version of the citation, on any account of what the original was, has travelled so far from that original; e.g. once *y'sh* read as Niph'al has been translated as *hētoimasen*, it would be easier to imagine the line found in 1 Corinthians 2.9b being added to the

citation. But we have already advanced far into the realm of conjecture. We must be content to say that we do not know at what stage the conflation was made, though the balance of probability lies on the side of its having been done at the Greek stage.

4. In what sort of milieu did the conflation take place? Prigent and Feuillet are confident that it took place in a liturgical context. Our knowledge of the synagogue liturgy of the first century A.D. is not very extensive. Moreover, if the conflation took place at the Greek and not the Hebrew stage, the question must arise how far Greek was actually used in the non-lection parts of the synagogue service among the Diaspora. This is a problem on which not very much light is to be had. Thackeray in his book on the Septuagint in Jewish worship confines himself entirely to an examination of lections.[35] G. F. Moore quotes passages from the Talmud to show that the *Sh'ma'* and the *T'fillah* may be said in any language; the priestly benediction must be said in Hebrew.[36] Professor Weingreen in a private communication says that both Aramaic and Greek could be used in the prayer part of the synagogue service of the Diaspora.[37] So it looks as if Prigent's and Feuillet's suggestion is quite a reasonable one, even if the conflation was made only at the Greek stage. But when they (severally) made this suggestion they were apparently both unaware of the reference in the *Biblical Antiquities*. After all, the two places in which the conflated citation certainly occurs in an original context are both much closer to midrash than to liturgy, and even the examples in the Fathers are by no means demonstrably liturgical.[38] All we know of Paul's methods of biblical exegesis argues in favour of his having encountered this conflated quotation in the context of midrash. As we shall be seeing, he uses it himself to drive home a centrally important point of doctrine. The strong probability must remain that the two citations were conflated in the first instance by someone who used them to expound the meaning of Scripture.

4

We must now ask the question which may be said to be behind

this part of our inquiry, what did Paul mean by using this conflated citation? Before trying to answer this we have to decide what he meant by saying that the powers failed to recognize the wisdom of God, and then decide where his citation came from and why it appears in the form in which Paul quotes it.

We may begin by looking at the evidence in rabbinic literature about how this text was used. We have indeed already begun this process in that we have noted the use of the text in the *Biblical Antiquities*. There certainly the citation is used as a description of the joys of the age to come, and this is also the way in which Isaiah 64.3 is used in our rabbinic sources. Thus in *Tractate Berakoth* 34b we find the words of the text applied to the world to come: 'What is meant by *Eye hath not seen*? R. Joshua ben Levi said: This is the wine which has been preserved in its grapes since the six days of creation.'[1] The text is applied in exactly the same way in *Abodah Zarah* 65a to the age to come in which the righteous will be rewarded.[2] Compare also K. G. Kuhn's edition of the Tannaitic *Midrash Sifre* on Numbers,[3] where the text is used to show how much God had already promised Moses in the world to come. Kuhn claims that this is characteristic of the way in which this text is understood by the rabbis.

In some rabbinic passages, however, a distinction is made between two stages in the happy future which lies before the righteous: first will come the days of the Messiah, and then the full enjoyment of the age to come. The question from Isaiah 64.3 is applied to the later stage. Thus in *Sanhedrin* 99a we read 'R. Hiyya b. Abba said in R. Johanan's name: All the prophets prophesied [all the good things] only in respect of the messianic era: but as for the world to come, *the eye hath not seen, O Lord, beside thee what he hath prepared for him that waiteth for him* ... R. Hiyya b. Abba also said in R. Johanan's name: All the prophets prophesied only for repentant sinners; but as for the perfectly righteous [who had never sinned at all], *the eye hath not seen, O Lord, beside thee what he hath prepared for him that waiteth for him.*'[4]

It is interesting to note that the editor of this Tractate, H. Freedman, has quite naturally translated *yʻśh* in the MT of Isaiah 64.3 with 'what he has prepared', even though this is not the meaning in the original context. It shows that, once these words were taken in an eschatological context as applying to the blessings of the age to come, *yʻśh* was bound to be understood in this sense. We need not seek any further for an explanation of Paul's *ha hētoimasen*. The same distinction is made in *Tractate Shabbath* 63a, and in the same way our text is applied to the world to come and not to the time of the Messiah.[5]

In *Pesikta Rabbati* 37.1 this point is made in an even more striking way, one which serves as an admirable transition to an examination of how Paul uses the citation.[6] First the Messiah suffers all sorts of troubles because he is a penal substitute for the sins of Israel. These sufferings are described in the language of the righteous sufferer of the psalms, especially Psalm 22. Then God says to him: 'My true Messiah has not yet been repaid for half his anguish. I have one more measure of reward which I will give him, one which no eye in the world has seen, as is said, *Neither hath the eye seen a God beside thee, who worketh for him that waiteth for him.*' This vindication takes place in the presence of all the righteous. This is very interesting indeed, for it shows us what Paul has done with the traditional time-scheme: in accordance with his belief in realized eschatology, he has telescoped the times; the citation applies to the end time. But what the rabbis said would happen to the triumphant Messiah in the remote future has now happened to the historical Messiah. The unimaginable glory has become visible in the cross and resurrection. In just the same way Paul has telescoped the two groups of the penitent and the absolutely righteous respectively whom R. Johanan distinguished. The Messiah came not to call the righteous but sinners, so there are no righteous, or rather righteousness consists in realizing that one is a sinner, and in approaching God in faith through Christ. Moreover the vindication of the Messiah has taken place in the presence of the righteous in the sense that only those who through faith are righteous can recognize the vindication.

In section 1 we came to the conclusion that the wisdom of God which the elemental powers failed to recognize was simply the whole design of God apprehensible in the life, death, and resurrection of Jesus Christ,[7] but centrally in his death on the cross. This is 'the weakness of God and the foolishness of God' which the world and its rulers cannot recognize. But, says

Paul in verses 9 and 10, God has revealed it to us Christians through the Spirit. Thus the purpose of the conflated citation which has given scholars so much trouble is really very simple indeed: it refers to nothing else but the life, death, and resurrection of Jesus Christ. This is what eye has not seen nor ear heard, what nobody could have imagined. Thus the incredible, unheard-of element is not the joys of heaven or the furniture of the world to come, but the glory (nature) of God manifested in the cross. This is the way in which God's design has exceeded all our expectations, not in its unimaginable splendour but in its unimaginable humility. Thus Paul has in fact in a most remarkable way turned the traditional exegesis upside down. He could not have done this if the two quotations had not already undergone a process of thorough futurizing at the hands of Jewish commentators. Paul takes the conflated citation, carrying as it does all the overtones of the age to come, and applies it to something which God has already done, but which most Jews have missed because it was so totally unexpected, the revelation of God in the shameful death of the Messiah.

> Now we have received not the spirit of the world, but the Spirit which is from God, that we might understand the gifts bestowed on us by God (*ta hupo tou theou charisthenta hēmin*).

No matter how much the force of the aorist may have been blunted in *Koinē* Greek, it is hard to deny that the aorist passive participle must apply to some definite event or events in the past. It means in fact the events of the total career of Jesus Christ, centring on the cross, and including the resurrection, and their consequences for us. Of course it is only because we are *en Christō/i* that we can understand these events; but in Pauline thought being in Christ and possessing the Spirit are two descriptions of the same condition.[8] Indeed, we might almost go a step further and say that what eye has not seen nor ear heard nor heart conceived is simply the revelation of God in Christ, and that therefore in some sense God has made himself visible, apprehensible, conceivable in Christ. The original quotation in Isaiah 64.3 concerned a plea for an epiphany. Paul uses it to show that the epiphany has taken place and has taken the form of an incarnation.

The earliest exponents of Paul's conflated quotation, the Fathers and other early Christian writers, missed this point entirely. One and all they understand the citation in a purely futurist sense. This is how Clement applies it: we are to 'strive to be found in the number of those who await God' (35.4). In II Clement we are to 'expect hourly the kingdom of God' (12). In *The Gospel of Thomas* the citation is understood as referring to the end time. Similarly in *The Testament of Jacob*, quoted on page 45 above, it is applied to the rewards of the righteous after death. We must, however, make an exception for the quotation in the interpolation in *The Ascension of Isaiah* which has been assigned to the fourth century A.D. (see page 38 above). Here the conflated citation is applied to Isaiah's vision of the ascended Christ after he had deceived and defeated the powers, an interpretation nearer to Paul's thought though by no means identical with it.

It is not surprising that the Fathers should misunderstand Paul's subtle and profound use of the citation. We have observed how Ignatius has reinterpreted 1 Corinthians 2.6-8 so as to make it apply to a theology of God incognito: and how the author of *The Vision of Isaiah* has misinterpreted Paul even further in a Docetic direction. Presumably we must put Hagner also in the category of those who believe that Paul meant his citation to refer to the joys of heaven, since he claims emphatically that there is no difference between Paul's interpretation and Clement's. But Clement certainly understands it in a futuristic sense.[9]

This futurizing of the meaning of the citation may very well account for a phenomenon of which Prigent makes a great deal, the fact that in many quotations from the Fathers the third line, ἃ ἡτοίμασεν ὁ θεὸς τοῖς ἀγαπῶσιν αὐτόν, is either quoted by itself or is put before the other two.[10] Prigent suggests that this is because these Fathers knew a form of the citation in which only the third line occurred. But it seems much more likely that this emphasis on the third line is to be accounted for by the fact that what most interested the Fathers in the citation was the element of future reward, and this is the element which comes out most clearly in 1 Corinthians 2.9c. There is really no reason

A Quasi-Gnostic Pauline Midrash: 1 Corinthians 2.6-16

to suppose that the citation was known to the Fathers in any other form.

There has always been a school of commentators who followed the same line as the Fathers at this point. Thus Robertson and Plummer think that the citation refers to 'the consummation of final blessedness'.[11] Strack-Billerbeck also maintain that Paul understands the quotation in the sense which traditional Jewish exegesis had already given it. And W. D. Davies writes: 'Just as Paul described the life of the age to come by saying that "eye hath not seen ... etc" ... so a saying of the first-century Rabbi is reported as follows',[12] and he proceeds to quote the saying of R. Johanan from *Sanhedrin* 99 as referred to on page 63 above. If our interpretation of Paul is correct, Paul does not apply the citation to some future age, but to what God has done in Christ. Wilckens also believes that Paul uses the citation to indicate the future blessings stored up for the elect.[13]

But other commentators are more discriminating. Eighty years ago a contributor to the *Expository Times* who signed himself 'M.D.' made the point that the things promised are only future from the point of view of the prophet.[14] Paul means to identify them with present realities. 'M.D.' defines them as 'the spiritual blessings in the heavenly places', by which apparently he means present Christian experience of God in Christ. Goudge's comment on the verse is also worth quoting: 'To wait for God is characteristic of God's people before the incarnation, to love him is their characteristic now.'[15] In much the same vein Weiss understands the quotation to refer to 'the blessedness of the kingdom of God, the glory of the contemporaries of the Messiah'. And Allo says that Paul is by means of the quotation speaking of 'la grâce et la gloire'. Clearest of all is Feuillet. He energetically rejects the futurist interpretation and expresses his own exposition thus: 'Paul wishes to speak in the first place of a profound apprehension of the religion of Christ, a mysterious wisdom inaccessible to human speculations; but it is quite certain that the celestial glory to which this wisdom leads is not totally absent from the perspective.'[16]

We should welcome this tendency to examine more carefully exactly what Paul does mean by this citation, and the consequent freeing of Paul from the imputation of using it merely in order to speak of the future reward of the faithful. But we must also question the alternative chosen, which is to make it refer to present Christian experience or even present Christian experience plus the hope of glory hereafter. The whole point of Paul's quotation is to show what the powers have missed, and what the powers have missed is simply the significance of the life, death, and resurrection of Jesus Christ as the revelation of God. It is true that in verse 7 Paul describes this wisdom of God as having been pre-ordained 'for our glory', and in verse 8 he calls Christ 'the Lord of glory' (these are Feuillet's two reasons for introducing a futurist element into the meaning of the quotation). But the fact that the revelation of God's wisdom is to lead to the glory of Christians does not in itself imply that what is revealed includes our glory; and we may suggest that the phrase τὸν κύριον τῆς δόξης in verse 8 is inspired more by ὁ βασιλεὺς τῆς δόξης in Psalm 24 than by any particular emphasis on the parousia or the joys of heaven. In fact commentators have perhaps missed Paul's meaning for much the same reason that, according to Paul, the elemental powers failed to recognize the wisdom of God: it is so very unexpected and radical, reversing so many ideas about what God was likely to do.

Thus Paul in this conflated citation is probably not indulging in 'a free handling of the text in accordance with his own immediate purpose'.[17] He is of course building on the exegetical tradition in which he was brought up; but he is applying the text with a full understanding of what he believed it meant when it was originally written; and indeed, compared with the way in which the Fathers and the rabbis use Isaiah 64.3, Paul is closer to the original intention of the author as far as we can recapture it than they are. But he has used it with great power and profundity to express the sheer scandal of the gospel, the unimaginable humility of God's revelation of himself in Christ. Paul therefore is saying in 1 Corinthians 2.6-10 very much the same thing as John says in a very different context and by a very different method in John 1.18: 'No one has ever seen God; the only Son, who is in the bosom of the Father, he has made him known.' God has in Christ made himself visible and is now in Christ apprehensible to those who have faith. Thus the humanity of Christ is not an ingenious incognito, nor 'a transparent veil',[18] but the indispensable and unique medium of revelation.

A Quasi-Gnostic Pauline Midrash: 1 Corinthians 2.6-16

Up to and including verse 9 Paul has concentrated on expressing the fact of revelation and the content of revelation. From verses 10 to 16 he occupies himself with the fact that Christians can apprehend this revelation. We might explain it by saying that in verses 6-9 he argues that God really has revealed himself in Christ. In verses 10-16 he argues that he really has revealed himself to us Christians. To this second half of Paul's argument we must now turn.

5

Just as his first scriptural citation in verse 9 has been used by Paul to show that God has in fact granted his unimaginable revelation of himself in Christ, so he uses the second one (also in origin a combined one) to show that only God can reveal himself and that he actually has communicated this revelation to us in Christ. The emphasis in verses 6-9 is almost entirely on what God has revealed[1] and on the fact that he has revealed it. The emphasis in verses 10-16 is on the fact of the revelation *to us Christians*, hence the frequent use of words for 'Spirit' and 'spiritual'. We hope to show that the climax of the argument comes in verse 16, especially when we view it in the light of the other passage in Paul's writings where this citation occurs. But in between, in verses 10-15, a number of points occur to which we must give some attention.

What is the purpose of these verses (10-15)? Why did Paul not go straight on from verse 10 to quote Isaiah 40.13? The reason seems to be that he wishes first to show that only *God* can make the revelation, and that God *can* make the revelation. He is also anxious to emphasize that Christians are the people who can understand the revelation through the Spirit. Only when he has made these points can he go ahead and give what he must have regarded as the crowning proof in verse 16.

Perhaps I should here mention two considerations which seem to me to apply throughout the entire passage that occupies us in this work:

a) Paul treats *pneuma* and *nous* here as synonymous.

b) Paul does not here distinguish between the risen Christ and the Spirit. As far as concerns the first point, Allo would modify

The New Testament Interpretation of Scripture

it by saying that, according to Paul, it is impossible to distinguish *pneuma* from *nous* in God, but that Paul does distinguish them in man. *Nous* in man means 'discursive reason' or 'faculty of moral choice'.[2] In man, he says, *pneuma* does not replace *psuchē*, as Reitzenstein and others of the *Religionsgeschichte* school imagine, but crowns it. It is added to the other faculties. This is why the *pneumatikos* can judge others: he has all the faculties common to man plus *pneuma*.[3] Conzelmann agrees that in verse 11 *pneuma* is practically identical with *nous*, and he remarks of verse 16: '*Nous* here has the same meaning as *pneuma*.'[4] The second point (b) will, I trust, be made clear as we study verse 16. I would not want to generalize this so as to say that Paul never distinguishes the two; I only claim that he does not do so in this passage.

The assertion in verse 10 that the Spirit searches even the deep things of God has raised suspicions among some commentators. This is one of the phrases that gives this passage its apparently Gnostic character. In later Gnosticism *bathos* was a familiar term. Compare *Gospel of Truth*, 23.25, Ménard's translation: 'A cause de la profondeur (*bathos*) de Celui qui entoure tous les espaces'; and 35.15f: 'Mais . . . la profondeur (*bathos*) du Père c'est multipliée.' Again in 37.7f we have a reference to both the *Logos* and the *Nous* existing in the *bathos* of the Father; and also 26.7, where the Son is described as 'he who has proceeded from the *bathos*'. According to Hippolytus, in the Valentinian system *Sophia*, a female aeon, is described as 'hastening back into the *bathos* of the Father' (Foerster, op. cit., vol. I, p. 187); and Clement of Alexandria in his *Excerpta ex Theodoto* tells us that *Sigē* is 'the mother of all those brought forth by "depth" ' (Foerster, ibid., p. 226). But this is not the same thing as *ta bathē tou theou* which probably refers to God's saving design, whereas in the Gnostic systems *bathos*, like *Sigē*, is used as a word for the primordial transcendence of God. St John the Divine in Revelation 2.24 commends the orthodox party in the church in Thyatira because they have not learned what is called 'the deep things of Satan'. It is possible that there was a party of gnosticizing Christians in Thyatira who claimed to know 'the deep things of God', and John calls this teaching 'the deep things of Satan'. Conzelmann says plainly that the

A Quasi-Gnostic Pauline Midrash: 1 Corinthians 2.6-16

use of *bathos* here points to *Gnosis*. God himself can be defined as *bathos*. Weiss, however, explains the phrase rather in terms of wisdom teaching.[5] He quotes Judith 8.14, a sentiment to the effect that we cannot know the depth (*bathos*) of the human heart, so how can we hope to search out God and understand his mind (*nous*)? He adds that Paul is thinking of God's knowledge of himself. We may remark that, if so, we are very close indeed to John's Logos; we shall find in our study of verse 16 that we are driven to very similar conclusions. Evans defines God's *bathē* here as God's 'hidden attributes and purposes'.[6] F. F. Bruce very relevantly suggests that the phrase may come from Job 11.7: 'Can you find out the deep things of God?'[7] In fact there does not seem to be justification for suspecting Gnostic influence here. The depth of God's wisdom was a very prominent element in the system associated with the wisdom tradition. Paul himself exclaims in Romans 11.33 (a verse which introduces one that is directly linked with our verse 16 here): ᾽Ω βάθος πλούτου καὶ σοφίας καὶ γνώσεως θεοῦ, and does so in order to emphasize God's unexpectedness and inscrutability. Unless therefore we are to identify the wisdom tradition with Gnosticism, a gross anachronism, we have no reason to find Gnosticism here. This conclusion is clearly endorsed by E. Schweizer in his article πνεῦμα, πνευματικός in *TWNT* (vol. VI, p. 422, Stuttgart 1959). He says that Paul's answer to the question: 'What is the content of this "pneumatic" teaching?' is formally Gnostic, τὰ βάθη τοῦ θεοῦ, but 'its content is totally unGnostic, God's saving action on the cross', and he identifies *ta bathē tou theou* with τὰ ὑπὸ τοῦ θεοῦ χαρισθέντα ἡμῖν.

In verse 11 the comparison drawn between God's self-knowledge and our self-knowledge could lead to confusion. Lietzmann remarks that the parallel between divine and human psychology is not followed completely through.[8] If it had been it would have led to considerable anomalies since Paul believed not only that God knew his own mind entirely, but also that he knew ours better than we did ourselves (see Romans 8.26-7). But in fact this is not the point that Paul is making here. He only wants to show that God can enable Christians to apprehend his revelation; God is competent to do so. This may seem obvious enough to us, but possibly the proto-Gnostic ideology of the Corinthians may have been in danger of representing God (as the revealer, less than God, an aeon) as a sort of sub-personal process.[9] Paul's doctrine of God's Spirit, far from originating in an Hellenistic notion of spirit as a fluid element like electricity, always tends to bring out the personal nature of God; and nowhere more insistently than here.

The parallel with Proverbs 20.27, pointed out by Robertson and Plummer, is not really pertinent:

> The spirit of man is the lamp of the Lord, searching all his innermost parts.

The verse from Proverbs teaches that man's ability to contemplate his own mind is God's gift, which is not what Paul is saying here. Weiss, commenting on Paul's use of *nous* in verse 16, claims that this usage has the advantage that it emphasizes the personal, individual character of Christ's dwelling in the Christian and guards against an unduly impersonal understanding of the Spirit, very much the point we are making here.

On page 65 above we have already commented on the phrase τὰ ὑπὸ τοῦ θεοῦ χαρισθέντα ἡμῖν, and claimed that it must refer to the whole revelation of God in the career of Jesus Christ, from creation to re-creation at his resurrection. Hodge seems to take the same view: he says this refers to 'the wisdom of God, the gospel, distinguished from the wisdom of the world'.[10] Weiss, however, refers it to the glories of the parousia. Allo takes a third view. It refers to 'tout ce que Dieu leur a accordé pour leur salut'; this would seem to enlarge the range of the phrase beyond the immediate context, which is the argument that God has enabled Christians to understand what the powers missed. Conzelmann is quite unable to make up his mind on this point: he asks whether *ta charisthenta* means the understanding of the *Heilsgeschehen*, cites a view which holds that *ta charisthenta* and *ha hētoimasen* (in verse 9) are identical; but ends by saying that 'the question is still completely open'. C. K. Barrett defines *ta charisthenta ktl.* as 'things proper (in ordinary Jewish eschatological thought) to the life of heaven, but already freely given to Christians'.[11] This seems to coincide with Allo's view. We have indeed argued on page 65 above that Paul, beginning from traditional Jewish eschatology, has modified it and adapted it to fit a gospel which proclaims that the unimaginable has already taken place. It is important to realize that in verse 12 Paul is thinking of the Christian's understanding or apprehension of the revelation, not primarily of his enjoyment or experience of salvation. Admittedly these two cannot be kept apart, since for Paul the means of understanding is faith, and faith stands on the borderline between cognition and existential experience. But the emphasis in this passage, with its crowning use of *nous*, is on the element of understanding.

The exact meaning of the phrase in verse 13, *pneumatikois pneumatika sugkrinontes* is difficult to determine; there is uncertainty about the right sense of *sugkrinontes* here, and also as to whether *pneumatikois* is neuter or masculine. The verb can mean either 'comparing' or 'interpreting', especially interpreting dreams. The older editors on the whole rejected the meaning 'interpreting', both because they were under the influence of classical usage and because they did not like the association of dream-interpretation. But neither of these considerations would have weighed with Paul, and most modern editors prefer the sense 'interpreting, expounding' here. I have encountered four distinct ways of translating the phrase:

1 'combining spiritual things with spiritual things'; this is Allo's translation, but it has very little to be said for it in this context. It suits Allo's theory that Paul was putting together a sort of systematic theology.

2 'explaining things of the Spirit in the words of the Spirit': this has strong backing. It is accepted by Hodge, Lietzmann, Héring,[12] and Bruce. It is also one of C. K. Barrett's two alternatives. It certainly fits in well with the first half of the verse, where Paul says 'we impart this in words not taught by human wisdom but taught by the Spirit'. But it is doubtful whether in Paul's thought the adjective *pneumatikos* could properly apply to *logos* or *logoi*. Could one envisage the opposite, *logoi psuchikoi* or *sarkinoi*? It hardly makes sense in a Pauline context.

3 'suiting spiritual matter to spiritual hearers' (Robertson and Plummer), or 'adapting spiritual words to spiritual things' (one

of Goudge's two alternatives): this avoids giving *sugkrinontes* the meaning of 'interpreting', but encounters other objections. Why should Paul have to do this? If his hearers were spiritual, they should not need to have the spiritual matter adapted to them; they would understand it naturally. And Goudge's modification carries the same difficulty as we noted in the last rendering.

4 'expounding spiritual things to spiritual people': this is supported by Schmiedel,[13] Weiss, Evans, and is the second alternative favoured by Goudge and C. K. Barrett. It certainly does seem to be the best; in the first place, expounding spiritual things to spiritual people exactly describes what Paul is doing in this passage; and in the second place *pneumatikos* in the masculine occurs in verse 15 and is implied in verse 14 by the occurrence of *psuchikos* in the masculine.

Who is the *pneumatikos* in verse 15? Lietzmann, very much under the influence of the *Religionsgeschichte* school, describes him as having 'a superhuman soul of divine substance'. This would certainly put Paul among the Gnostics. But there is no justification for this in the text. Even Conzelmann, who is not slow to detect traces of Gnosticism in Paul, dissents from this. He says that what makes the difference between *pneumatikos* and *psuchikos* is not something in the created nature of the two types, but their reaction to revelation. Allo, who has devoted a long excursus to the subject in his commentary, points out pertinently that the adjective *pneumatikos* is found outside Scripture in this sense once in a papyrus and once in a late Hermetic writing.[14] There is no evidence, he says, that it was used in the Gnostic literature of Paul's day; nor does *pneuma* mean 'a portion of divine essence'. In Paul's view all baptized Christians were capable of becoming *pneumatikoi*.[15] The trouble with the Corinthians was not that they were constitutionally incapable of being anything but *psuchikoi*, but that they were not making use of the *pneuma* which could be theirs in Christ. In 1 Corinthians 3.1 Paul describes them as both *sarkinoi* and *nēpioi en Christō/i*. The latter term suggests that they were capable of growing up in Christ; if he has to give them only milk now, it is in order that later on he may be able to give them the strong meat suitable for *pneumatikoi*. So, in drawing the contrast between *pneumatikoi* and *psuchikoi* among the Corinthian Christians, Paul was not separating off himself and an elect few into an esoteric group which alone could hope to understand spiritual matters. He was trying to encourage the Corinthians to make use of the heritage which could be theirs in Christ in order that they might grow in the Spirit. In 3.3 he makes it plain that the signs of being a *sarkinos* were primarily moral: envy, friction, strife. This entirely agrees with our thesis that the failure of the powers to recognize Christ was fundamentally a moral one; they were disobedient beings. So the quality of being a *pneumatikos* is closely connected with faith in Christ, and this is primarily an act of moral and spiritual self-commitment.[16]

Paul uses *pneumatikos* with *charisma* and with *nomos* (Romans 1.11; 7.14); he also applies it to the manna and the water from the rock in the wilderness (1 Corinthians 10.3-4). He uses it of *sōma* to describe the resurrection body. Galatians 6.1 is a good example of *pneumatikos* meaning 'a Christian who is behaving and believing as he ought to'. It runs: 'Brethren, if a man is overtaken in any trespass, you who are spiritual (*pneumatikoi*) should restore him in a spirit of gentleness.' All these instances conform to Schweizer's definition of *pneumatikos* as 'belonging to God's world and originating from it' (art. cit., p. 435). In 1 Corinthians 14.37 the word is used somewhat differently: 'If anyone thinks that he is a prophet or *pneumatikos*, he should acknowledge that what I am writing to you is a command of the Lord.' Here *pneumatikos* does mean 'possessing certain gifts not necessarily available to all'. But this is not a Gnostic usage. I omit the occurrences of the word in Colossians and Ephesians because of the doubt about Pauline authorship of these works; *pneumatikos* is certainly used in a different sense in these Epistles, though not in a Gnostic sense.

The properly Gnostic use of *pneumatikos* is clearly differentiated from Paul's use by the fact that in the Gnostic systems one is by nature a *pneumatikos*. It is not normally something which anyone can become by pursuing the right discipline. Thus according to Hippolytus, Basilides taught that there was a class of pneumatics whose task it was to train and perfect their own souls (Foerster, op. cit., vol. I, pp. 69, 73); he also taught that inside the psychic man was an inner spiritual man, a doctrine which we do not find in the authentic Pauline letters. Irenaeus tells us that in the teaching of the Valentinians there is a category of 'spiritual men who possess the perfect knowledge of God and are initiated into the mysteries of Achamoth'. They will be saved 'not by means of good conduct, but because they are spiritual by nature' (Foerster, p. 138). Clement of Alexandria in his *Excerpta ex Theodoto* also tells us that in the Valentinian system 'the spiritual are saved by nature', a special class and few in number (ibid., p. 150). Epiphanius in his *Excerpta ex Theodoto* says that Jesus Christ 'was brought forth for no other reason than to come and save the spiritual race from above. . . . There are three classes of men, pneumatics, psychics, and fleshly . . . [the pneumatics], being spiritual, will be saved entirely' (ibid., p. 237). Heracleon, in his commentary on the Fourth Gospel as reflected in Origen, interpreted John 4.24 to mean that 'those who have the same nature as the Father are themselves spirit'. Conversely he took John 8.44 to mean 'you are of the substance of the Devil' (ibid., pp. 172, 179).

It is interesting to compare Philo's use of the word. In *De Opif. Mundi*, vol. I, 67 Philo, describing the process of conception, says that when the semen enters the womb the creative power 'moulds into life (ζωοπλαστεῖ) the moist element so as to form the various parts of the body; but the spiritual element (*tēn pneumatikēn ousian*) it moulds into the powers of the soul, intuitive and perceptive' (my translation). Similarly in *De Abrahamo*, vol. IV, 113 he describes the angels who visited Abraham and Sarah at the oaks of Mamre as 'having been changed from a spiritual and psychic substance into a human-seeming shape' (ἀπὸ πνευματικῆς καὶ ψυχοειδοῦς ἰδέας εἰς ἀνθρωπόμορφον ἰδέαν). Again in *De Praem. et Poen.*, vol. V, 48 he uses *tous pneumatikous tonous* to mean something like 'spiritual energies'. At the same time it must be emphasized that Philo did not use *pneumatikos* in at all the same anthropological sense that Paul did. This is made clear in *De Opif. Mundi*, vol. I, 134 ff., where he draws a contrast between man in the two creation accounts: the first man is νοητός, ἀσώματος, ἄφθαρτος; the second is composed of a union of earthly substance and the spirit of God, γεωδὴς οὐσία καὶ πνεῦμα θεοῦ. He then expounds

A Quasi-Gnostic Pauline Midrash: 1 Corinthians 2.6-16

the familiar Platonic contrast between the earthy part, which is mortal, and the soul, *psuchē*, which is immortal. Here *psuchē*, far from being contrasted with *pneuma* as in Paul, is identified with it.

We have now reached the last verse of our passage, but we are still far from the end of our study, since this last verse when carefully examined yields a great deal of information about Paul's Christology and forms an essential conclusion to his argument. Commentators on 1 Corinthians 2.16 have been on the whole strangely blind to what lies behind it, and in particular have almost entirely ignored the other place where Paul uses this citation: Romans 11.34. They confine themselves for the most part to two questions: Who is referred to by the word *kuriou* in the citation? And why does Paul use *nous* here instead of *pneuma*?

The majority of scholars answer the first question by saying that *kuriou* in this context must be meant to refer to Christ the Son and not to the Father. This identification is made by Hodge,[17] Schmiedel, Lietzmann, and Bultmann.[18] Weiss, however, notes that *kuriou* here must refer to God and not to Christ. One would have imagined that a glance at Romans 11.34 would have settled this question. There, after an exclamation of praise for the depth and unexpectedness of God's wisdom, Paul quotes τίς γὰρ ἔγνω νοῦν κυρίου κτλ. It is impossible to deny that God is referred to by *kuriou* here; only someone who regarded Paul as a surrealist theologian freed from the trammels of logical thought would argue that he uses the same citation in two places to refer to two different persons of the godhead. The word *kuriou* in 1 Corinthians 2.16 must refer to God and not to Christ.

As to the second question, the obvious answer is that Paul uses *nous* and not *pneuma* in 2.16a, despite the fact that the original Hebrew is *rwaḥ*, because that is how the LXX translates it and Paul feels bound to follow the LXX.[19] This is Schmiedel's explanation and also that of Bultmann.[20] This is a perfectly reasonable explanation. Weiss points out that *pneuma* would have suited Paul's sense better. But some editors have suggested other reasons. We have already noted Weiss's suggestion. Allo believes Paul used *nous* quite deliberately here because it is a question of discernment. But Weiss is right when he remarks that *nous* in the citation is used by Paul to mean the content of the intellect, not the organ. As we shall be seeing, Paul was not the first to understand this text that way. We must, I think, leave this question open. As our investigation proceeds we shall see, I hope, that Paul read a great deal into the phrase 'the mind of God', and also that in this context the Hebrew phrase *rwaḥ YHWH* had more than a touch of intellectual content in it.

Paul quotes Isaiah 40.13 twice in his extant letters. The second occasion is Romans 11.34-5, where he quotes it as follows:

τίς ἔγνω νοῦν κυρίου;
ἢ τίς σύμβουλος αὐτοῦ ἐγένετο;
ἢ τίς προέδωκεν αὐτῷ
καὶ ἀνταποδοθήσεται αὐτῷ;

In this second quotation Paul has added to the Isaiah citation a half-verse from Job 41.3 (41.11 in EVV). This means of course that we must investigate the Job citation. We should observe that LXX in effect divides Isaiah 40.13 into three sections:

a) who has known the mind of the Lord?
b) or who has been his counsellor?
c) who shall instruct him?

Paul follows this division, quoting 13ac in 1 Corinthians 2.16 and 13ab in Romans 11.34. On the other hand, in his Job citation in Romans 11.35, he differs from both the LXX and the MT.

On the whole, commentaries on Romans 11.33-6 throw very little light on this composite quotation. Nearly all of them emphasize that Paul is dilating on the inscrutability of God and the impossibility of man ever fathoming his designs. In fact, however, what Paul is doing here is glorying in the fact that God, inscrutable though he be to human knowledge, has revealed his designs to us Christians. Most commentators go out of their way to emphasize that the questions in both the quotations are purely rhetorical and imply the answer 'no'. Thus Michel finds here 'three rhetorical questions';[21] Leenhardt says the message of the text is 'there has never been a

A Quasi-Gnostic Pauline Midrash: 1 Corinthians 2.6-16

counsellor or a creditor for God';[22] Eltester claims that the answer to the question in Romans 11.34 is 'no one';[23] and van Roon writes: 'Both to the prophet and to Paul there is no counsellor who has instructed God.'[24] Other commentators simply elaborate the theme of God's inscrutability. Lipsius writes: 'Human speculation cannot reach God's designs';[25] true enough, but this is not all that Paul is saying here. Karl Barth finds here a splendid example of the doctrine of the *deus absconditus*: 'What is searched out in the deep things of God is his unsearchability' and 'There is no direct knowledge of God. He decides without the assistance of counsellors.'[26] Bultmann interestingly renders the first line of the citation in Romans 11.34 with: 'Who has recognized God's wondrous plan of salvation?', but does not proceed to make the obvious link with 1 Corinthians 2.8, 16.[27] C. H. Dodd indulges in a meditation which owes more to Schleiermacher and Otto than to Paul: 'The vision of the future which has been given us is not knowledge but faith, and faith set against a background of ignorance. . . . The religious consciousness, after its highest flights of speculation, returns to the simple "numinous" feeling of awe before the Mystery.'[28] Paul, far from eschewing knowledge, believed that faith could give us knowledge of God's designs, hence his acceptance of the word *nous*. He did not regard himself as indulging in speculations in this or previous passages in Romans; he believed he was making explicit what the Scriptures had told him. He did believe that God had a counsellor; he did not regard these questions as rhetorical; nor was he the first to approach the Isaiah passage in this way.

Two scholars must be regarded as remarkable exceptions to this unanimity about Paul's emphasis on the inscrutability of God. W. L. Knox writes *à propos* this passage: 'The words of Isaiah 40.13 proved the folly of trying to teach God: His purpose in creation was entirely above man's comprehension. But that purpose in creation was simply the divine Wisdom.' And again: 'Thus Isaiah 40.13 appears to be quoted with a reference to its original context: it would naturally be useful as a Christian proof-text, implying that God had a counsellor in creation, namely Wisdom.'[29] Here we have the true significance of the citation from Isaiah in both places: God has indeed a counsellor who knows his mind, the pre-existent Christ.

The New Testament Interpretation of Scripture

The other commentator is Ernst Käsemann; he does make use of 1 Corinthians 2.16 to interpret Romans 11.34, something which no other commentator that I have read does. He says that 'what eye has not seen, etc.' is the contents of Romans 9-11; he states that Paul is not here emphasizing the basic unknowability of God; Romans 1.20 makes this plain. Unfortunately, however, he has not grasped the implicit reference to the pre-existent Christ here, and can thus describe the unsearchability of God as consisting in the fact that God brings about the justification of the godless instead of the pious, as is implied in 1 Corinthians 1.19. He can thus claim that this fact breaks any 'scheme of historical continuity or rationally apprehensible development'. He adds: '*sola fide* is the only answer to this.'[30] Just because Käsemann has missed the reference to the pre-existent Christ, he is driven to represent the content of the revelation of God's design as too much of a divine intrusion. Dare one say that he has here over-Lutheranized Paul? Once accepted the dimension of pre-existence,[31] and salvation history becomes the content of the revelation; we are not confined to the one vertical event of the justification of sinners. But we must now turn to an examination of how both the Isaiah passage and the Job passage were understood in traditional Jewish exegesis.

In the MT Isaiah 40.13 runs as follows:

my tikēn 'et rwaḥ YHWH
w'yš "ṣatw ywdy'enw

The LXX offers:

τίς ἔγνω νοῦν κυρίου,
καὶ τίς αὐτοῦ σύμβουλος ἐγένετο
ὃς συμβιβᾷ αὐτόν;

Kittel on the basis of the LXX translation suggests that the Hebrew originally read *wmy 'ys*, which would give the sense: 'Who shall measure the spirit of the Lord, and who shall advise him as his counsellor?' This seems to be how Theodotion understood the verse, with his rendering of 40.13b: καὶ ἀνὴρ βουλὴν αὐτοῦ καὶ ἐγνώρισεν αὐτόν. *egnō* is a most extraordinary translation for *tikēn*. There are only three other instances of *tkn* in the Pi'el to be found in the NT: Psalm 75.4, Isaiah 40.12.

and Job 28.25; the first of these the LXX translates with *estereōsen*, and in the other two avoids translating the verb altogether. But in Psalm 93.1 (LXX 92.1); 96.10 (LXX 95.10), and 1 Chronicles 16.30 *tikēn* may with great probability be restored for MT *tikwn*; here LXX offers *estereōsen*, *katorthēsen*, and *katorthōthēto* respectively.[32] The Vulgate is also remarkable: 'Quis adjuvit spiritum Domini?' One can only speculate that the LXX translator, seeing the language in verses 13 and 14 about counselling and instructing, decided that the whole passage was concerned with knowledge or lack of it, and translated accordingly. We consider the question of why he rendered *rwaḥ* with *nous* below (pp. 89 ff).

It is certain that by *sumbiban* the LXX translator meant 'instruct, communicate knowledge', since he uses the verb twice elsewhere to render the Hiph'il of *yd'*; in Exodus 18.6 Moses describes himself as communicating the instructions of the Lord to Israel; and in Deuteronomy 4.9 Israel is told to instruct his children in the story of salvation.

Delitzsch claims that *tikēn* means not 'to test' but 'to bring into orderly shape'.[33] He describes verse 13b as 'an attributive clause', and therefore claims that the LXX translation is correct. Duhm on the other hand suspects that the LXX's translation *egnō* indicates a reading *hēbyn* instead of *tikēn*. The word *tikēn* means 'Who judges Jahweh?' not 'Who searches his spirit?'[34] Jahweh is not to be influenced by any counsellor. The spirit here is the organ of the divine knowledge. Here *rwaḥ* in Jahweh equals *lēb* in man; so he concludes that the LXX's *nous* for *rwaḥ* is by no means astray. Westermann, on the other hand, argues that by *rwaḥ* is meant not the being of God nor the organ of his knowledge, but 'God's wonderful, active power'.[35] Elliger rejects Rignell's suggestion that 13b refers to Cyrus.[36] Cyrus is only the organ of God's design; he does not have any inner understanding of it.[37] We do, it is true, meet a council of Jahweh in Job 1; but in Deutero-Isaiah God's servants only carry out his will, they do not give him advice. My colleague, Professor R. N. Whybray, has greatly extended this thought of a counsellor in a learned monograph.[38] He claims that in Babylonian mythology there was the belief that each god had a junior attendant-counsellor. The prophet is concerned to deny that Jahweh has any need for such a counsellor.

The New Testament Interpretation of Scripture

He thinks that 'Who has comprehended the mind of the Lord?' is probably the right translation, and adds: 'We therefore suggest that the content of the supposed knowledge taught to Yahweh is the practical knowledge required to create the world.'[39] He admits that Deutero-Isaiah did have the conception of a heavenly court, but 'the function of its members was not to assist Yahweh in making his decisions, but simply to carry out his commands'.[40]

Thus, those scholars who have claimed that the correct answer to the questions posed in Isaiah 40.13ab is 'No one' are right as far as the meaning of the prophet himself is concerned. But it is very different when we come to examine how the verse was understood in subsequent tradition. Elliger points out that the masoretic punctuation of verse 13b seems to favour the meaning: 'And he [Yahweh] has informed his counsellor.' This sense also seems to be behind Symmachus's rendering (as preserved by Jerome in Latin): 'Et virum consilii eius quis ostendit ei?' Elliger is no doubt right in rejecting this as Deutero-Isaiah's meaning, but this is on the whole the way the Targum takes it. Indeed the Targum drastically changes the meaning of the verse, as follows:

> Who hath directed the holy spirit in the mouth of all the prophets? is it not the Lord? and to the righteous who perform his commands hath he made known the things of his good pleasure.[41]

Here are no rhetorical questions at all. The meaning has been changed from the thought of someone informing Jahweh (which tradition no doubt dismissed as blasphemous) to the question of who it is to whom God imparts knowledge. The *rwaḥ YHWH* is interpreted in terms of the Holy Spirit. The righteous are in effect the counsellor of whom the prophet speaks; and the means of revelation (or at least the ground for revelation) is the Torah. One might reasonably claim that the part played in this text by Christ in Paul's theology is in the theology of the Targumist played by the Torah.

We can indeed cite an earlier witness to this interpretation of Isaiah 40.13, the author of the Book of Wisdom. We quote Wisdom 9.13,17 in the Greek, as follows:

τίς γὰρ ἄνθρωπος γνώσεται βουλὴν θεοῦ;

A Quasi-Gnostic Pauline Midrash: 1 Corinthians 2.6-16

ἢ τίς ἐνθυμήσεται τί θέλει ὁ κύριος;
... βουλὴν δέ σου τίς ἔγνω εἰ μὴ σὺ ἔδωκας σοφίαν
καὶ ἔπεμψας τὸ ἅγιόν σου πνεῦμα ἀπὸ ὑψίστων;

For what man can learn the counsel of God?
Or who can discern what the Lord wills?
... Who has learned thy counsel, unless thou hast given wisdom
and sent thy holy Spirit from on high?

Verse 18 runs:

And thus the paths of those on earth were set right,
And men were taught what pleases thee,
and were saved by wisdom.

It is the habit of the author of Wisdom to paraphrase Scripture rather than to quote it verbatim, so few will deny that he has Isaiah 40.13 in mind here. He certainly seems to have the same interpretation as that which the Targumist reproduces. Like the Targumist, he identifies the *rwaḥ YHWH* with the Holy Spirit, and also like him he says that by the Spirit men learn what is God's good pleasure. Indeed 9.18b might almost be a Greek version of the last clause in the Targum of Isaiah 40.13: 'To the righteous he hath made known the things of his good pleasure.' Like the Targumist, he does not regard the prophet's questions as rhetorical; there is an answer to them. The counsellor is in fact Wisdom. Talbert points out that in Wisdom 9.17-18 the Holy Spirit and Wisdom are identified.[42] Larcher makes the same point.[43] When we recollect the way in which the author of the Book of Wisdom traces the activities of the divine Wisdom in the course of salvation history, we realize that we are only a step away from Paul's interpretation of Isaiah 40.13, and equally that Paul's interpretation is intimately bound up with the activity of the pre-existent Christ.[44]

Goodrick in his commentary on Wisdom sees that the author is quoting Isaiah 40.13.[45] He writes, with Paul in mind: 'Both writers have drawn from the same source; but it must be noticed that in our author it is implied that by means of Wisdom man is enabled to understand God's will. In any case St Paul is nearer to Isaiah than to Pseudo-Solomon.' In other words Goodrick has realized that the author of Wisdom thinks there is an answer to Isaiah's questions, but not that Paul also thinks so. In this respect Paul is not nearer to Isaiah. Oesterley has the perspicacity to make cross-references here not only to Isaiah but also to Romans 11.34; 1 Corinthians 2.16; and he comments in verse 17: 'With this identification of Wisdom with the holy spirit (not, of course, in the Christian sense) cp. 1.4-7; 1 Cor. 2.7,8.'[46] This would seem to support our contention that Paul does not distinguish Christ from the Spirit in 1 Corinthians 2. More than eighty years ago Grafe devoted a whole article to a study of the relation of the Pauline writings to the Book of Wisdom.[47] He admits that in 1 Corinthians 2.16 Paul comes very close to echoing Wisdom 9.13-14, except that Paul is here following the LXX word for word, and is concerned with quoting Isaiah 40.13. He concludes therefore that we cannot claim 1 Corinthians 2.16 as a verse in which Paul echoes the Book of Wisdom. No doubt this is a perfectly correct conclusion, and for our purpose the significance of Wisdom's treatment of Isaiah 40.13 lies in the fact that in Wisdom as in 1 Corinthians 2.16 Isaiah's questions are regarded as both answerable and answered. On the other hand, we have no right to claim that Wisdom is not quoting Isaiah 40.13 just because his language differs from Paul's. His technique of quotation is not the same as Paul's, since he prefers paraphrase to actual citation.

We now turn to Paul's second citation, Job 41.3 (EVV 41.11). He quotes it thus:

ἢ τίς προέδωκεν αὐτῷ καὶ ἀνταποδοθήσεται αὐτῷ;

This coincides exactly neither with the MT nor with the LXX. The MT runs as follows: *my hiqdymāny wa'ašalem taḥat kol hašāmaym ly hw'*. This will hardly make sense as it stands. Literally translated it would mean: 'Who has opposed me and I shall repay? Everything under the heavens he (is) to me.' Beer, in Kittel's *Biblia Hebraica*, follows the emendation originally suggested by Gunkel and reads: *my hw' qidmw wayšlom taḥat kol hašāmaym lo' 'eḥad* (others suggest *lo' hw'* for *lo' 'eḥad*). This gives the sense: 'Who can stand before him and be safe? Under the whole heavens not one' (or 'there is not one'). This emendation is partially supported by the LXX, which translates:

καὶ τίς ἀντιστήσεταί μοι καὶ ὑπομενεῖ,
εἰ πᾶσα ἡ ὑπ' οὐρανὸν ἐμή ἐστιν;

A Quasi-Gnostic Pauline Midrash: 1 Corinthians 2.6-16

The Vulgate seems to render the MT but with Paul's meaning:

Quis ante dedit mihi, ut reddam ei?
Omnia quae sub caelo sunt, mea sunt (41.2)

This may have been influenced by Paul's citation, but in Romans 11.35 it offers: 'Aut quis prior dedit illi, ut retribuetur ei?' Gunkel's emendation would make excellent sense in the context. The verse occurs in a poem on the crocodile and the verse would simply emphasize the beast's invincibility. It may even be that Gunkel has recovered what the poet originally wrote. But it is obvious that very soon exegetical tradition got to work on this text. Just as pious minds could not tolerate even the thought that anyone could give advice to God, so it was quite unacceptable to learned commentators among the Jews that the inspired Scriptures were only describing a beast such as the crocodile. There must be profound truths hidden in the text. So we find that tradition discovers here a reference to what God did at the creation. Paul would certainly not have quoted the text if he had thought that it merely referred to the crocodile: he too must have associated it with the creation. In fact the form in which he quotes it is formally not very far from the MT; *qdm* in Pi'el can mean, 'to anticipate'[48] and if we can allow that *antapodothēsetai* is a reverential periphrasis for God's action,[49] it could render *'šlm* well enough. The Targum offers:

> Who has been beforehand with me in the works of creation, that I have to pay him back? Is not everything under the heaven mine?[50]

This might account for the rendering of the second half of the verse in the LXX, but certainly not of the first half.[51] Dhorme suggests that the phrase in the Targum 'in the works of creation' (*b'bdy br'šyt*) is an attempt to make sense of the MT *hqdymny* and to impart a reference to the creation.[52] At least we can say that by the time the Targum was written this verse was no longer regarded as simply concerned with the crocodile; it was already being interpreted as giving us information about what happened at the creation. As we shall be seeing, not even here was the poet allowed to employ a purely rhetorical question; there was an answer to it.

D

Ewald points out that the two animals referred to in Job 40 and 41, the hippopotamus and the crocodile, have often been allegorized. He writes: 'These two marvellous animals have often been interpreted symbolically, and the strangest things have been imported into the description. As early as the Book of Enoch lx. 1-10, 24, 25, this allegorical interpretation commenced.'[53] Pope elaborates this theme, referring to 'the supernatural character of Leviathan' (who is mentioned in 40.25, EVV 41.1).[54] He continues: 'If the author of the present composition wished merely to exercise his poetic abilities on the subject of the power and ferocity of the crocodile, he surpassed his goal at the start by the use of the term Leviathan.' And on our passage he comments: 'These things are difficult, and it is apparent that the text has suffered some sabotage intended to obscure gross pagan mythological allusions.' Gunkel's emendation has been very widely adopted, being accepted by Dhorme, Driver-Gray,[55] Hölscher,[56] and Fohrer.[57] This last scholar remarks in a footnote that Paul has changed the corrupted text by means of a free rehandling. This seems most unlikely. As we shall be seeing, there is evidence that the thought of someone being in God's credit was found in this text by the rabbis. Paul is only using traditional exegesis of the passage. Weiser has a somewhat different explanation of the verse;[58] he renders it:

> Who has brought about a confrontation with me so that I should permit it? Under the whole heaven, he is mine;

and he comments that Job's pride in challenging God is like the pride of the chaos monster in fighting against the God who had created him. If this is the original sense, then there is some justification for the traditional exegesis: from the very beginning this passage referred to God's action in creation.

The history of the exposition of Job 41.3 in early rabbinic exegesis is interesting. In *Pesikta Rabbati* the text is used to remind those in Israel who are under obligation to tithe that 'all things come of God', i.e. they do not possess anything which God has not already given them.[59] The verse is understood as meaning 'Who has given me anything beforehand, that I should repay him?', precisely the sense in which Paul takes it. Then follows a series of questions, all emphasizing that God does not ask anything of a man until he has first given the man something, e.g. no one is required to circumcise his son till God has given him one. God is represented as saying: 'I have not asked for a portion of that which is yours: I have asked for a portion of that which is mine.' This agrees well enough in general with Paul's thought in Romans: we have no ground on which we can of ourselves establish a claim against God. But in fact Paul uses the citation to say more than that: he implies that there is a means whereby we can justify ourselves before God; we can do so in Christ. In Paul's interpretation the question in 11.35 is not rhetorical. We can actually find a similar interpretation in the rabbis.

In the *Pesikta de Rab Kahana* an interpretation is attributed to R. Tanhuma (an Amoraite living in Palestine c. A.D. 300) which understands the verse thus:[60]

> Whoever, without being required to, bestirs himself [to help provide instruction in the Torah which] under the whole heaven was [first] mine, I will repay him [by not turning a deaf ear to his prayer for male children].

The prayer for male children has been brought into the interpretation of this verse by running on into verse 4a (EVV 41.12a) and adopting a somewhat artificial exposition: 'I will not keep silence concerning his boastings' (*lo' 'aḥᵃryš badayw*). The word for 'boastings' could be translated 'limbs' (as in the RSV) or 'branches', and hence can be taken to mean 'offspring'. This interpretation is significant for our purpose because it introduces into the text an allusion to the pre-existent Torah, the first of God's creatures. God's reward is connected with the Torah.

But R. Tanhuma himself gives a further interpretation in the name of R. Jeremiah ben Eleazar (Palestinian, c. A.D. 200). He expounds the verse as follows:

> Whosoever without being required to bestirs himself [to provide instruction in the Torah which] under the whole heaven was [first] mine, I will repay him [by having a Voice proclaim] under the entire heaven [that such a man has wrought as I have wrought].

And R. Jeremiah comments on the verse thus:

'Some day in the future a divine voice [it refers to the *Bath Qōl*] reverberating on the mountain tops will declare, "whosoever wrought with God [as the unmarried man wrought by providing for children to be instructed in the Torah even though he had no children of his own], let him come and receive the reward due to him". Of this it is said "At the due season shall it be told to Jacob and to Israel: Who hath wrought with God" (Numbers 23.23): "Whosoever wrought with God, let him come and receive the reward due to him".' Braude explains that R. Jeremiah has pointed the text of Numbers 23.23 so as to give the sense 'Who has wrought with God?' instead of the sense of the MT, which is 'What hath God wrought!'[61] Braude goes on to compare Isaiah 40.10cd: 'Behold his reward is with him, and his recompense before him.' This brings in the idea of reward, which is absent from the text of Numbers 23.23.

This refinement of R. Jeremiah's is interesting for our subject because he has so interpreted Job 41.3 as to bring in not only the idea of there being the possibility of putting oneself in the right with God, or even on a credit basis with him, but also the thought of working together with him. Now this, as we have seen, is what one tradition in Judaism seems to have understood by Isaiah 40.13: God does have a counsellor who understands the secrets of his creative action. Though we cannot provide any positive evidence that Isaiah 40.13 and Job 41.3 were connected in rabbinic tradition, we can show that one rabbinic interpretation of Job 41.3 also made use of the thought which Paul, the Targumist, and the author of the Book of Wisdom found in Isaiah 40.13.

Of course the evidence from *Pesikta de Rab Kahana* and from *Pesikta Rabbati* is late. It comes from a period when Judaism had emerged as a tradition opposed to, and anxious to distinguish itself from, Christianity – hence no doubt the emphasis on the importance of the Torah. But we do not need to argue that the interpretation of Job 41.3 as we find it in these rabbinic works is what Paul received as his tradition. It is quite enough to have shown that the rabbis connect Job 41.3 (and Isaiah 40.13) with a pre-existent something. It may even be that the notion of the pre-existence of the Torah (created before anything else, etc.) was brought into Judaism, or received

A Quasi-Gnostic Pauline Midrash: 1 Corinthians 2.6-16

emphasis in Judaism, after Paul's day specifically in order to counterbalance the emphasis on the pre-existent wisdom of God of which early Christian theology had made so much use. Paul has in fact made Christ do duty both for the Torah and for the righteous in Jewish tradition. According to the rabbis, God did disclose his mind to the righteous by means of the Torah; he did in some secondary sense put himself in their debt if they obeyed the Torah, or at least voluntarily bound himself to them. This is what the combined citation of Romans 11.34-5 meant to Judaism. But Paul finds only Christ here: it is Christ who knows God's mind, indeed he is God's mind. It is Christ who has established a claim on God by his life and death, so that his resurrection and exaltation are not merely the events which happened to follow his crucifixion, but are the necessary consequences of it. This is not to say that Paul has in mind no group corresponding to the righteous. But, just because of his doctrine of justification by faith (by no means his invention), the righteous in his theology can only be described as such *in Christ*. Far from ignoring them, Paul is much concerned to show how they fit into God's design, especially in 1 Corinthians 2.6-16. Unless, however, we realize that at the very heart of his scriptural citations, whether in 1 Corinthians 12.16 or in Romans 11.34-5, lies the interpretation that finds Christ here; unless we acknowledge that none of these questions is taken by Paul to be rhetorical (and there are three of them, by any reckoning, in the two citations); unless we accept that according to Paul and his tradition correct answers could be found to these questions, we shall never understand what these passages from Scripture meant to Paul.

Before we bring this study to a close, there are four questions of a more technical nature that present themselves, on the analogy of those which we considered at the end of section 3. They are as follows:

1 Why did the LXX translator render *rwaḥ* in Isaiah 40.13a with *nous* and not *pneuma*? We have referred to this problem before, but not yet posed it directly. We may begin by observing that apparently the translator was uncertain about the exact sense of the Pi'el of *tkn*. On two occasions he avoids translating it altogether: on the four occasions when he does translate it,

other than Isaiah 40.13, he uses either *stereoun* or *katorthoun*.⁶²
Neither of these verbs would have made any sense in the context of Isaiah 40.13. He was therefore thrown back on the context to find a clue as to the meaning of the verb here. The context is strongly intellectual and cognitive. He therefore concluded that *egnō* was the safest rendering of *tikēn* here. Having once written *egnō* it would be more natural to translate *rwaḥ* with *nous* rather than *pneuma*, unique though that translation actually is. This does mean indeed that the LXX translator apparently had a somewhat different tradition of interpretation for this verse compared with that utilized by the author of the Book of Wisdom and the Targumist. These two took the reference to *rwaḥ* as an indication of the presence of God's holy Spirit; this could easily lead them on to find an emphasis here on the communicability of God rather than his incomprehensibility, since the holy Spirit was the means *par excellence* of his communicating himself. Paul in fact seems to make use of both traditions. We have noted above that several scholars maintain the accuracy of the LXX's translation: *rwaḥ* here, they say, does mean the mind of God.

2   Why does Paul quote Isaiah 40.13ac in 1 Corinthians 2.16 and Isaiah 40.13ab plus Job 41.3a in Romans 11.34-5? In 1 Corinthians 2.16 Paul is mainly interested in the cognitive aspect of the citation, though, as we have seen, the element of salvation history is certainly there in the background. He wanted to show that because Christians are in Christ they can comprehend God's revelation of himself in the events of Christ's entire career from creation to exaltation. For that purpose Isaiah 40.13ac was certainly most relevant, since these two lines express exactly what Paul wanted to prove: we can know God's mind or design because Christ has interpreted him to us. In the context of Romans 11, however, we can detect two main preoccupations: the first is the desire to summarize all he has been concerned with in the preceding chapters, that is the whole Gospel, all that God has done for us in Christ in its widest aspect. The second concern was the doctrine of justification by faith, which figures prominently in Romans but hardly at all in 1 Corinthians. Both these concerns were met by the form of the citation which he uses in Romans 11.34-5: the

A Quasi-Gnostic Pauline Midrash: 1 Corinthians 2.6-16

specific mention of the counsellor would remind those familiar with Paul's theology of his doctrine (not his exclusively, of course) of the pre-existent wisdom which Paul saw personified in the pre-existent Christ; and the Job citation would certainly remind his readers not (as some commentators have mistakenly suggested) that nobody can be justified with God, but that Christ was, and we in Christ. At the same time both citations are heavily endowed with overtones of God's creative activity. This would be particularly appropriate in Romans, which begins with a consideration of God as creator. We can naturally only give a conjectural answer to this question, but our conjecture is not without foundation in what we know of Paul's methods of scriptural interpretation.

3 When were Isaiah 40.13 and Job 41.3 combined? This question is quite complex, since we must try to decide whether it was Paul who combined them, or, if they were already combined when Paul used them, when was it done and at what linguistic stage (in Hebrew or in Greek). It seems to me very unlikely indeed that Paul was the first to couple these texts: though we know that Isaiah 40.13 could be quoted alone by Paul, Job 41.3 on its own would seem to have little point; it would require some mention of God to go before it (which is not to be found in the text of Job 41.1-3). The context of the works of the creation, which alone can qualify this verse to be considered relevant to God's action in saving history, is much clearer in Isaiah 40.13 than in Job 41.3. It is much more likely that the two verses were already associated in the Jewish exegetical tradition when Paul used them.[63] Moreover both texts are connected with the pre-existent Torah in later rabbinic tradition at least. Had they been only associated by the Christians, it seems very unlikely that the later rabbis would have been so free in using them.

As for the question of language, we must probably admit the same inability to decide as we had to concede in the case of the conflated citation of 1 Corinthians 2.9. At first glance there would seem to be a probability in favour of the association having taken place at the Greek stage, because both the LXX of Isaiah 40.13 and Paul's Greek version of Job 41.3a favour an interpretation in terms of the pre-existent Wisdom more than

The New Testament Interpretation of Scripture

does the MT as we have it. But we have seen very good reason to believe that Jewish tradition had already read the pre-existent Torah into Isaiah 40.13 at the Hebrew stage, and also that later tradition had no difficulty in extracting from the Hebrew of Job 41.3 references to the creation and the pre-existent Torah; so the Greek does not really appear to have very much advantage over the Hebrew as far as concerns speculative theology either Jewish or Christian. About the year 180 B.C. Jesus ben Sira emphasizes very strongly that God has no need of a counsellor. See Ecclesiasticus 42.21bc:

Nothing can be added or taken away, and he [God] needs no one to be his counsellor.

This is certainly an echo of Isaiah 40.13-14. In the same book we have quite an advanced doctrine of the divine wisdom; speculation on such passages as Isaiah 40 was already beginning. A hundred years later or so it had developed further, as we can see from the Book of Wisdom. Also the allegorical interpretation of Job 40-41 was already in evidence by at least the first Christian century. Hence the most likely conclusion seems to be that the quotations were associated at the Hebrew stage rather than the Greek.

4 In what context were the citations originally combined? This admits of a relatively simple answer: they must have been combined in a milieu where there was a strong interest in speculation about God's attributes and creative activity. The combination must come from the tradition of wisdom speculation in Judaism and this means midrash rather than liturgy. Martin Hengel in his book already referred to has argued effectively that we must look for the origins of Paul's Christology, and indeed for the Christology of the early Church, in the area of such wisdom speculation, merging at one end of the spectrum into *Merkabah* mysticism, rather than to Gnosticism, Hellenistic cults, mystery religions, or any of the other sources which have been so often suggested.[64] The two texts which we have been examining fit very appropriately into such a context. The occurrence of the word *sumboulos* in Isaiah 40.13 points towards a form of messianic speculation, since the Messiah was identified with the 'wonderful counsellor' of Isaiah

9.5d.⁶⁵ The Job citation is so far from whatever the original text of the author of Job was, that one must allow, apart from any other evidence, for a considerable period of exegesis and speculation.⁶⁶ To transform what was originally (we must assume) a description of the crocodile of the Nile into a piece of information about God's employment of an intermediate agent in creation demands a process extended over more than one or two generations, no matter how much we must allow for the initial impetus to the process given by the use of the mythological name Leviathan.

We conclude then that the combined citation in Romans 11.34-5 is in fact an implicitly christological statement. Paul has ended his exposition of the whole design of God, and exclaims with admiration at the depth and unexpectedness of that design. But, far from suggesting that God's intention has always been inscrutable, he implies by his two citations that it has always been known to God's counsellor, the pre-existent Christ, or Son, to whom God disclosed his whole mind and in whom his whole plan for the redemption and justification of man has been carried out. It is in fact a superb example of Paul's conception of God-in-Christ.⁶⁷ The three prepositional phrases which he uses in 11.36 are not indeed a formal statement of Trinitarian doctrine, since the concept of God as three in one had certainly not dawned on Paul's intellectual horizon. But they are all christological as well as theological: we are from Christ because he was the agent in creation; we are through Christ because he is the agent of our redemption; we are to Christ because he is our goal and purpose in life. And all three phrases apply equally to God the Father because he is at work in Christ.

If with this understanding of what Paul is saying in Romans 11.33-6 we now turn back to 1 Corinthians 2.16, we ought to be in a position to understand Paul's argument more adequately. Paul, we have claimed, is anxious to show, first that God is able to reveal himself to us, and next that he actually has done so (and is doing so) in Christ. Up to verse 16 he has used the word *pneuma* to describe the means by which God reveals himself to us Christians, partly no doubt because it was a word which was freely used among the Corinthian Christians, and Paul was probably anxious to rescue the word *pneumatikos* at least from the hands of proto-Gnostics. But now he produces a quotation from Scripture where the significant word is *nous*, not *pneuma*. We must not imagine that Paul was embarrassed by this, as if he had been a professor of theology who has to be careful not to disturb the naive literalism of the congregation to which he is preaching. On the contrary Paul probably welcomed the LXX's use of the word; he must have known that the original Hebrew was *ruaḥ*, but the translation *nous* here enabled him to stress that element of cognition which is important to his argument. We really do know the mind of God, because Christ, the one referred to in the scriptural quotation, is ours. The counsellor, the one who was God's agent in creation, confidant and executor of God's whole design, is available to us Christians because we are 'in him'. It is not a question of belonging to an esoteric group within the Church, nor of undergoing some special ecstatic experience, but of making use of that knowledge and power which are ours as Christians. It seems to me quite impossible that in this passage Paul distinguishes between the Spirit and Christ. The transition from *to pneuma to ek tou theou* in verse 12 to *noun kuriou* and *noun Christou* in verse 16 depends on the assumption that the Spirit of God and Christ are identical. Whether this identity is maintained throughout Paul's writings is another question with which we are not concerned here.[68] Verse 16 then crowns Paul's entire argument in chapter 2 of 1 Corinthians: the words of Scripture narrate both what God has done in Christ (verse 9) and how he has communicated the knowledge of his activity to us (verse 16). These quotations, obscure and irrelevant to Paul's argument though they may appear to us moderns, were to Paul (and no doubt to his readers) luminous proofs of the truth of what he was saying. We may regard what lies behind the citations as a form of theological speculation: to Paul they constituted the strongest possible assurance that what had happened in Christ had all been planned by God beforehand, and that therefore the events of the cross and resurrection, unexpected and indeed scandalous as they might appear to some, were in fact God's chosen means of self-revelation and redemption, and could be in some sense authenticated for themselves by those who chose to enter the fellowship of the Christian Church.

A Quasi-Gnostic Pauline Midrash: 1 Corinthians 2.6-16

As we look back over the whole passage which has been the subject of our study, 2.6-16, we can now realize how important a part the scriptural background plays in the development of Paul's argument. Indeed we might well claim that an understanding of Paul's approach to Scripture provides the key to an understanding of what Paul is trying to convey in this chapter. Perhaps I might be allowed to repeat what I have underlined more strongly in a previous book;[69] we may regard Paul as in some respects a speculative theologian, but he believed himself to be a biblical exegete. At every step in the argument of this passage Scripture is there, either in the background or explicitly quoted, to undergird the movement of his thought. It is, we have suggested, an interpretation of Psalm 24 that inspires his account of the powers' failure to recognize Christ in verse 8. In verse 9 it is a compilation from Scripture which both describes God's revelation in Christ and underlines its unexpectedness and unimaginable quality. Finally it is Scripture which proclaims that God has communicated his revelation to us in Christ. At every stage Paul appeals to Scripture to back up his argument.

We have described 1 Corinthians 2.6-16 as a 'quasi-Gnostic Pauline midrash'. The word 'quasi-Gnostic' was deliberately used so as not to prejudge the question whether this passage is Gnostic or not. In the course of our study, however, we may well conclude that this question has answered itself. As we have gone through these eleven verses in 1 Corinthians 2, we have encountered a whole series of phrases and concepts that appear at first sight to be redolent of Gnosticism: wisdom in a mystery, world-rulers misled by the appearance of the redeemer, the deep things of God, the contrast between the spiritual men and the natural, even *nous* itself, which as an aeon played a big part in many a subsequent Gnostic system.[70] But on examining these phrases and concepts we have invariably found that in Paul's hands they pointed away from Gnosticism. It may seem unlikely that he could use so many apparently Gnostic terms and yet not be a Gnostic himself. But we must constantly remember that full-blown Gnosticism is a phenomenon which belongs to a period more than a generation after Paul's death. It is in part a product of Christianity rather than Christianity being a product of Gnosticism.

The New Testament Interpretation of Scripture

We must also allow something for the fact that Paul was actually struggling with something like proto-Gnosticism among some of his Corinthian converts. His technique is always to carry the war into his enemy's territory; he makes use of some of the terms which they use[71] and converts them to what he regards as the true usage. None of the characteristically Gnostic concepts which appear on the surface to be present in this passage proves to be really there on closer examination, neither the disguised descent of the redeemer, nor the deep secrets of God known only to the group of the elect, nor the distinction between those whose souls are composed of *pneuma* and those who are by nature merely *psuchikoi*, nor the idea of *nous* as a world-soul or an intermediary aeon. All such language is far more satisfactorily explained in terms of Jewish Wisdom speculation applied to the event of Christ. One could with as little justification accuse Paul of being a Gnostic as one could accuse Hegel of being a Nazi. Our conclusion must be that, as far as the passage we have been studying is concerned, Paul cannot properly be described as a Gnostic at all.

3

John 1. 14-18 and Exodus 34

Since at least the beginning of this century the suggestion has been made by Johannine scholars that behind the important passage in John's prologue 1.14-18 there lies the whole narrative of the theophany in Exodus 33-4 and, in particular, that John's phrase *plērēs kharitos kai alētheias* is in fact a deliberate citation of *rab ḥesed we'ᵉmet* in Exodus 34.6. The purpose of this chapter is to bring together the evidence which can be found for this theory and to examine a recent article which would reject it altogether.

1

In examining the views of scholars on this question we can divide them into three main groups: (a) those who do see a reference to Exodus 34 in this passage – by far the largest number of those scholars whom I have consulted; (b) those who are doubtful about a reference to Exodus 34, but who allow that *kharis kai alētheia* in 1.14 and 17 does reproduce the familiar phrase *ḥesed we'ᵉmet*; (c) those who deny any connection at all, a very small group indeed. Among the first group we may begin with Westcott, who writes: 'The combination recalls the description of Jehovah Exod. 34.6.'[1] Similarly Holtzmann sees a reference to Exodus 34.6, though he denies a formal dependence.[2] Lagrange also sees an echo of Exodus 34.6, and adds that John's phrase means that *ḥesed* is what God is in himself.[3] Hoskyns refers us to the whole passage Exodus 33.7-34.7,[4] and Barrett says that the pair of nouns in 1.14, 17 recalls Exodus 34.6.[5] Two years earlier Boismard had devoted a great deal of attention to Exodus 34 as the background to this passage, from which he draws important theological conclusions. But he seems to make things unnecessarily complicated by insisting on a connection with the narrative of the transfiguration also, of which I can find no trace in John's Gospel.[6] Kuyper in an article written in 1962 believes that Exodus 34.6 is one of the passages lying behind John's phrase.[7] Among the very recent commentators, Schnackenburg refers it primarily to Exodus 34.6;[8] and so does Brown.[9] Sanders likewise sees the equivalence of *kharis kai alētheia* with *ḥesed we'ᵉmet* and the reference to Exodus 34.6, and suggests that John may be translating direct from the Hebrew.[10] Finally, Lindars writes: 'The whole phrase recalls the theophany to Moses at Mt. Sinai, Exodus 33.12-34.8'; and also believes that John has rendered the Hebrew for himself.[11]

In the second group we must put Strack-Billerbeck, who simply equate *kharis kai alētheia* with *ḥesed we'ᵉmet*.[12] Here also belongs Bernard, who only gives Exodus 34 a bare mention; much preferring Psalm 85.7-11 as a likely source.[13] We consider this interesting suggestion below and hope to show that in fact it brings us back to Exodus 34. Dodd underlines the connection of *kharis kai alētheia* with *ḥesed we'ᵉmet* but traces no particular connection with Exodus 34.[14] R. H. Lightfoot adopts the same position,[15] and Schlatter takes it for granted.[16] In this group also should be Strachan, who contents himself with saying that John's phrase is reminiscent of *ḥesed we'ᵉmet*.[17]

The third group is a very select one indeed, since it only includes three scholars (apart from the article to be discussed below). Loisy in 1903 wrote: 'The connection between "mercy and faithfulness", *ḥesed we'ᵉmet*, so often mentioned in the Old Testament, has therefore more appearance than reality.'[18] Even more weighty is Bultmann's opinion: he rejects in two lines of a footnote any connection between *kharis kai alētheia* and *ḥesed we'ᵉmet* on the grounds that John does not use *alētheia* in the sense of *'ᵉmet* and that the LXX does not use *kharis* but *eleos* to translate *ḥesed*.[19] We may also refer to Marsh's commentary; he has no mention whatever of Exodus or any other OT passage in his exposition of these verses, so presumably denies any connection.[20]

We must now turn to the recent article in which the Loisy-Bultmann rejection of any connection between John 1.14-18 and Exodus 34 has been upheld. The article is by Professor Ignace de la Potterie, and it appears in a *Festschrift* for Professor Kümmel called *Jesus und Paulus*.[21] De la Potterie is concerned

John 1.14-18 and Exodus 34

to distinguish Paul's use of *kharis* from John's. In Paul, he says, *kharis* means 'the gift of salvation' ('le don du salut', p. 269), whereas in this passage in John (the only one in the Gospel in which *kharis* occurs) it means 'the gift of revelation', an objective reality. He goes on to identify the revelation with Jesus Christ, and actually translates the phrase *ekeinos exēgēsato* in verse 18 as 'il fut, lui, la révélation' (p. 277). The reason why he is unwilling to assent to the suggestion that *kharis kai alētheia* is equivalent to *ḥesed we'ᵉmet* in Exodus 34.6 is that in the Exodus passage 'mercy and faithfulness' plainly connote the content of the revelation: this is God's character as revealed. But de la Potterie understands *kharis kai alētheia* in 1 John as an announcement of the fact that a revelation has taken place, not an analysis of what the revelation communicated. In fact he even goes so far as to claim that in 1.17, instead of writing ἡ χάρις καὶ ἡ ἀλήθεια ἐγένετο, John might just as well have written ἡ ἀλήθεια ἐχαρίσθη.

De la Potterie supports his argument by reference to 2 John 1-3, where he claims he finds *kharis* and *alētheia* used in the same way as he believes they are used in John 1.14-18. He traces a chiastic pattern in this passage from 2 John: the two extremes (A and A') are οὓς ἀγαπῶ ἐν ἀληθείᾳ in verse 1 and ἐν ἀληθείᾳ καὶ ἀγάπῃ in verse 3c; then come B and B', διὰ τὴν ἀλήθειαν τὴν μένουσαν ἐν ἡμῖν (verse 2a) and χάρις ἔλεος εἰρήνη in verse 3b; the two middle members are μεθ' ἡμῶν ἔσται εἰς τὸν αἰῶνα in verse 2b and ἔσται μεθ' ἡμῶν in verse 3a. He is thus able to claim that B corresponds to B', i.e. that *tēn alētheian* in 2a is the equivalent of *kharis* in 3b; his comment is: 'Malgré la différence de vocabulaire, ces deux membres sont eux aussi parallèles' (p. 272). He thus concludes that here also *alētheia* means 'revelation' and *kharis* means 'gift of revelation'.

2

In deciding this particular question the lexicographical evidence must weigh heavily. Both Bultmann and de la Potterie have emphasized the fact that the LXX only very rarely uses *kharis* as a rendering of *ḥesed*; de la Potterie adds that *kharis kai alētheia* are never found as a translation of *ḥesed we'ᵉmet* (p. 258). It is true that there is only one clear example in the LXX of the canonical books of *kharis* for *ḥesed* (Esther 2.9); but the translator of Sirach's Book of Wisdom certainly uses *kharis* for *ḥesed* twice (Sirach 7.33, 10.17); in 17.22, though the Hebrew is not extant, R. H. Charles believes that the Greek χάριν ἀνθρώπου renders *ḥesed* in the original Hebrew.[22] When we turn to the remains of the other Greek translations, we find much less restraint in using *kharis* for *ḥesed*: Symmachus uses it in 2 Samuel 2.6, 10.2; and in Symmachus's version of Psalm 89.24 he renders *'mwnh wḥsd* with βεβαίωσις καὶ χάρις, a translation for *ḥsd* in a context where *ḥsd* and *'mwnh* come together.[23] Four other examples can be quoted: Theodotion's rendering of Proverbs 31.26; Quinta's of Psalm 33.5; and Sexta's of Psalms 30.7, 33.18.[24] In addition we may refer to an article by J. A. Montgomery in which he points out that *kharis* in the New Testament is regularly translated by *ḥsd'* in the Syriac. This is certainly the case with the Syriac translation of *kharis* in John 1.14, where he says that text is 'reproducing the Hebrew of Exodus 34.6'.[25] Two years later Matthew Black wrote an article on the phrase χάριν ἀντὶ χάριτος in John 1.16 in which he postulated an Aramaic source behind the passage;[26] he pointed out that the Jewish Palestinian word for grace is *ḥsd'* and suggests a play on words (in the original) on the two meanings of *ḥsd'*.

One other point with regard to vocabulary should be added; if it is correct to say that *plērēs kharitos kai alētheias* in John 1.14 renders *rab ḥesed we'ᵉmet* in Exodus 34.6, then *rab* is translated by *plērēs*. For such a translation I can find no parallel anywhere else. From this, however, I would conclude, not that the equivalence is mistaken but that the author of the Fourth Gospel has translated the phrase for himself direct from the Hebrew. It is, all the same, a perfectly reasonable translation of the Hebrew phrase. As Lindars points out, it is a more literal rendering than that which the LXX offers.

De la Potterie lays great stress on the point that according to his interpretation *kharis kai alētheias* is a hendiadys. He would take it to mean 'the gift of truth' or 'the gift of revelation'. The term 'hendiadys' has often been used in this connection; Bultmann calls the phrase a hendiadys, and Glueck, in his magisterial exposition of the phrase *ḥsd we'ᵉmet* comes very near to claiming it is a hendiadys when he writes: 'Whenever *ḥesed* appears together with *'emeth* or *'emunah*, the quality of loyalty inherent in the concept *ḥesed* is emphasized.'[27] Thus the term 'hendiadys' is open to various interpretations.

As we have seen, de la Potterie supports his arguments by citing what he regards as a parallel from 2 John 1-3. But it is by no means clear that this passage does afford a real parallel to John 1.14-18, and his argument depends on the conclusion that there really is a chiastic structure in the opening verses of 2 John. In fact the language of 2 John 1-3 would seem closer to that of a passage such as 1 John 4.7-12, 19-20. There also we find the emphasis on the invisibility of God and the suggestion that God is revealed as love. If there is a link between 2 John 1-3 and John 1.14-18, it would point towards the conclusion that in both these passages we are dealing with the *content* of revelation (God revealed as grace, mercy, or love) rather than with the fact of revelation ('the gift of truth') as de la Potterie maintains. Again, the chiastic structure which de la Potterie traces in the 2 John passage breaks down at the very point where, if he is right, it should be clearest: in his schema διὰ τὴν ἀλήθειαν τὴν μένουσαν ἐν ἡμῖν is parallel to χάρις ἔλεος εἰρήνη. But this is no parallel, and de la Potterie's mere assertion (quoted above) that they are parallel does not make up for the deficiency in his argument. The chiastic structure, it must be added, is weakened when one includes the two phrases καὶ οὐκ ἐγὼ μόνος ἀλλὰ καὶ πάντες οἱ ἐγνωκότες τὴν ἀλήθειαν and παρὰ θεοῦ πατρὸς καὶ παρὰ Ἰησοῦ Χριστοῦ τοῦ υἱοῦ τοῦ πατρός. It is also doubtful whether the author of 2 John uses *alētheia* in an entirely uniform manner throughout the three verses: οὓς ἐγὼ ἀγαπῶ ἐν ἀληθείᾳ does not seem to have exactly the same meaning as διὰ τὴν ἀλήθειαν τὴν μένουσαν ἐν ἡμῖν in the next clause. In any case surely the idea of *kharis* and *alētheia* forming a hendiadys can hardly be said to be found in the 2 John passage, where *kharis* is clearly separated from *alētheia* and can only be associated by assuming a chiastic structure.

When one looks at 2 John without any assumptions concerning a connection with John 1.14-18, it seems quite natural to explain the language as mostly that of conventional greeting. When Holtzmann paraphrases ἐν ἀληθείᾳ καὶ ἀγάπῃ as 'rechte Glaube und Bruderliebe', one suspects that he is probably right,[28] fairly conventional though the sentiment be. Several editors have pointed out that χάρις ἔλεος εἰρήνη occurs as a greeting in 1 Timothy 1.2, 2 Timothy 1.2,[29] and Bultmann describes the phrase as 'an adaptation of the traditional greeting formula'.[30] Indeed, an honest appraisal of 2 John makes one wonder whether there may not be some truth in Bergmeier's contention that in 2 and 3 John 'truth' simply means 'Christian doctrine' and ἐν ἀληθείᾳ has no greater force than ἀληθῶς.[31] The author of 2 and 3 John, he maintains, is only using language 'with a Johannine colouring', but not in the true Johannine sense. He compares the relation of 2 and 3 John to the rest of the Johannine literature with the relation of the Pastoral Epistles to the genuinely Pauline Epistles.[32]

3

Any adequate exposition of John 1.14-18 must include an explanation of why the author lays such stress on the invisibility of God in verse 18. A great weakness of de la Potterie's account is that he never comes to terms with the phrase θεὸν οὐδεὶς ἑώρακεν πώποτε. In fact he totally ignores this phrase throughout his article. It must surely refer to some occasion when someone claims to have seen God. This means we must turn back to Scripture, the author's primary theological source. In the series of events narrated in Exodus 33.12-34.8 we have a Scripture passage in which (a) Moses is allowed to see God, however partially; (b) this vision is represented as a vision of God's glory; (c) the content of the vision is described in terms of a revelation of God as (literally) 'full of mercy and truth'; and (d) the revelation is associated with, though not identified with, the giving of the Law through Moses. It would be impossible to find a Scripture passage which contains more fundamental elements in common with John 1.14-18. I find it inevitable to conclude that the one is the basis of the other.

But we still have to determine two important questions: first, how does John reconcile the narrative in Exodus, wherein Moses does see God at least imperfectly, with his statement that no one has ever seen God? and second, what sort of a contrast is John drawing in verse 17 when he says the law was given by Moses but grace and truth came by Jesus Christ? It is not surprising that in attempting to answer the first of these questions several editors have been content to conclude that, according to John, Moses saw God so very imperfectly on Sinai that it can hardly count as seeing God at all. Thus Westcott says that, compared with the appearance of the Word made flesh, previous Christophanies were 'partial, visionary, evanescent'. Similarly Lagrange describes the Old Testament visions of God as 'of an inferior order, or still enveloped in images'; and Hoskyns writes: 'No theophany had vouchsafed the much desired . . . vision of God.' Lindars follows the same line. The objection to this exegesis is that John does believe in a revelation under the old dispensation. Any explanation that suggests that John did not take the passage in Exodus 33-4 completely seriously is most improbable. Moses really did see Adonai, according to John. We must look elsewhere for an explanation of θεὸν οὐδεὶς ἑώρακεν πώποτε.

Bultmann suggests that what John really means is that God can only be known by faith: not a Greek meaning of intellectual apprehension, nor the Gnostic one of transcendent mystic communion, but the claim that God is only apprehensible by faith.[33] This is no doubt true, but it does not solve our problem. It does not explain how Moses can have been described as seeing Adonai. Equally unsatisfactory is Schlatter's solution: 'Man may not see God, but he can hear him, because the mediator between God and the world is the Word.' In 5.37b we read οὔτε φωνὴν αὐτοῦ ἀκηκόατε οὔτε εἶδος αὐτοῦ ἑωράκατε. God has never been either audible or visible. It would seem to be a direct challenge to much in Scripture: what is John implying here?

It seems to me there can only be one answer: according to John, on those occasions in Israel's history when God is described as being seen, it was not in fact God who was seen, but the Logos. John says this *totidem verbis* in 12.41, where he describes Isaiah's vision in the Temple as Isaiah having seen Jesus's glory; in other words, Jahweh Sabaoth is the Logos. It is significant that throughout the passage in Exodus 33-4 with which we are concerned the Tetragrammaton is used for God and not *'lhym*. This conclusion has been accepted by several commentators, notably Holtzmann, Loisy, Boismard, and Sanders.[34] This last writes: 'In later Judaism it was held not just that no man could see God and live (cf. Exodus 33.20), but that it was not in fact God whom the recipients of the Old Testament visions had seen.' It therefore follows that in John's theology the Word is the visibility (as well as the audibility) of God; whenever God has been described as appearing in Israel's history, it has always been the Word who appears. Consequently, far from disparaging or denying the reality of the revelation on Sinai, John regards it as a genuine revelation of God's character as full of mercy and truth, but it is a revelation, as all revelation must be, mediated by the Word.[35]

We can now see more clearly what John means by the contrast between the law given by Moses and grace and truth occurring in Jesus Christ, as described in verse 17. He does not mean to say that the Sinai event was inferior or obsolete contrasted with the incarnation of the Word. On the contrary he distinguishes two elements in the Sinai event, the giving of the Law and the revelation on the rock. The giving of the Law is certainly regarded as temporary, obsolete, and above all indirect (cf. Galatians 3.19). But the revelation on the rock is none of these: it was the revelation of God in Christ. It only differs from the revelation in the incarnate Word in so far as it was temporary and limited to Moses.[36] This conclusion will also help to clarify the debate about the meaning of χάριν ἀντὶ χάριτος in verse 16: John does not mean that the grace of Christ has been received in the place of the grace of the Law; still less does he mean that Christians received grace corresponding to the grace of Christ. He means that the revelation of God, full of grace and truth, has been continuous since the revelation on the rock at Sinai culminating in the revelation in the incarnate Word.[37] This means that, following Bultmann, we must take χάριν ἀντὶ χάριτος as the equivalent of χάριν ἐπὶ χάριτι. The passage in Philo (*De Post. Caini* 43) to which all appeal who take this view does go a long way towards vindicating it. Philo speaks of a succession of charisms, 'new ones always being supplied in place of the old' (καὶ ἀεὶ νέας ἀντὶ παλαιοτέρων). Here the sense seems to be very close to John's: the new supplies, renews, maintains the line of the old. In John the new revelation in the incarnate Word has just this relation to the old revelation on Sinai.

John 1.14-18 and Exodus 34

4

The word *exēgēsato* used in verse 8 has prompted some comparison with other parts of Scripture, in particular with Job 28.27 and with two passages in Sirach. The Job passage runs in the LXX: τότε εἶδεν αὐτὴν καὶ ἐξηγήσατο αὐτήν, ἑτοιμάσας ἐξιχνίασεν. The object is of course wisdom, and καὶ ἐξηγήσατο αὐτήν translates the Hebrew *wysprh*. The passages from Sirach are Sirach 1.9b, 43.31a. In 1.9 the author is speaking of the universal diffusion of wisdom among men:

κύριος αὐτὸς ἔκτισεν αὐτήν,
καὶ εἶδεν καὶ ἐξηρίθμησεν αὐτήν,
καὶ ἐξέχεεν αὐτὴν ἐπὶ πάντα τὰ ἔργα αὐτοῦ.

This verse is based on Job 28.27. Though the Hebrew is not extant, it is almost certain that ἐξηρίθμησεν αὐτήν renders an original *wysprh*. Sirach 43.31a is nearer to John 1.18; it refers to God: τίς ἑόρακεν αὐτὸν καὶ ἐκδιηγήσεται; There is no line corresponding to this in the Hebrew, though the Hebrew of verse 30 and verse 32 in the LXX has been recovered. Charles believes that verse 31 is a later interpolation, perhaps originally written in Greek.[38] This does not mean of course that the author of the Fourth Gospel could not have known this verse and perhaps drawn inspiration from it. Certainly John 1.18 forms a very suitable commentary on it: who has known God and will declare him? The Word has always known him, says John, and has declared him in Jesus Christ.[39] In other words, the hidden Wisdom has now been revealed in Christ. B. L. Mack in a recent work on Wisdom and Logos has distinguished three forms of Wisdom to be found in Jewish religious literature.[40] He calls these 'the hidden Wisdom', 'the available Wisdom' (*die nähe Weisheit*), and 'the vanished Wisdom', respectively. The hidden Wisdom is referred to in such passages as Job 28.27, Sirach 1.9. The latter passage might seem to contradict this, since God pours Wisdom out on all his works; but, says Mack, Wisdom still has to be sought. He also brings under consideration Sirach 17.11: 'He established with them an eternal covenant, and allotted to them the law of life.' Here he follows the reading 'knowledge' (*epistēmēn*) for 'covenant' (*diathēkēn*), and comments as follows: 'It is in the Sinai revelation and in the possibility, granted by God to man, to know and observe the law, that the author finds the solution to the problem of hiddenness.'[41] The 'available Wisdom' is described in the famous Wisdom chapter, Sirach 24. Wisdom, far from being hidden, seeks a dwelling place for herself among men. The 'vanishing Wisdom', a concept confined to apocalyptic literature, pictures Wisdom as having descended to earth, found no place ready to receive her, and then having returned to heaven.

It is interesting that one could find traces of all three types of Wisdom in the Prologue to the Fourth Gospel. Not, of course, that the author is to be regarded as having deliberately included all three types by way of completeness, but that the ideas about revelation implied by all three types are to be found in the Prologue. We find the 'hidden Wisdom' concept in the emphasis on the invisibility of God, and the fact that it is God who is revealed in the incarnate Logos. He needed to be revealed, and man needed the revelation. The 'available Wisdom' concept comes out in the fact that the Logos did decide to become flesh and dwell among us (the parallel between John 1.14, ἐσκήνωσεν ἐν ἡμῖν and Sirach 24.8, ἐν Ἰακώβ κατασκήνωσον is a significant one); and the 'vanished Wisdom' concept finds an echo in John 1.11: 'He came to his own home, and his own people received him not.' It seems that in his account of the incarnation of the Logos John is attempting to make a takeover bid for all that Wisdom meant to Israel of old. The relevance of this evidence for our subject is that it clearly demonstrates the connection of John 1.14-18 with the revelation of God. But, if this passage is concerned with revelation, the question must arise: revelation of what? Or, what is God revealed to be? And once we have reached this point we can hardly escape a reference to God revealed on Sinai as full of grace and truth. Thus de la Potterie's emphasis on the fact of revelation is quite justified, but it must raise the question of the content of revelation; and here we are inevitably brought back to Exodus 33-4.

We have noticed above (page 98) that J. H. Bernard insists on Psalm 85 rather than Exodus 34 as the main scriptural inspiration behind John 1.14-18. It is certainly true that, as one reads Psalm 85.7-10, whether in the Hebrew or the Greek, one

John 1.14-18 and Exodus 34

cannot help being impressed with the way in which it appears to fit in with the thought of John 1.14-18 – or rather the passage in John would seem to be God's response to the plea of Psalm 85.7-10 (MT 85.8-11; LXX has 84.8-11). Verse 7 runs:

δεῖξον ἡμῖν τὸ ἔλεός σου (ḥsdk)
καὶ τὸ σωτήριόν σου δώῃς ἡμῖν.

Here is a request for the revelation of God's character which is itself the eschatological act of salvation. Verse 9 continues:

πλὴν ἔγγυς τῶν φοβουμένων αὐτὸν τὸ σωτήριον αὐτοῦ
τοῦ κατασκηνῶσαι δόξαν ἐν τῇ γῇ αὐτοῦ.

Here we have the notion of 'tabernacling' (MT liškwn) reproduced in John 1.14. Then comes verse 11, where the famous phrase occurs:

ἔλεος καὶ ἀλήθεια συνήντησαν,
δικαιοσύνη καὶ εἰρήνη κατεφίλησαν,

eleos kai alētheia of course rendering the Hebrew *ḥesed we'ᵉmet*. The verse in between, verse 8, might seem to have little bearing on this theme, but this is in fact the verse that is referred to in a rabbinic document in a way very relevant to our topic. In the *Pesikta Rabbati* this verse and Exodus 34.1-8 are brought together in the context of the feast of Hanukkah.[42] On the feast of Hanukkah the Torah reading is from Numbers, wherein Moses is described as completing the setting-up of the tabernacle. In this discourse Psalm 85.5 and Exodus 34.6 are brought together. Moses is represented as uttering Psalm 85.8: 'Let me hear what God the Lord will speak, for he will speak peace to his people, to his saints, to those who turn to him in their hearts.'[43] Moses wants to see whether God is still angry with Israel because of the incident of the golden calf: 'Hence in reply to Moses' question (in Psalm 85.8) the Holy One, blessed be He, at once reassured Moses that there was nothing against Israel in his heart, as it is written, *And the Lord passed by before him and proclaimed: The Lord, the Lord, God merciful and gracious.*' Thus this exposition of Psalm 85 is used in order to illuminate the narrative of Exodus 34. The same association of Psalm 85.8 with the setting-up of the tabernacle is quoted by Bacher from Rabbi Jehuda ben Simon.[44]

The New Testament Interpretation of Scripture

We should also note those passages in which the revelation narrated in Exodus 34.1-8 is described as being essentially a revelation of the mercy of God: 'Thirteen qualities of mercy are ascribed in Scripture to the Holy One' is how one rabbi refers to this passage.[45] In this connection we might bear in mind the rabbinic tradition that the name '*lhym* for God indicated his quality of justice, whereas the Tetragrammaton *YHWH* indicated his quality of mercy. This is actually referred to in the passage from Piska 5.11 mentioned above (page 107). The phrase *h'l YHWH* occurs in Psalm 85.8 (MT 85.9), and this is understood as meaning God's two attributes of justice and mercy respectively. Now in the whole of the passage Exodus 33.12-34.8 God is never mentioned under any other name but that of *YHWH*. It is therefore by no means farfetched to suggest that, according to the author of the Fourth Gospel, *YHWH* was the Logos, and that consequently God, when he revealed himself to Israel of old, revealed himself as essentially the God of mercy. This is surely true of the revelation of Sinai narrated in Exodus 34. We must not forget that, as we have pointed out above, the revelation of Jahweh Sabaoth narrated in Isaiah 6 is specifically described by John in 12.41 as a revelation of the glory of Jesus.

In view of the connection in *Pesikta Rabbati* between Exodus 34, Psalm 85, and the feast of Hanukkah, it is very tempting to speculate as to whether the occurrence of this lection at this feast had any significance for the author of the Fourth Gospel. It is true that Aileen Guilding in her book on the topic of the connection of the Fourth Gospel with the synagogue lectionary readings does not mention this particular link.[46] But after all, the feast of Hanukkah is one which John specifically mentions in 10.22. In the ensuing passage Jesus is concerned with just the question of his relation to God which would be implied by the connection of the Word with the revelation on Sinai. However, the evidence is too scanty, and the pursuit of this question would take us too far from our theme; so we must leave it as an intriguing possibility.

We may hope, however, to have shown that John 1.14-18 is best understood against the background of Exodus 33-4. One could claim without undue exaggeration that these are the two passages in the Old Testament and the New Testament respec-

John 1.14-18 and Exodus 34

tively which treat most explicitly of the particular revelation of God to man. It is not therefore altogether surprising that they should prove to be so closely connected.

4

The Theme of Christ as the True Temple in the Fourth Gospel

1

The logion in John 1.51: 'You will see heaven opened, and the angels of God ascending and descending on the Son of man' has occasioned a great deal of discussion and has called forth a wide variety of theories, ranging from the view that we have here a reference to a Gnostic 'image-concept', to the outright denial that there is any reference intended to Jacob's vision at Bethel. My intention is to put forward an interpretation that associates the logion very closely indeed with Genesis 28 on the one hand, and on the other links it with a number of other similar Scripture references in the Fourth Gospel, all having in common the theme of Christ as the true Temple.

I would begin by claiming that it is a mistake to limit the influence of Genesis 28 too strictly to verse 51 and the verses which immediately precede it.[1] I believe that the first trace of the Bethel narrative is to be found in 1.30-31: 'This is he of whom I said, "After me comes a man who ranks before me, for he was before me". I myself did not know him; but for this I came baptizing with water, that he might be revealed to Israel.' The phrase 'I did not know him' is repeated for emphasis in verse 33: now this phrase, κἀγὼ οὐκ ᾔδειν αὐτόν, appears to be an echo of the LXX of Genesis 28.16. Jacob, waking from his dream, exclaims: 'Surely the Lord is in this place, and I did not know it' (ἐγὼ δὲ οὐκ ᾔδειν). Moreover, the Baptist says in this same passage that the reason why he came baptizing with water was that Christ might be manifested to Israel. But the Genesis 28 narrative describes a manifestation of the Lord to Israel, and a few verses later in the Johannine narrative (1.47) Nathanael is greeted by Jesus as 'an Israelite indeed, in whom is no guile'. It is thanks to John the Baptist that Nathanael has come to recognize Christ, and if Nathanael is to be identified with the true Israel, then it is by John's activity that the Christ has been manifested to Israel.

We may now trace the outlines of a quite extensive midrash on the scriptural account of Jacob's vision in Bethel. But we must note carefully which New Testament characters correspond to which Old Testament ones. In the first place, Jesus is not here represented as the true (or new) Israel.[2] That role, as we have seen, is given to Nathanael. Nor does Nathanael exactly correspond to Jacob; he is rather what Jacob should have been but was not, at least when he came to Bethel, an Israel without guile. If anyone corresponds to Jacob it is John the Baptist, who, like Jacob, found himself in the presence of the Lord, but did not recognize him, or at least did not recognize him at first sight. Nathanael here again corresponds to Jacob as he should have been, for he does recognize Jesus at first sight as Son of God and king of Israel. It follows naturally that in this schema Jesus corresponds to the Lord who appeared in the vision to Jacob. He is, however, more than this just because of the incarnation, which indicates the significant difference between the old dispensation and the new. Jesus corresponds both to Yahweh, who stood at the top of the ladder,[3] *and* to the ladder itself. Thus the meaning of the logion in 1.51 will be that, after his death and resurrection, Jesus Christ will be the permanent place where God is to be found. The angels are there simply because they identify the ladder vision and indicate the true link between heaven and earth. Windisch is fully justified when he says that in the Fourth Gospel the Son while on earth does not need the ministry of angels. In 12.29-30 the Father speaks directly to him, though the bystanders mistakenly think an angel has spoken to him.[4]

This means of course that John sees in the Bethel vision an appearance of the pre-existent Logos. This is no novel feature in the Fourth Gospel, and was indeed almost a commonplace in the early Fathers until the extensive use of the pre-existent Logos concept by the Arians induced most orthodox theologians to drop the attempt to distinguish the activity of the pre-existent Christ in Israel's history. We find precisely this identification in Justin. In his *Dialogue* at one point he is going through the career of Jacob finding appearances and foreshadowings of Christ in every episode.[5] When he comes to

Genesis 28, he identifies Christ with the appearance of Yahweh at the top of the ladder; but he goes further than this. The LXX renders Genesis 28.13, 'the Lord stood above it', with *ho kurios epēstērikto ep' autēs*, literally 'the Lord was fixed on it'.[6] Justin eagerly seizes on this as a foreshadowing of the cross.

Among the rabbis Jacob is treated as a completely righteous man (that this was no late development is shown by Wisdom 10.10). There is a tendency to universalize and magnify the significance of Jacob's experience. Jeremias (quoted in Bultmann, op. cit., p. 74n) brings evidence to show that some rabbis identified Jacob's stone with the rock on which the creation was originally based. In the *Midrash on the Psalms* there is an elaborate account of how, when Jacob had set up the stone pillar, oil came down from heaven and he poured the oil on the pillar, whereupon God drove the stone into the earth and it became the spindle-stone, the navel of the earth.[7] The Targum of Palestine has the tradition, witnessed to elsewhere, that the likeness of a man in Ezekiel's chariot vision was in fact the likeness of Jacob and that therefore the revelation at Bethel was the manifestation of a heavenly and an earthly image of Jacob.[8] R. H. Lightfoot and C. H. Dodd are both attracted by the theory that John is here reproducing another rabbinic interpretation which turns on the meaning of *bw* in the MT of Genesis 28.12.[9] It originally meant 'on it', i.e. on the ladder; the angels of God are represented as ascending and descending on the ladder. But some rabbis took it to mean 'on him', i.e. Jacob, and Jacob is thus represented as the prototype of the ideal Israel, the recipient of divine communications. In the context of John 1.51 and the phrase *epi tou huiou tou anthrōpou*, this would mean that Jesus is the new Israel, the perfect recipient of God's guidance. But we have already shown reason for denying that Christ is regarded by John as typified by Jacob. The pre-existent Logos was present at Bethel and therefore cannot be represented by a type.

More to the point are those rabbinic passages in which Bethel is regarded as an anticipation of the Temple. Thus in the *Sifre to Numbers* R. Eleazar ha Kappar is reported as saying that God had shown beforehand to Jacob the building, history, and destruction of the Temple, all indicated by the ladder in the vision.[10] This element in John's treatment of the story is emphasized by Léon-Dufour and by Fawcett.[11] In the *Pesikta de Rab Kahana* we find a tradition, which is traced back to R. Meir, that Jacob at Bethel was encouraged to climb up the ladder and remain in heaven, but lacked the courage to do so.[12] Consequently his people Israel must remain still under the yoke of history. This confirms the suggestion that the Bethel story conveyed very much the sense of God's real and abiding presence with men. Philo is, I suppose, in the same tradition, though in his treatment of the Bethel episode he shows a strong tendency to interpret it in such a way as to avoid altogether the suggestion that God can ever be located in one place.[13] He takes great liberties with the biblical text, making it say in fact the exact opposite of what it really means. The LXX of Genesis 28.17 runs: *ouk estin touto all' ē oikos theou* ('this is none other than the house of God'). Philo takes it as: 'This is not the case, God is not here, because he cannot be located in space.' In another work he explains the same text thus: 'The House of God is not this that is all round me, consisting of things that ... fall under sense perception ... no, not such is God's House, but invisible, withdrawn from sight and apprehended only by soul as soul.' Essentially the same tradition appears in the *Pesikta Rabbati*: Jacob attempts to comfort Jerusalem, but she replies: 'How can I receive comforting from you, who envisioned my obliteration in saying of God's House in Jerusalem, *This is none*?'[14] This passage also assumes that in Genesis 28.17 Jacob is speaking of the Temple. R. J. McKelvey, in his book *The New Temple*, well writes: 'The desire to depict Christ as the new temple may be in mind at 1.51.'[15]

It follows that the rabbinic conceit of Jacob's double image, whether it springs from a Gnostic milieu or not, is not relevant to this passage. Windisch emphatically rejects the 'double-image' theory (as does Bernard). John, he says, means by this passage that Jesus on earth was a man to whom heaven was always open. Only for a moment on the cross was it shut. Quispel elaborates this point, and maintains that the open heaven corresponds to Ezekiel 1.1: 'The heavens were opened and I saw visions of God.'[16] He is thus able to connect 1.51 with *Merkaba* mysticism. Nathanael is promised a vision of the heavenly Christ even in this life. The language of 'ascending and descending' was used in *Merkaba* mysticism to describe the mystic's approach to God. Michaelis takes almost the opposite point of view: the connection with the OT, he says, is 'not late Judaistic and certainly not un-Jewish Gnostic'.[17] In fact he tends to isolate this pericope, to suggest that the connection with the OT is as much one of unlikeness as of likeness, and finally even tends towards the opinion that it is perhaps a mistake to see any reference at all here to Jacob's dream, a conclusion which, I imagine, he shares with almost no one else. On the point of the open heaven Schlatter is interesting.[18] He claims that the open heaven means not the vision of God, but the descent of his gifts: 'Jesus does not say that the heavens were opened, but that they are open': what is meant is continual fellowship between God and man. The essential point of the reference to Jacob's vision at Bethel, as it seems to me, is God's presence at a certain place. In the new dispensation (as in fact in the old, if the truth had been perceived) that place is Christ.

Reim in his interesting study seems to come reluctantly and hesitatingly to this conclusion.[19] He remarks that in the circle to which the author of the Fourth Gospel belonged they liked to compare Jesus to Old Testament characters, just as in 1 Corinthians 10.4 Christ is compared ('gleichgesetzt') to the following rock in the wilderness. This is a strange way of expressing it, rather as if this comparison with OT figures was a hobby or special interest of John. It is in fact common to nearly all the writers of the NT. Again, in 1 Corinthians 10.4 Christ is not compared to the rock, he is identified with it. However, a little later on, Reim wonders whether ('es fragt sich') behind John 1.51 there may not stand a similar interpretation to that which stands behind John 8.56f. There Abraham is described as having seen Christ: perhaps the same thought occurs in 1.51 with regard to Jacob. In a note on p. 155 he refers to Justin's acceptance of this view. I would defend this view with much more confidence: if we once grasp that according to John the pre-existent Logos it was who appeared to Jacob at the top of the ladder in his vision, we are, I believe, in a much better position to understand what John is trying to say in this pericope.

2

We now turn to 2.17f. In the middle of an account of the

cleansing of the Temple that has much in common with the Synoptic accounts, John inserts the sentence:

> His disciples remembered that it was written, 'Zeal for thy house will consume me'.

And in 2.22 John adds:

> When therefore he was raised from the dead, his disciples remembered that he had said this, and they believed the scripture and the word which Jesus had spoken.

It is my contention that this is another passage in which a quotation from Scripture is used to present Jesus as the true Temple, the House of God. It is important to notice that John does not say that the citation of Psalm 69.9 was made by Jesus or his disciples at the time of the cleansing. The verse was only applied afterwards by his disciples, when his resurrection had opened their eyes to the full implications of Scripture. Nevertheless I think we must assume that John regards Psalm 69.9 as an utterance of the pre-existent Christ. As editors have often pointed out, Psalm 69 is a favourite psalm with early Christians in general and with John in particular. He quotes it again of Jesus in 15.25 and 19.29, in both places claiming that Jesus is fulfilling Scripture. The very next line in the psalm to that quoted here is cited by Paul in Romans 15.3, a context in which it is extremely likely that Paul understands the pre-existent Christ as speaking. It is a psalm of the righteous sufferer, and an early Christian would see in it not only various incidents of the passion, but quite likely Christ's resurrection as well; see verse 33:

> For the Lord hears the needy,
> and does not despise his own that are in bonds.

Compare Acts 2.24, where Peter claims that it was not possible that Christ should have been held by the bonds of death.

This conclusion is scouted by Freed, who writes that we cannot be sure that 'this verse of the psalm was generally accepted and used messianically when these citations were made'.[20] This seems to presuppose an unjustifiably atomistic approach to the use of Scripture in the early Church. Seeing that Psalm 69 is quoted so extensively in the NT, we have no

The New Testament Interpretation of Scripture

reason to suppose that each author, so to speak, discovered the psalm for himself. It must have been in general use as a quarry for messianic texts, even though different authors cite it on different occasions. At any rate a number of modern scholars can be quoted in favour of the view that in John 2.17 the psalm is being used as a messianic proof-text, notably Hoskyns, Sanders,[21] and Léon-Dufour.[22] The meaning of the verse from the psalm is that Jesus's zeal for God's house will lead to his death at the hands of the Jews. C. K. Barrett regards this interpretation as 'strained',[23] and Bernard turns it into concern for Jesus's health ('the fiery energy . . . will wear him out at last'); but there can be little doubt that this is how John understands it. It is interesting that in the *Midrash on the Psalms* Psalm 69.6 is applied to David, and his vindication is seen in terms of resurrection.[24] David's enemies say: 'Where is thy God?'. 'Then the Holy One, blessed be he, said to David: "If you are reproached because of me, I will free you from reproach." As scripture says: *He will swallow up death for ever.*'

I have assumed that the Scripture referred to in verse 22 (*tēi graphēi*) is the psalm quoted in verse 17. It is true that in 20.9 *tēn graphēn* is used in what appears to be a general reference to those parts of the Scriptures which foretold Jesus's resurrection; but every other instance of *hē graphē* in John applies to one particular passage of Scripture. And after all John has here gone out of his way to quote the passage. Nevertheless this argument has not convinced all commentators by any means: Bultmann writes (op. cit., p. 90 n.) that we are unable to guess which passage John has in mind; or it might be a general reference, like *kata tas graphas* in 1 Corinthians 15.3. This last suggestion has the approval of C. K. Barrett, R. H. Lightfoot, and Lagrange.[25] Bernard supports the view, which apparently he found in Westcott, that the Scripture referred to is Psalm 16.10, because it is quoted twice in Acts as a proof-text for the resurrection. But it seems quite unnecessary to have recourse to a proof-text that John never uses elsewhere when he has already given us one which, by his criteria, is perfectly sound. One may suspect that those who look elsewhere than Psalm 69.9 for the reference do so because they have not really understood John's approach to Scripture. Hoskyns, Sanders, Léon-Dufour,[26] and McKelvey[27] all agree that the Scripture of verse 22 must be that quoted in verse 17. Lindars seems to have shifted his position slightly: in 'New Testament Apologetic' written in 1961,[28] he suggests that verse 22 refers to the final verses of Psalm 69 (in which the psalmist looks confidently forward to God's coming salvation). But in his commentary on the Fourth Gospel, published in 1972, he contents himself with the statement that the Scripture referred to is Psalm 69.9.[29] It is surely significant that those who have studied John's method of scriptural interpretation most closely are most firmly convinced that Psalm 69.9 is intended in verse 22.

It follows from all this that in this passage also Jesus is seen as the true Temple. I cannot do better than quote McKelvey's paraphrase of the meaning of the passage, which seems to me to be quite correct: 'Even though you (Jews) by your unbelief destroy this temple, that is the tabernacle of the Word (and thereby destroy the temple of Jerusalem), in three days I will raise it up again, but (we may well fill out the thought of the text) your temple will never be restored, for the new temple of my body will become the rallying point of the true worshippers of God.'[30] Léon-Dufour claims that the double reference to the rebuilding of the Temple (part of the Jewish eschatological programme) and the resurrection of Christ's body does not imply any suggestion that the Church is Christ's Body,[31] but this is probably because he is anxious to defend the historicity of the narrative as presented in the Fourth Gospel, and very naturally believes that the Jews can hardly be expected to understand a reference to the Church here. Dubarle, on the other hand, sees here not only a link with 1.51, but also a reference to the Church and to the eucharistic Body of Christ.[32] Once one has admitted a conscious reference to Christ as the place where God is to be found and worshipped, it is difficult not to take the next step of contending that John is thinking of the Church as that place. Whether there is also a eucharistic reference here or not does not really concern our purpose. We have indicated another place where John uses Scripture to show that Christ is the new Temple. As the Scripture passage cited here calls the temple God's house, we may perhaps suggest that the transition from 1.51 to 2.17 is the transition from Christ as the *place* of God's presence to Christ as the House of God.

The New Testament Interpretation of Scripture

3

The third passage which we examine seems to confirm the suggestion that when John thinks of Christ as the place where God is to be encountered and worshipped he means the Church. The passage is 12.1-8, though I think that we must take the whole of chapter 12 into consideration and also that if there is one verse which echoes Scripture more decidedly than any other it is verse 3, and in particular the apparently insignificant detail (though one peculiar to John): 'And the house was filled with the fragrance of the ointment.'

I suggest that behind the account in the Fourth Gospel of the anointing in Bethany lie four verses from Haggai: Haggai 2.6-9. Before quoting them, however, I must point out that they are addressed to Zerubabel and Joshua. In Greek 'Joshua' is of course indistinguishable from 'Jesus', so an early Christian might well believe, as he read Haggai in Greek, that this passage concerned Jesus Christ. I give my own translation of the LXX of Haggai 2.6-9:

> For thus says the Lord almighty, 'Yet once again
> I will shake the heaven and the earth and the sea
> v.7 and the dry land; and I will make all the Gentiles
> tremble; and the chosen things of the Gentiles will
> come, and I will fill this house with glory
> (*plērō ton oikon touton doxēs*),' says the Lord
> v.8 almighty, 'Mine is the silver and mine the gold,'
> says the Lord almighty. 'for greater shall be the
> latter (*eschatē*) glory of this house than the former,'
> v.9 says the Lord almighty, 'And in this place shall I
> give peace,' says the Lord almighty, 'and peace of
> soul for a possession to every one who lays foundations
> in order to raise up this shrine (*tou anastēnai
> ton naon touton*).'

The phrase rendered 'chosen things of the Gentiles' in verse 7 no doubt referred originally to the treasures which the Gentiles would voluntarily bring to the renewed Temple. The Vulgate (probably because of Christian interpretation) translates it with 'desideratus cunctis gentibus', thus making it a definitely messianic allusion.[33] The last clause in verse 9, from 'and peace of soul' to the end, is not found in the MT. But it

The Theme of Christ as the True Temple in the Fourth Gospel

was probably originally a gloss in Hebrew rather than in Greek, and we have no reason to think that it may not have been in John's bible.[34]

The points of contact between these verses from Haggai and John 12 are quite remarkable. We have already pointed out that they are associated (in Greek) with *Iēsous*. Then comes the shaking of the house; this might correspond to the heavenly voice, interpreted by the crowd as thunder, in 12.28-9. The Gentiles bringing their desirable things reminds us of 12.20f, where certain Greeks desire to see Jesus. God's filling the house with glory is paralleled by the fragrance of the ointment filling the house in Bethany. The reference to the silver and the gold reminds us of 12.4-6, where Judas is represented as making a hypocritical plea that the ointment should be turned into money, which would come into his keeping. And of course the very last phrase in the Greek, 'to raise up this shrine', would be to John a pretty clear reference to Christ's resurrection, especially in the light of his treatment of the 'temple-body' theme in 2.17-22. Thus John would see this passage from Haggai as a prophecy of the death, burial (and anointing) of Jesus, his resurrection, and the accession of the Gentiles. It seems to me quite possible that the narrative throughout chapter 12 has been influenced by this prophecy.

In *Sanhedrin* 97b in the Babylonian Talmud[35] the shaking of the heavens in Haggai 2.6 is taken as a sign of the coming of the messianic age (cf. Hebrews 12.26-7) and in 103b we have a piece of interesting Haggada *à propos* Haggai 2.8: 'The silver is mine and the gold is mine': King Jehoiakim is represented as saying that he has no need for God, nor even for the sun, for he has plenty of gold. His courtiers quote to him this verse (thereby perpetrating a considerable anachronism!), and he replies: 'He has long since given the silver and the gold to us.' Similarly in *Abodah Zarah* 2b[36] at the great assize the kings of the Gentiles will claim that their accumulation of wealth was only undertaken in order to enable Israel to have leisure to study the Torah. God in reply will quote Haggai 2.8. There is a certain parallel between the hypocrisy of the Jehoiakim and the Gentiles in these two instances and Judas's hypocrisy in John 12.4-6.

The well-known reference to the anointing incident by

Ignatius of Antioch is relevant here. In Ephesians xvii, he writes:

> This is why the Lord received myrrh on his head, that he might breathe incorruption over the church (*hina pneē/i tē/i ekklēsia/i aphtharsian*).

It might be disputed whether Ignatius has this passage in mind, since John only records an anointing of the feet. But it is certainly significant that Ignatius draws a symbolical meaning from the detail of the fragrance: it indicates that the risen Christ will communicate his own incorruption to the Church. At the very least we can say that both John and Ignatius, writing some considerable time after the event, have probably seen a symbolic significance in the fact of the fragrance of the myrrh filling the house. Both have connected it with Christ's resurrection and, we may conclude, both have seen the Church as the place where the effect of the resurrection is to be encountered. In other words, in this incident the house symbolizes the Church.

Those commentators who have taken any notice of the detail of the fragrance filling the house may be divided into three main groups as far as their understanding of the detail is concerned. The first group denies that any symbolical significance is intended. In this group are Lagrange, Bernard, Barrett, Schnackenburg,[37] and Lindars.[38] The second group believes that there is a symbolical meaning and that it corresponds to Mark 14.9; Matthew 26.13, the statement that the story of the anointing will be proclaimed throughout the world. In other words, for this group the house is the world; this group includes Bultmann[39] and Strachan.[40] The third group holds that the detail is symbolical but that it symbolizes the new life of the Lord available in the Church; the only other commentator that I can point to as belonging to this group is Hoskyns, and even he modifies this position by saying that 'the action of Mary is of universal significance and its odour permeates the church and reaches the extremities of the world.'

However, if the connection of Haggai 2.6-9 is valid, this third view is strongly supported. We may suppose that one of the features that attracted John to this Haggai passage is the contrast it exhibits between the present mean state of the house of God and its future glorious state. This would fit in well with the actual circumstances of the anointing: the incident looks forward both to the lowest point of Christ's humiliation, his actual death, and to the glorious risen state to follow. We may therefore relate this third passage in the Fourth Gospel to the other two which we have examined, by saying that it brings the Church onto the stage. All three set forth the theme of Christ as the new Temple: the first emphasizes Christ as the *place* of God's presence. The second brings out Christ as the new and truer Temple, where God is henceforth to be encountered and worshipped. The third indicates that Christ, the new Temple, is at the same time the locus of the Church, the community which is to be filled with the glory of the risen Lord.

5

The Scriptural Background to the Doctrine of the 'Descensus ad Inferos' in the New Testament

A great deal has been written about the doctrine of the *Descensus ad Inferos*, especially in connection with that passage in the New Testament where this doctrine seems to figure most prominently, 1 Peter 3.18-4.6. This chapter will not attempt a large-scale examination of the doctrine in itself, but will concentrate on the scriptural background. I believe that the scriptural sources for the doctrine have not yet been fully explored nor have they been brought together and presented in one survey. To do these two things is precisely the intention of this chapter.

1

In an article written in 1962 W. Diezinger traced a connection between Romans 6.1-11 and Psalm 88.[1] In a book published in 1974 I took that comparison further and included in it the passage in 1 Peter already referred to, 1 Peter 3.18-4.6.[2] The obvious point of comparison is the resemblance of Romans 6.7 to 1 Peter 4.1, a point which has not, of course, escaped the notice of commentators. I begin this investigation therefore by juxtaposing Romans 6.1-11 and 1 Peter 3.18-4.6. To bring out the comparison, I have kept the verses in Romans 6.1-11 in their original order and have transposed the materials in 1 Peter 3.18-4.6 so that they come opposite the verses that resemble them in the Romans passage.

Scriptural Background to the Doctrine of the 'Descensus ad Inferos'

ROMANS 6.1-11	1 PETER 3.18-4.6
3 ... all of us who have been baptized into Jesus Christ were baptized into his death.	3.20–21 (they) were saved through water. Baptism, which corresponds to this, now saves you.
4 We were buried therefore with him by baptism into death, so that as Christ was raised from the dead by the glory of the Father, we too might walk in newness of life...	3.21–2 through the resurrection of Jesus Christ, who ... is at the right hand of God.
	4.2 so as to live for the rest of the time in the flesh no longer by human passions but by the will of God.
6 ... our old self was crucified with him so that the sinful body might be destroyed, and we might no longer be enslaved to sin. 7 For he who has died is freed from sin (ὁ γὰρ ἀποθανὼν δεδικαίωται ἀπὸ τῆς ἁμαρτίας).	4.1 for whoever has suffered in the flesh has ceased from sin (ὁ παθὼν σαρκὶ πέπαυται ἁμαρτίας).
10 The death he died he died to sin, once for all, but the life he lives he lives to God.	3.18 For Christ also died for sins once ... being put to death in the flesh but made alive in the spirit
11 So you also must consider yourselves dead to sin and alive to God in Christ Jesus.	(θανατωθεὶς μὲν σαρκὶ ζωοποιηθεὶς δὲ πνεύματι).

This does not in itself provide a particularly striking comparison. Certainly no one should suggest that one passage is based on the other; all one can claim so far is a general resemblance: both passages trace a death and resurrection of Christ, which is reproduced in the lives of Christians by means of baptism. What is lacking in the Romans passage as compared with the 1 Peter one is any overt reference to the *descensus ad inferos*. Lundberg, however, does find a reference to the *descensus* here: in 6.4 we are described as having been *buried* with Christ. He very reasonably links this with the reference to Christ having been buried in 1 Corinthians 15.4. This, he claims, implies entry into the realm of death (see note 19, page 128; this passage occurs on p. 219).

In the diagram on page 124 I have juxtaposed these two

The New Testament Interpretation of Scripture

New Testament passages with certain verses from Psalms 88 and 89 (LXX 87 and 88). In this case I have preserved the order of verses in the psalms and have transposed the NT material so as to bring out the comparison. I hope to show thereby that in fact the reference to the *descensus* is basic to both the NT passages.³ I have made my own rendering of the Greek of the LXX:

ROMANS 6.1-11	PSALMS 88 and 89	1 PETER 3.18-4.6
7 For he who has died is freed from sin . . . 10 The death he died he died to sin, once for all, but the life he lives he lives to God.	88.4–6 My life has come close to Hades. 5 I was reckoned with those who go down to the pit (εἰς λάκκον). I have become as a man without help, free among the dead (ἐν νεκροῖς ἐλεύθερος) 6 like wounded men cast away sleeping in the grave (καθεύδοντες ἐν τάφῳ)	3.18 being put to death in the flesh but made alive in the spirit. 4.1 whoever has suffered in the flesh has ceased from sin.
4b Christ was raised from the dead by the glory of the Father.	7 They placed me in the lowest pit . . . 10b I cried out unto thee, Lord, all the day, I stretched forth my hands unto thee. 11 Wilt thou do wonders among the dead? Or shall physicians⁴ rise up (ἀναστήσονται) and praise thee? . . . 14 And I, Lord, have cried to thee, and early shall my prayer come before thee.	3.19 he went and preached to the spirits in prison (τοῖς ἐν φυλακῇ πνεύμασιν ἐκήρυξεν). 3.21 through the resurrection of Jesus Christ.

	16 I am poor and in labours from my youth; having been exalted, I was humbled (ὑψωθεὶς ἐταπεινώθην) and was in dire straits.[5]	
4a We were buried therefore with him by baptism into death.	18 They came round about me all the day like water... 89.2 Thy mercies, oh Lord, will I sing for ever... 3 because thou hast said, For ever will mercy be built up.	3.20–1 (they) were saved through water. Baptism, which corresponds to this, now saves you.
	In the heavens shall thy truth be prepared... 7 For who in the clouds is equal to the Lord, who among the sons of God shall be compared to the Lord?	3.22 who has gone into heaven and is at the right hand of God, with angels, and authorities and powers subject to him.

At first glance the parallels between these three passages are not very striking, but I believe Psalm 88 (and perhaps the beginning of Psalm 89) does provide the framework which lies behind both Romans 6.1-11 and 1 Peter 3.18-4.6. The crucial phrase comes in Psalm 88.6 (LXX 87.5) which in the MT runs: *bamētym ḥophšy*, rendered by the LXX ἐν νεκροῖς ἐλεύθερος. ἐλεύθερος is also used to render *ḥophšy* here by both Aquila and Symmachus. Commentators on the psalm have found it a difficult phrase, and many have sought to emend it.[6] Several editors compare Job 3.19:

> The small and the great are there,
> and the slave is free (*ḥophšy*) from his master.

Oesterley remarks: 'The use of the word free may be an audacious and bitter parody and perversion of the phrase in

Job 3.19.'[7] Gunkel also sees a link here with the Job passage.[8] Certainly in Job 3.19 it is death that has enabled the servant to escape from his slavery.[9] We may follow Diezinger here in suggesting that ἐν νεκροῖς ἐλεύθερος was originally understood by Christians of Christ and taken as the equivalent of ἐκ νεκρῶν ἐγερθείς. When we start looking at this psalm with the eyes of an early Christian, we can see other features that would be taken as applying to Christ. It is possible that verse 11, though in fact it denies the possibility of resurrection, might be taken by an early Christian as saying exactly the opposite. In sacred writings rhetorical questions expecting the answer 'No' can be taken literally and understood as implying the answer 'Yes'. Compare Paul's treatment of Hosea 13.14 in 1 Corinthians 15.55. In the *Midrash on the Psalms* 'early shall my prayer come before thee' in Psalm 88.13 is interpreted by some rabbis as God's reply to the psalmist's plea and is paraphrased as 'in the morning shall my prayer come to meet thee', i.e. in the morning will deliverance come.[10] This would, of course, fit in very well with a reference to Christ's resurrection.

There are two points at which we might trace a link between this psalm and the 1 Peter passage. The first I have already expounded in my work referred to (page 122);[11] Rabbi Helbo understood the phrase 'free among the dead' to refer to the generation before the flood, which of course provides a link with 1 Peter 3.18f. The other point concerns the phrase τοῖς ἐν φυλακῇ πνεύμασιν in 1 Peter 3.19. In Psalm 88.5, 7 we have a reference to 'the pit' (EVV 88.4, 6); in verse 5 the psalmist says, 'I am reckoned among those who go down to the pit' and in verse 7: 'Thou hast put me in the depths of the pit.' In both places the Hebrew word is *bwr*, which the LXX translates with λάκκος. This word λάκκος is used extensively in the Greek versions of the Hebrew Bible to give the meaning 'prison'. Thus it is used by the LXX of the female slave in 'prison' (MT *bēyt habwr*) whose firstborn died (Exodus 12.29). In Genesis 40.15 it refers to the prison in which Joseph was confined after the episode of Potiphar's wife (MT *bwr*). In Jeremiah 44.16 (MT 37.16) the place in which the prophet is imprisoned is called οἰκία τοῦ λάκκου (MT *bēyt habwr*). Even more interesting is the fact that in Isaiah 14.15 Aquila uses λάκκος for the MT *š"wl*, where it is Lucifer who is to be brought

Scriptural Background to the Doctrine of the 'Descensus ad Inferos'

down to She'ol (LXX εἰς ᾅδου). So λάκκος could be used of the place of imprisonment of a rebellious angel. And in Isaiah 24.22 Symmachus uses λάκκος for *bwr* where it refers to the place where the rebellious host of heaven will be confined (LXX offers δεσμωτήριον). It is therefore by no means fanciful to suggest that an early Christian exegete, finding λάκκος in Psalm 88, should interpret it as meaning the place where departed spirits (whether angels or men) were confined. The word φυλακή would be a perfectly reasonable synonym for this. J. N. D. Kelly is therefore mistaken when he writes *à propos* 1 Peter 3.19: 'The abode of the dead is nowhere else depicted as a gaol in biblical or extra-canonical literature' (*A Commentary on the Epistles of Peter and Jude*, London 1969). MacCullagh well points out (op. cit., p. 51) that *phulakē* is used in Revelation 20.7 of the prison in which Satan is confined for a thousand years (see note 19, page 128).

Psalm 88.6 is echoed in the Dead Sea Scrolls in *Hodayoth* viii. 28-9 as follows: *w'm mtym yhpś rwḥy*. M. Delcor translates this with 'avec les morts mon esprit a cherché'.[12] Mansoor offers 'and with the dead he setteth my spirit adrift';[13] and Vermes has 'my spirit is imprisoned with the dead',[14] the exact opposite of the sense which I believe the NT writers extracted from the quotation. As far as our purpose is concerned, the interesting point is the context in which the citation occurs rather than the exact meaning of the citation. The author of this hymn applies it to himself and thereby identifies himself with the sufferer in the psalm.

The next verse in the psalm is quoted in 1 QS iv.13. In the course of an account of the state of the evil or damned, they are described as being *bmḥškym*. P. Wernberg-Møller in his edition of *The Manual of Discipline*[15] renders this phrase with 'in the fire of murky hell' and comments '*mḥshkym* is used in the OT (Psalm 88.7) as referring to Sheol'. Vermes offers for this phrase 'in the fire of the dark regions'.[16] It is remarkable that the Qumran sectaries can use Psalm 88 to apply both to the individual leader of the community and to the irrevocably damned. It shows us that it would be perfectly possible for early Christians to use the psalm in a similar way, both for Christ as one who has undergone the paradigmatic experience of death and descent into the realm of the dead, and as applying to those who are in the realm of the dead already, though not, as in the grim predestinarian theology of Qumran, without hope.

Fazekaš has examined Romans 6.3f in an interesting article.[17] He points out that in the OT you can be enveloped ('baptized') in waters which represent hostility to God, and he compares Psalm 18.16 and Jonah 2.5 and points out that Matthew 12.40 uses the image of the prophet in the fish's belly as a parallel to the death of Christ. These are passages which we examine further below. E. Klaar has also noted that in Romans 6.7 the word used is ὁ ἀποθανών not ὁ νεκρός.[18] The phrase seems to mean, he says, 'freedom from the obligation to slavish obedience to the power of sin has been won'. He agrees that the reference is undoubtedly christological.

We must now turn to 1 Peter 3.18-4.6 and determine how far our suggestion that behind it lies the framework of Psalms 88.1-89.7 illuminates our understanding of the passage. A very great deal has been written about this. I will try to limit myself to a discussion of those points which are relevant to our topic.[19]

The problems inherent in this passage may be summed up under five headings, not all of which are equally important for our topic.

1 *What is the meaning of ἐν ᾧ in 3.19?*

Scholars fall into two camps: one group holds that ἐν ᾧ refers to πνεῦμα and therefore means that it was in the dimension or realm of spirit that Christ preached to the spirits in prison. To this group belong von Soden, Bigg, Lundberg, MacCullagh (op. cit., p. 51), Beare, Windisch-Preisker, Schweizer, Kelly, Schelkle, Cranfield, and Dalton (p. 138). So also does Bieder (op. cit., p. 105), but he takes it to mean the Holy Spirit and zō(i)opoiētheis of the resurrection. According to this interpretation the author is still maintaining in verse 19 the σάρξ-πνεῦμα distinction which he makes in verse 18, and is saying that Christ's death deprived him of flesh, but that his life continued in the Spirit, in which he rose on the third day. As Lundberg puts it: 'Christ as a spiritual being has preached in this form to the spirits in prison' (see pp. 105-6). It might even be that we have here the germ of the later two natures doctrine, which would maintain that the incarnate Word being immortal could not undergo death in the spirit. The other group of scholars holds that ἐν ᾧ means something like 'in these circumstances'. Selwyn suggests 'in which process'; Reicke (pp. 111-13) argues that Christ being ἐν πνεύματι does not mean the same thing as the πνεύμασιν in verse 19; ἐν must therefore be either a temporal or a causal conjunction. 1 Peter uses ἐν ᾧ four times elsewhere as a conjunction, so he concludes that we have here a temporal conjunction indicating the period during which Christ preached to the spirits. Dalton, though he takes ἐν ᾧ as 'in which Spirit', would make the phrase apply not to the *descensus* but to the resurrection of Christ (pp. 124ff; 138). He lays much stress on ζῳοποιηθείς, claiming that this must refer to resurrection and not just to continued existence in the world of the dead. Lundberg agrees that the word refers to the resurrection, but merely concludes that it is mentioned out of order, since there is certainly a reference to the *descensus* here (pp. 106-7). Bieder (op. cit., p. 107), who denies that there is a conscious reference to a *descensus* at all in this passage, claims that, had the author meant to imply a *descensus*, he would have used *katabas* not *poreutheis*. But we may point out that in 3.21, where he certainly means a going up, he uses *poreutheis* not *anabas*, so no capital can be made for Bieder's view from the word-usage here. As for Lundberg's argument, ζῳοποιηθεὶς πνεύματι is a strange way to describe the resurrection of Christ's body. In fact our author is probably rather embarrassed as to what language he is to use to describe the mode of existence of Christ during the *descensus*. The σάρξ-πνεῦμα contrast was all he had; a Platonic σῶμα-ψυχή contrast was quite alien to his thought-world. I incline to think that ἐν ᾧ probably should be taken as meaning 'in which dimension of Spirit', despite Reicke's well-marshalled arguments. The parallel with Romans 6.1-11, and perhaps the Christian interpretation of Psalm 88.6 (87.5 LXX) ἐν νεκροῖς ἐλεύθερος, suggest that our author thought of Christ as having died to the flesh (and thereby to sin) but as continuing to live in the Spirit as he enters the abode of the dead. We may note also that the author of the *Hodayoth*, when he echoes Psalm 88.6 in 1 QH viii.28-9, can say that his spirit (*rwḥy*) is among the dead.

The New Testament Interpretation of Scripture

2 Who are the spirits in prison?

We can distinguish three schools of opinion here: that they are rebellious angels, or men (sinners either from before the time of the flood or from some later epoch), or that they consist of both elements. Schweizer, Dalton, Kelly, and Best maintain that the spirits comprise only rebellious angels. Friedrich,[20] Lundberg, Beare, Cranfield, and Brooks believe that the spirits are only men and not angels. Friedrich would limit the men to the generation before the flood; because they were particularly sinful, they were assigned to a different prison. Selwyn, Reicke, Bieder, Windisch-Preisker, and Schelkle all believe that the spirits in prison must include both angels and men. On the whole this last view seems the most probable, though either of the first two is quite consistent with the claim that Psalm 88 is in the background. The presence of rebellious angels is made very likely by 1 Peter 3.22, where the whole process of the *descensus* and the resurrection has as its result the subjection of 'angels, authorities, and powers'. On the other hand I agree with Reicke that the purpose of the *descensus* was not just to overcome the hostile powers but also to manifest the range of God's redeeming love, in which case it is likely that the author of 1 Peter wished to show that no one among the living or the dead was beyond the range of redemption. But this discussion has already impinged on the area covered by our fourth question.

3 Where did the preaching take place?

On this point Dalton finds himself in a relatively small minority. But he does have the support of H. Schlier in *Christus und die Kirche im Epheserbrief* (Tübingen 1930), p. 15. Most scholars conclude that this passage does intend to describe a *descensus ad inferos*, and that therefore the preaching must have taken place in the land of the dead, the underworld.[21] Dalton (p. 33) holds that ζωοποιηθείς πνεύματι in 3.18 refers to Christ's bodily resurrection at the end of the *triduum*, and hence that the preaching to the spirits took place after that, that is during the forty days between the resurrection and the ascension (p. 186). This preaching took place in the realm of the air, which, according to him, is where the rebellious angels were confined (pp. 165ff). We have already argued the point about the meaning of ζωοποιηθεὶς πνεύματι, but we might add here that Dalton's view seems to depend on an acceptance of the Lukan schema of a forty days' interval between resurrection and ascension, of which there is no sign in 1 Peter. Also, Dalton is led by his argument to deny that the concept of the Church as the ark of salvation is to be found in verses 20-21; this is because he wants to avoid any suggestion of Christians dying with Christ in baptism, as that would point too clearly towards a *descensus* scheme here (p. 207). Moreover he himself points out certain parallels between this passage and Jonah 1.2; 3.4, where the words πορεύθητι, κήρυξον, and ἐκήρυξε in the LXX seem to have an echo in 1 Peter 3.19 (pp. 150-51). But if there is a link with the story of Jonah this is a strong argument in favour of a *descensus* being intended here, as we shall be seeing below. It seems therefore a hopeless enterprise to argue that a *descensus ad inferos* is not intended in this passage.

4 What was the content of Christ's preaching?

The great majority of editors believe that Christ preached the message of salvation to the spirits in prison; this view is held by Friedrich, MacCullagh (op. cit., p. 53), Reicke (op. cit., p. 130), Bieder, Windisch-Preisker, Schweizer, Cranfield, Schelkle, Best, and Brooks. Synge has a modified version of it: the good news preached by Christ, in his view, is the information that being drowned in the flood meant that the spirits in prison had already undergone the first half of baptism: 'Their drowning had been turned by the death and resurrection of Christ into baptism.' As it stands this is a grotesque concept, envisaging the flood-generation as existing for centuries in the underworld in a condition of semi-baptism. But it may serve to point towards the concept which I believe is present in this passage, that Christ in his *descensus* turned the waters of chaos into the saving waters of baptism. If I am right in my conjecture that the opening verses of Psalm 89 may have been part of the background to this passage, perhaps we can see in Psalm 89.2 a hint that Christ's message of salvation was preached to the angelic powers: 'In the heavens shall thy truth be prepared.' Only Dalton and Kelly maintain that what Christ proclaimed to the spirits in prison was a message of damnation. Both are influenced by inter-testamental literature,

The New Testament Interpretation of Scripture

in which a figure such as Enoch is sent to proclaim doom to the rebellious angels in captivity. But we must allow for the fact that we are dealing with a Christian text. The redeeming mission of Christ is all-important here; this must surely have been the content of Christ's message to the spirits in prison, according to our author. One might also suggest that Psalm 89.10 (EVV 89.9), 'Thou dost rule the raging of the sea', could be taken by a Christian writer as an indication of Christ's conquest of the waters of death (see Lundberg, op. cit., p. 66).

5 *What does νεκροῖς εὐηγγελίσθη mean in 4.6?*

The temptation to associate this verse with 3.19 is very strong, and has not been resisted by many editors. Jeremias, Reicke (pp. 205ff), Cranfield, Synge, and Best all view it as a reversion to what has been already said in 3.19. Schweizer arrives at this conclusion by taking ἵνα κριθῶσιν as indicating consequence, not purpose, which was apparently possible in *koinē*, and offers the rendering: 'This is why it was preached to the dead, because they were in human fashion judged in the flesh, but that they should live after God's fashion in the Spirit.' But this does demand an unusual construction in an epistle which exhibits almost the best Greek style in the NT. To this group also belong MacCullagh (p. 58) and Windisch-Preisker. But Selwyn, Dalton, Schelkle, and Kelly think that some other explanation must be found, since the preaching to the dead would not be in place in the context of 4.6. From the point of view of this study it does not make very much difference which view we accept. The only alternative is that lucidly set out by Selwyn. It must mean 'the gospel was preached (while they were alive) to Christians who are now dead'. Dalton (p. 268) holds that 4.5b refers to the parousia, and 4.6 refers to the fact that there are already among the dead those who have heard and accepted the gospel while alive, so that Christ's judging the dead at the parousia will not be without significance. On the other hand a passage in the *Shepherd of Hermas* referred to by Lundberg (p. 71) would seem to suggest that 4.6b refers to the same topic as 3.19. It runs: 'These apostles and teachers who proclaimed (κηρύξαντες) the name of the Son of God fell asleep (κοιμηθέντες) in the power and faith of the Son of God and preached (ἐκήρυξαν) also to those who had already fallen asleep (τοῖς προκεκοιμένοις) . . . They therefore descended with them into the water and came up again. But the first group [sc. the apostles] went down while alive . . . whereas those who had already fallen asleep went down [sc. into the water] while already dead (νεκροὶ κατέβησαν), and came up alive' (text from J. B. Lightfoot, *Apostolic Fathers* S. 9. xvi, 5-6 (London 1898), my translation). Here the author of *Hermas* attributes to the apostles exactly the activity which the author of 1 Peter attributes to Christ, if the first view of 4.6b is correct. The waters of baptism are identified with the waters of death. This seems to me to incline the balance of probability towards this view.

Bieder (op. cit., p. 156) believes that this passage in *Hermas* supports his view that νεκροῖς in 1 Peter 4.6 means 'spiritually dead', but I cannot see that this follows. However, he does agree that the author of *Hermas* attributes to the apostles the activity which a doctrine of *descensus* attributes to Christ. MacCullagh (p. 64) actually suggests that the *Hermas* reference is a gloss on *euēggelisthē* in 1 Peter 4.6.

A number of editors do make cross-references to Romans 6 and even to Matthew 12.40, but any recognition that Christ is regarded as in some sense undergoing the waters of baptism while in the underworld is rare. Reicke, however, in his commentary observes that 'the suffering and death of Christ were regarded as a baptism'; and in his longer work (p. 245) he does mention the 'waters of death' theme in the Psalms and does list Psalm 88 as one such passage. And Dalton interprets 4.1b in the light of the Pauline doctrine that baptism brought the believer into mystical union with the death and resurrection of Christ (p. 114). But he has no suggestion of a scriptural background. Lundberg is of course the great champion of the view which sees in this passage the descent of Christ into the waters of death identified with the waters of baptism. It seems to me he makes out a very strong case which has not been refuted.

At this point it is relevant to compare some passages from the *Odes of Solomon* in which a clear doctrine of the *descensus ad inferos* occurs. Charlesworth maintains that they are actually a first-century Jewish-Christian work, but it seems to me that a date early in the second century is more likely: their connection with the tradition of the Fourth Gospel and with Ignatius

The New Testament Interpretation of Scripture

seems to suggest this. They are not, as far as I can judge, to be fairly described as Gnostic – at least the characteristic features of Gnosticism do not appear in them, though one certainly can discern signs of incipient Docetism. Ode 22.4-8 runs as follows (translation from J. H. Charlesworth, *The Odes of Solomon* (Oxford 1973), p. 89); Christ speaks:

> He who gave me authority over bonds
> So that I might unbind them;
> He who overthrew by my hands the dragon with seven heads,
> And set me at his roots that I might destroy his seed;
> Thou wert there and helped me,
> And in every place thy Name surrounded me.
> Thy right hand destroyed his evil venom,
> And thy hand levelled the way for those who believe in thee.
> And it chose them from the graves
> And separated them from the dead ones.

Here certainly is an account of Christ descending to the underworld, overcoming the powers of evil by God's help, and calling to himself some of the dead. See also Ode 42.11-17 (op. cit., pp. 145-6); Christ speaks:

> Sheol saw me and was shattered,
> And Death rejected me and many with me . . .
> And I made a congregation of the living among the dead;
> And I spoke with them by living lips
> In order that my word may not be unprofitable.
> And those who had died ran towards me;
> And they cried out and said, Son of God, have pity on us,
> And deal with us according to thy kindness,
> And bring us out from the lands of darkness,
> And open for us the door by which we may come out to thee.
> For we perceive that our death does not touch thee.

We may observe that in this account Christ is naturally immortal, in much the same way as we have interpreted the phrase *zō(i)opoiētheis de pneumati* in 1 Peter 3.18 (see page 129 above). It is interesting that MacCullagh (p. 132) says that this Ode is actually based on Psalm 88. See also Ode 28 (Charlesworth, op. cit., pp. 109-10), which says in effect that

Christ's enemies could not kill him because he was pre-existent. This contrasts with Acts 2.25-8, which we discuss below. I would conclude from this that the dating and affinities of 1 Peter are more with the *Odes of Solomon*, whereas the material which Luke is handling in Acts 2 is earlier. This does not mean, however, that the connection between the *Odes* and the Qumran documents (especially the *Hodayoth*) is to be denied. Charlesworth himself suggests that the author may even have been 'un Essénien converti'. See his article 'Les Odes de Salomon et les Manuscrits de la Mer Morte' in *RB* 77 (1970), p. 549. W. Bauer believes that the *Odes* were originally written in Greek, and he describes them as 'a Gnostic hymnbook from the second century', though he presently qualifies this by adding: 'Here "Gnostic" must be understood in a broad sense' (see W. Schneemelcher, ed., *New Testament Apocrypha* (London 1965), vol. II, pp. 809-10).

2

We now turn to two passages in the NT in which the descent-ascent pattern is securely based on exegesis of the Scriptures, Romans 10.6-8 and Ephesians 4.7-10.

It should by now be generally admitted among scholars that in Romans 10.6-8 Paul is using both Moses and Jonah as types of Christ. His modification of Deuteronomy 30.13, 'Neither is it beyond the sea, so that you should say "Who will go over the sea for us?"' so as to make it run: 'Who shall descend into the abyss?' is in fact found in the newly discovered *Targum of Palestine*. This is how that Targum renders Deuteronomy 30.12-13:[22]

> The law is not in the heavens, that thou shouldest say, O that we had one like Mosheh the prophet to ascend into heaven, and bring it to us ... Neither is the law beyond the great sea, that thou shouldest say, O that we had one like Jonah the prophet, who could descend into the depth of the sea, and bring it to us.

Le Déaut's comment is perfectly just: 'Paul bears in mind the Targumic rendering and applies to Jesus what was said of Moses and of Jonah, and that all the more easily because, from the Christian point of view, both were considered as figures of Christ.'[23] McNamara on the same theme suggests that 'the great sea' in the Targum is a reference to Jonah 2.6, where Jonah says that the *t'hwm* has surrounded him, which the LXX renders with ἄβυσσος.[24] He concludes that 'Paul knew of this paraphrase of the text of Deuteronomy and adapted it for his own purpose'. A. M. Goldberg would modify this claim to the extent that he believes that Paul was acquainted with the traditional interpretation that lies behind the Targum rather than with the Targum itself.[25] He believes the gloss on the text of Deuteronomy may have been in origin a polemic against *Merkaba* mysticism, and even that Paul may have intended his gloss in a similar sense. But these modifications do not affect our argument. What is important is to note that, since a *descensus* is explicitly referred to in this passage, we may legitimately assume that it is implicit in Romans 6.1-11. This strengthens the link between that passage and Psalm 88. Lundberg (p. 136) well points out the parallel with 1 Corinthians 10.1: there the Red Sea corresponds to baptism. Hence the absence of a reference to baptism in Romans 10.6-8 is fortuitous, not deliberate. Lundberg would associate διὰ τῆς θαλάσσης in 1 Corinthians 10.1 with the sea of death (p. 143).

The same pattern appears in Ephesians 4.7-10, which we take to be deutero-Pauline. But the claim that there is a *descensus ad inferos* here has often been challenged, so we must give it rather more attention.

As in the case of Romans 10.6-8, it has now become clear that in Ephesians 4.7-10 the author is basing his exegesis of Psalm 68.18 on the Targumic interpretation or on the tradition that lies behind it. M. Harmon claims that Paul is not indebted to any Targumic tradition, but has made a 'deliberate alteration' to the text of Psalm 68 for the sake of his exegesis. But his conclusion seems motivated as much by a desire to dissociate Paul from any contact with rabbinic exegesis as by consideration of the evidence (see M. Harmon, 'Aspects of Paul's Use of the Psalms', in *Westminster Theological Journal* 32 (1969), 1-23). Likewise Bieder's statement (op. cit., p. 82) that it was Paul who changed ἔλαβες to ἔδωκεν is not supported by any examination of the evidence from the Targums. The Targumist had already altered the *lqḥt* of the MT 'thou hast received' to

Scriptural Background to the Doctrine of the 'Descensus ad Inferos'

ḥlqt 'thou hast inherited (and hence bestowed)', from motives of reverence, according to Rubinkiewicz.²⁶ The Targumist also altered *b'dm* literally 'in man' to 'to men', so as to be able to make the passage apply to the giving of the Torah through Moses. There is undoubtedly an implied Moses typology in this passage in Ephesians, as in Romans 10.6-8. The question we have to decide is, can we detect a Jonah typology also? Does the passage refer to a *descensus ad inferos*?

The answer depends on the interpretation of verse 9 and in particular of the phrase τὰ κατώτερα [μέρη] τῆς γῆς. Those who deny that there is a reference to the *descensus ad inferos* have here to take the meaning, 'this lowly earth of ours', from this phrase. There is also a tendency among this school of interpreters to understand the 'coming down' in verse 9 not of the incarnation, but of the descent of the Spirit at Pentecost. Hodge, however, takes κατέβη of the incarnation and τὰ κατώτερα τῆς γῆς as simply 'this earth', referring to Isaiah 44.23, where *taḥtywt 'ereṣ* is used of the earth as opposed to the heavens.²⁷ Von Soden holds that κατέβη is not necessarily to be taken as coming chronologically before ἀνέβη; he understands verse 9 to refer to Christ's indwelling in the Church.²⁸ T. K. Abbott belongs to this school of interpreters; but only adds the dubious argument: 'St Paul would hardly have given such a material local designation to the place of the departed spirits.'²⁹

J. Schmid, in 'Der Epheserbrief des Apostel Paulus' (in *Biblische Studien*, ed. O. Bardenhewer (Freiburg 1928), pp. 356-7) argues thus: 'As in the Psalm passages Jahweh mounts not from Hades but from the earth to heaven, so Christ has mounted up not from Hades but from earth to heaven' (my translation). But we have seen that the psalm passage that lies behind the *descensus-ascensio* theme is from Psalms 88-9 rather than from such psalms as 24 or 47. Christ in the psalms is represented by the innocent sufferer rather than by Yahweh. H. Schlier, in his important study already referred to (see page 130), *Christus und die Kirche im Epheserbrief*, argues that this passage is based on a descent-ascent pattern such as we meet in Gnostic writings, and hence the phrase in verse 9 refers to the earth and not to Hades. He is able to show that the author of Ephesians believed that the demonic powers dwelt in the air, *en tois epouraniois*, and hence to overcome them Christ would not need to descend to Hades. He also points out that in Ephesians 1.10, 3.15 things in the heavens and on earth are mentioned, but there is no word of things under the earth (see Schlier, op. cit., pp. 3-5). To this we may reply that since Schlier wrote, it has become clear that the author's master Paul believed in a *descensus*. Secondly, it is not certain that in either 1.10 or 3.15 a reference to Hades would be appropriate, certainly not in 3.15, since we would hardly look for a 'family' in the underworld. Thirdly, we must not take *en tois epouraniois* in too literal a sense as indicating a position in space, since in 2.6 God has seated us there. It is more like a dimension than a place. This does not suggest the later Gnostic notion of graded heavens. Fourthly, quasi-Gnostic ideologies are not inconsistent with a belief in a *descensus*, witness the quotations from the *Odes of Solomon* given above. And lastly we note 3.18, where one dimension of Christ's love is *to bathos*, 'the depth'. This is associated with fulfilling, as is Christ's descent in 4.10.

We must also take note of Caird's article.[30] He believes that the descent in verse 9 is Christ's return at Pentecost, and he links this passage with Acts 2.33 where he takes ἐξέχεεν as the counterpart of κατέβη here. He points out that Psalm 68 was used at the feast of Pentecost, and he suggests that the passage in Acts 2 is also based on Psalm 68. Since there is no suggestion of a *descensus ad inferos* in Acts 2, there is no reason to see one in Ephesians 4, he maintains. He concludes: 'The probability is that Ephesians represents an early stage in the theological process which was ultimately to produce the Pentecost story of Acts' (p. 544). He also argues that Christ cannot have conquered the powers of evil in the underworld, since the author of Ephesians locates them in τὰ ἐπουράνια (6.12).

These arguments admit of a ready reply: in the first place, it is not accurate to say that there is no *descensus ad inferos* in Acts. I shall be arguing in the last section of this chapter that the concept of the *descensus* is to be found in Acts 2.24-8. Next, Caird's view implies an over-elaborate pattern of divine action: descent for the incarnation, ascent for the resurrection-ascension, descent at Pentecost, ascent to fill all things. Also pouring out gifts cannot be equated with a descent. I hope to show in the next section that in chapter 5 the author of Ephesians manifests a belief in the *descensus* quite independently of this passage. As for the argument that the author could not believe in a conquest of the powers in the underworld because the powers dwell in τὰ ἐπουράνια, Paul found these two beliefs quite compatible. Romans 10.6-8 shows that he had a doctrine of the *descensus*, but in Romans 8.39 ὕψωμα is one of the powers that has been rendered harmless to Christians, and in Philippians 2.10 τὰ ἐπουράνια are to bow to Christ.

Caird has also ignored the evidence about the meaning of τὰ κατώτερα τῆς γῆς. As long ago as 1898 Bröse argued that τὰ κατώτερα τῆς γῆς is in contrast with ὑπεράνω πάντων τῶν οὐρανῶν, and must therefore mean 'under the earth' not 'on the earth'; he compares καταχθονίων in Philippians 2.10.[31] He claims that Paul never uses καταβαίνειν for the incarnation as John does, and adds that ἵνα πληρώσῃ τὰ πάντα must include Hades. J. Armitage Robinson uses a similar argument in *St Paul's Epistle to the Ephesians* (London 1914, 2nd edn in loc.). Selwyn claims that τὰ κατώτερα τῆς γῆς must mean the *inferi* in view of Psalm 63.9 and Psalm 139.15.[32] In both these places the MT has *taḥtywt ha'ereṣ* in a context which must refer to the underworld; LXX renders with τὰ κατώτατα τῆς γῆς in each case. He rightly claims that the phrase ᾐχμαλώτευσεν αἰχμαλωσίαν in Ephesians 4.8 must refer to Christ's conquest of the powers in the underworld and sees a close parallel with the τοῖς ἐν φυλακῇ πνεύμασι in 1 Peter 3.19. Büchsel also concludes that verse 9 refers to Christ's journey to the underworld, because the Epistle speaks of Christ's resurrection from the dead, not from death.[33] In any case Christ could not fill all things unless he had been through all things including Hades. McNamara points out that the hymn of 5.14 favours the view that 4.9 refers to the *descensus*.[34] He suggests that 'both 4.8 and 5.14 may well have formed part of the same hymn'.

It is amusing that C. L. Mitton in his book *The Epistle to the Ephesians* (Oxford 1951, p. 22) can quote Goodspeed's argument that the existence of a doctrine of *descensus* in Ephesians 4.7 is a proof of non-Pauline authorship, since 'it is almost impossible to suppose that such a view had any place in Paul's thought. In fact he virtually excludes it by what he says in Rom. x.6-7.' But F. F. Bruce, writing only ten years later than Mitton, claims that there is a reference to the *descensus* here just because of the parallel with Romans 10.6f (see Bruce's

The Epistle to the Ephesians (London 1961), in loc.). The difference of opinion is due of course to the fact that Bruce was aware of the version of Deuteronomy 30.11-13 in the *Targum of Palestine*, whereas neither Goodspeed nor Mitton shows any knowledge of it. We should add that Mitton inclines to the opinion that there is no reference to a *descensus* in Ephesians and that Paul did not hold such a doctrine either (pp. 205, 239-40).

There is, as we have seen in the case of Schlier, a school of commentators who use the argument that the Gnostic background to Ephesians proves that τὰ κατώτερα τῆς γῆς must mean 'this lowly earth', since Gnostics believed that the redeemer degraded himself by coming into contact with physical matter. Of these is Bultmann and also Lindars,[35] whose argument is that verse 10 'has a Gnostic ring about it'. It is remarkable that a certain proportion of those who deny a reference to the *descensus* have done so for *a priori* reasons, either because Paul could not use mythological concepts or because the author of Ephesians is a Gnostic and therefore must take a low view of the earthly sphere.[36] As a matter of fact, belief in the *descensus ad inferos* is by no means incompatible with Gnosticism; see for example *Acts of Thomas* 10, where Christ is addressed as 'ambassador that was sent from the height and reached Hades, thou who hast also opened the doors and led up thence those who were for long times shut up in the treasury of darkness' (Foerster, op. cit., vol. 1, p. 347). Hence the mere suspicion of Gnosticism (which Bieder and Lindars for example detect in Ephesians) is not in itself an argument that there cannot be a doctrine of *descensus* in it. It is only fair to add that MacCullagh suggests that in this *Acts of Thomas* passage 'Hades' may mean not the underworld but the earth itself (p. 305).

The right interpretation seems to be that the author of Ephesians had no difficulty in finding in Psalm 68 a typological reference to the resurrection and ascension of Christ, but that he could not find any obvious reference to the *descensus* there, and therefore wrote verses 9-10. Rabbinic exegesis had already interpreted the psalm in terms of Moses receiving the Torah on Mount Sinai and bringing it down as God's gift to Israel. Our author was well aware of this, and can accept the Moses typology exactly as Paul accepts it in Romans 10.6-8. As a matter of fact our author could probably find two other features in the traditional interpretation of the psalm that would help to produce the exegesis he intended. There was quite strong rabbinic emphasis on the opposition which Moses encountered in heaven when he proposed to bring the Torah down. This is referred to in Strack-Billerbeck's commentary on this passage,[37] but we can also cite *Shabbath* 89a, where Satan encounters Moses.[38] Even more emphatic is *Pesikta Rabbati*, where a troop of angels of destruction meet Moses and attempt to burn him with a breath of their mouths, and where he even overcomes the angel of death. This would confirm our author in the belief that the psalm refers to Christ's conquest of the powers. The other feature is the reference to resurrection which occurs in the traditional exegesis. Psalm 68.10 (EVV 68.9) seems to mean: 'Rain in abundance, O God, thou didst shed abroad.' This was taken as a reference to resurrection. In *Tractate Hagiga* 12b we read that one of the heavens is called '*Araboth*.[39] It contains 'the dew wherewith the Holy One, blessed be He, will hereafter revive the dead, for it is written, *A bounteous rain didst thou pour down, O God*.' This is explained in *Pesikta Rabbati*[40] thus: 'When Israel heard the first of the commandments, "I am the Lord thy God", their souls at once departed from them. Thereupon the Holy One, blessed be He, made descend the dew which at the resurrection will quicken the souls of the righteous and revived them, as it is said, *Thou, O God, didst send a bounteous rain, whereby thou didst restore thine inheritance when it fainted away*.' If our author knew that the reference to rain in verse 10 was traditionally understood as a reference to God's power in raising the dead, he would the more easily see in this psalm a reference to the resurrection of Christ from the dead.

3

So far we have traced the pattern of descent-conquest-ascent in Paul, in 1 Peter, and in Ephesians. We have limited ourselves to indicating three Scripture passages which lie behind the *descensus* doctrine: Psalms 88-9, Deuteronomy 30.11-13, and Psalm 68. But in the background has been hovering the figure of Jonah. In this section we bring him into the foreground

The New Testament Interpretation of Scripture

and examine three passages in the NT where he is mentioned or seems to be implied. Two of them are in Ephesians itself. The first is Ephesians 5.14:

ἔγειρε, ὁ καθεύδων,
καὶ ἀνάστα ἐκ τῶν νεκρῶν,
καὶ ἐπιφαύσει σοι ὁ Χριστός.

No one who wishes to examine this passage can afford to ignore Noack's valuable study.[41] He considers nearly all the possible scriptural sources for the passage. He thinks the nearest is Isaiah 60.1:

Φωτίζου, φωτίζου Ἰερουσαλήμ,
ἥκει γάρ σου τὸ φῶς,
καὶ ἡ δόξα κυρίου ἐπί σε ἀνέταλκεν.

60.2b runs:

ἐπί σε δὲ φανήσεται κύριος.

Other possible passages are Isaiah 26.19 and 29.19, but neither is really at all reminiscent of Ephesians 5.14. Noack is sure that we have here a piece of baptismal liturgy. We need not pursue his speculation that the original hymn referred to the parousia.

Isaiah 60.1, 2b is no doubt the nearest parallel in Scripture, but it is sufficiently remote and lacks in particular two very important elements in Ephesians 5.14, the command to arise and the reference to sleep. I would like to bring forward a suggestion originally made by my brother R. P. C. Hanson to the effect that this passage is influenced by Jonah 1.5-6:[42] 'But Jonah had gone down into the inner part of the ship and had lain down and was fast asleep. So the captain came and said to him, "What do you mean, you sleeper? Arise, call upon your god!"' The Hebrew rendered 'was fast asleep' with *wayiškal wayērādam*, LXX καὶ ἐκάθευδεν καὶ ἔρεγχεν. The phrase 'you sleeper, arise' is a translation of *nirdām qwm*, LXX τί σὺ ῥέγχεις; ἀνάστα. Now it is true that the Greek here does not immediately suggest the ἔγειρε, ὁ καθεύδων of Ephesians 5.14, but it does contain ἀνάστα, which occurs in the next line in Ephesians 5.14. Moreover, we would hardly expect the phrase ἔγειρε ὁ ῥέγχων in a liturgical hymn ('Arise, you snorer!'), and we do have ἐκάθευδεν in the previous verse. The verb *rdm*

Scriptural Background to the Doctrine of the 'Descensus ad Inferos'

used in the Niph'al can mean 'to sleep heavily'. Elsewhere it means 'to be in a faint, unconscious' or even 'to throw a fit', and LXX translates it accordingly. It is interesting that in Psalm 76.6 (LXX 75.7) MT *hirdām w'rekeb wāsws* ('horse and rider lay stunned') LXX translates with ἐνύσταξαν οἱ ἐπιβεβηκότες τοὺς ἵππους. Also Psalm 88.5, the very verse in which we have detected a reference to the *descensus ad inferos* on the part of Paul, contains the phrase *šok'bēy qeber*, which the LXX renders with καθεύδοντες ἐν τάφῳ.[43] Finally we may point to Matthew 25.5, 'the parable of the foolish virgins', where 'they all slumbered and slept' translates ἐνύσταξαν πᾶσαι καὶ ἐκάθευδον. It looks very like an accurate rendering of *wayiškal wayērādam* in Jonah 1.5 (*mutatis mutandis*). Could it be that this parable has in fact the parousia in mind? Not only the foolish virgins but *all* of them slumbered and slept. Do the virgins represent the dead generally, and the wise ones Christians who have accepted Christ in this life, and who can therefore enter into the joy of the Lord at the parousia? (Compare our discussion of 1 Peter 4.6 on page 132 above.) In that case 'slumbered and slept' will be a phrase describing the condition of those who are dead, and will echo the Jonah story. MacCullagh (p. 48n) makes the remarkable suggestion that this hymn-quotation 'may represent Christ's triumph-song on entering Hades'. R. R. Williams in F. L. Cross, ed., *Studies in Ephesians* (London 1956), p. 93 describes the verse as 'a quotation from the formula of baptism'. F. F. Bruce thinks it is probably 'a primitive baptismal hymn', and tells us that 'in the Hellenistic world this precise rhythm was specially associated with religious initiation-chants'. The connection with baptism can hardly be denied. The hymn will naturally therefore have overtones of the resurrection, and will have definite reference to Jonah, the Old Testament figure who foreshadowed Christ in having gone down to the depths of Hades and having been delivered from thence by God. But this connection of baptism with Christ's paradigmatic death and *descensus* brings us to our next passage.[44]

This is Ephesians 5.25-7. The problem raised by these verses is, when is Christ understood as having washed the Church in baptism? And, to what does ἐν ῥήματι refer? We may look at the second question first. There are really only three possible answers to this: (a) the gospel: this is supported by Hodge, Oepke,[45] and Houlden, though these last two give equal support to the second answer, as does J. Armitage Robinson; (b) the baptismal formula: this is supported by Von Soden, Abbott, Gore,[46] Hauck, Kittel, and (very doubtfully) Dibelius-Greeven; and (c) the baptismal confession: only Gore and Bruce support this, and Gore lends equal support to (b). I hope to show that there is more to be said for it.

The first question indicates the really difficult element in this passage. Is the author suggesting that Christ underwent a sort of archetypal baptism on behalf of the Church? If so, the time when this happened can only be at his death and burial, i.e. during the *triduum* in which the *descensus* took place. Or does the author merely mean 'the baptismal purification of all the individual members of the Christian body' (Gore)? The difficulty with this solution is that it hardly agrees with the past tense καθαρίσας. Von Soden compares Titus 3.5 and John 15.3. The first could quite reasonably refer to the baptism of those to whom the letter is addressed, but Ephesians refers to the whole Church. Abbott quotes Augustine: 'Accedit verbum ad elementum et fit sacramentum', which makes ῥῆμα refer to the baptismal formula, but does not answer our first question. Oepke suggests that the participle καθαρίσας does not have a reference to a past event, but to the means whereby Christ's cleansing of the Church was fulfilled. But it would seem necessary to make καθαρίσας refer to a past event however we take it, either to the archetypal baptism in Christ's death, or to the baptism of the actual members of the Church, also a past event. Houlden writes of our author: 'It may be that he sees lying behind the baptism of individuals in an archetypal (quasi-Gnostic? . . .) way the death of Christ, of his body (cf. v.30), as the fount of saving action'; and he well compares Mark 10.38. Dibelius-Greeven seem to be moving in the same direction when they write: 'The presupposition of the cleansing in baptism is the self-giving of Christ. Baptism is the image (*Abbild*) of Christ's sufferings.'

This passage comes in the context of a marriage metaphor to describe the relation of Christ to the Church. It seems consistent therefore to regard the bath referred to in verse 26 as being in the figure the ceremonial bath which in eastern countries the bride is given before the wedding. It was also a Roman custom. See *The Wealth of the Roman World*, eds. J. P. C. Kent and K. S. Painter, published as a catalogue to the 'Wealth of the Roman World Exhibition' (London 1977), p. 44, exhibit 88. The 'Casket of Projecta' from the Esquiline Hill, Rome represents 'the bathing and dressing rituals which took place on the eve of a Roman wedding'. There is no indication of date, but Secundus and his bride Projecta were Christians. Admittedly in Ephesians 5.26 it is Christ the bridegroom who gives the bath to the bride, a proceeding which would be highly irregular, but we must allow perhaps that the metaphor has rather run out of control at this point. If the bridal figure is applicable here, then we must imagine Christ as having died for the sake of the Church, baptized her in the waters of the underworld (the waters of death are transformed into the saving waters of baptism), and having actually married her in his resurrection, when he rose in his spiritual Body which is the Church's proper sphere. Compare a phrase from Ignatius that connects Christ's baptism by John with his suffering and death, Ephesians xviii.2: '[Christ] who was born and baptized that by his suffering he might cleanse water ($\tau\grave{o}$ $\mathring{v}\delta\omega\rho$ $\kappa\alpha\theta\alpha\rho\acute{\iota}\sigma\eta$)'. J. B. Lightfoot comments: 'It was the death of Christ that gave this purifying effect to the baptismal water.' It is even possible that we can find this pattern in Psalms 88–9. We have already noticed the reference to the waters of enmity in Psalm 88.18 (EVV 88.17): 'They surround me like a flood all the day long.' Psalm 89.2 (EVV 89.1) could well be taken as the joyful confession that the Church makes in baptism:

> I will sing of thy steadfast love, O Lord, for ever; with my mouth I will proclaim thy faithfulness to all generations.

We are reminded of Romans 10.8–9:

> 'The word ($\tau\grave{o}$ $\acute{\rho}\hat{\eta}\mu\alpha$) is near you, on your lips and in your heart (that is, the word of faith which we preach); because, if you confess with your lips ($\acute{\epsilon}\nu$ $\tau\hat{\omega}$ $\sigma\tau\acute{o}\mu\alpha\tau\acute{\iota}$ σov) that Jesus is Lord, and believe in your heart that God raised him from the dead, you will be saved.'

The reference to John 15.3 which Houlden makes is relevant here: the disciples are pure because of the word which Jesus has spoken to them.⁴⁷ Ephesians 5.25-7 connects that word with baptism. Romans 10.8-9 both refers to it in a context where the *descensus ad inferos* is certainly in mind, and connects it with the convert's confession of faith. It seems to me therefore very likely indeed that Ephesians 5.25-7 does refer to Christ's archetypal baptism of the Church in the waters of the underworld, and that ἐν ῥήματι in verse 26 refers both to the word of proclamation and to the convert's baptismal confession. Naturally, if my interpretation of Ephesians 5.14 and of 5.25-7 is correct, there can be no question at all but that Ephesians 4.9-10 refers to the *descensus ad inferos*.

I confess that I cannot see anything particularly Gnostic about this last passage which we have been examining. But Schlier finds here an example of the marriage between *Sophia* and the *Logos* (or some other suitable aeon) which is a familiar feature of later Gnosticism. He writes on p. 62: 'She, the Church, is also the wisdom of God in the Body of Christ', and he claims that the epithet *polupoikilos* ('manifold') applied to the wisdom of God in 3.10 is to be equated with *polumorphos*, an adjective that applied to all sorts of deities in contemporary Hellenistic religion and in later Gnosticism. But in fact the Church is not identified with the wisdom of God in Ephesians. On the contrary, the wisdom of God applies to God's whole design, precisely as it does in 1 Corinthians 2.7. As for the *manifold* wisdom of God, we can find excellent parallels to this idea in Romans 11.33 and Hebrews 1.1. It would seem more scientific to seek affinities for the thought of Ephesians in earlier or contemporary Christian literature than to range far afield in Gnostic literature of the second century.

The third passage that concerns us here is Matthew 12.38-41, the sign of Jonah. A great deal has been written on this subject from the form-critical or source-critical point of view. We must try to avoid concerning ourselves too much with the question: 'Is Matthew 12.40 an authentic logion of Jesus?' Whether the logion is authentic or not only concerns us in as far as it indicates an approximate dating for the reference to the sign of Jonah. Scholars differ widely in their conclusions here, though the great majority would say that the Matthaean addition to the narrative of the other two Synoptists is not authentic.⁴⁸ Some scholars besides Jeremias believe that Jesus did see his death and resurrection as a sign, even though they do not believe that Jesus uttered the logion about Jonah in the whale's belly. Thus Linton points out that according to the Fourth Gospel (John 2.17-21) the sign is the death and resurrection of Jesus,[49] and there is strong evidence that Jesus did utter a mysterious saying about the Temple being rebuilt. A reasonable conclusion would be that in fact Jesus simply refused to give a sign. Early Christian reflection saw two quite different resemblances between Jonah and Jesus: (a) at Jonah's preaching the Gentiles repented and listened to God's word; this was happening in the early Church; (b) Jonah's descent into the whale's belly and subsequent deliverance is a type of Christ's death, descent to the realm of the dead, and resurrection. Luke reproduces (a) only; Matthew reproduces (a) and (b). Meyer suggests that (a) orginated 'in the Q community'.[50]

There is, however, a group of scholars who describe Matthew 12.40 as an actual interpolation, not composed by the author of the First Gospel. The material of Matthew 12.39-41 occurs in Justin without verse 40. This view is defended by Holtzmann, McNeill, Stendahl, and Cope.[51] But there is no textual evidence to suggest that Matthew 12.40 is an interpolation, and in the passage in the *Dialogue with Trypho* which is cited as a proof that there is an interpolation here, Justin shows himself to be fully aware that the sign of Jonah consists in Jonah's being delivered from the belly of the whale. He does not actually quote Matthew 12.41 either: 'The men of Nineveh shall rise up in judgement with this generation', but no one suggests that Matthew 12.41 is an interpolation. There is indeed a tendency to describe this Matthaean addition as later than the Q material. Thus Green claims that it 'belongs to a later stage of Christian reflection, familiar to us from early Christian art'.[52] But we have no reason at all to label this tradition as later. On the contrary, it is actually witnessed to at an earlier date than the Q explanation, since we know that Paul reproduces the typology of Jonah. We are not justified therefore in treating Matthew 12.40 as if it belonged to the category of Matthaean legendary additions such as Matthew 14.28-31; 17.24-7; or 27.52-3.

It is very interesting that Origen provides a link between Matthew 12.40 and Romans 6.7. In his commentary on Matthew

12.40 he writes: 'Jonah was alive in the belly of the monster, and Christ when he encountered death (*en thanatō/i genomenos*) was free of it (*eleutheros ek toutou*)' (*Die Griechischen Christlichen Schriftsteller der Ersten Drei Jahrhunderte; Origenes* 12th vol., (Leipzig 1941) p. 124). Unfortunately this is only a fragment: Origen's continuous commentary is only extant from Matthew chapter 13. But it does suggest that Origen knew of the interpretation of Psalm 88.6 in terms of the *descensus*.

We must insist that Matthew 12.40 does definitely imply a *descensus ad inferos*, not just a lying inert in the tomb during the *triduum*. This point is made by Holtzmann, Seidelin (p. 130), and Klostermann.[53] This last writer says that the verse means not just that Jesus was 'in the grave', but that he was 'in Hades'. It definitely refers to the *descensus*.

In order to appreciate the full significance of this overt reference to the *descensus*, we must realize that in Jewish tradition Jonah was something of a saviour figure. There are disparaging references to him in the rabbis, it is true,[54] but on the whole he emerges as a righteous man, anxious for Israel's welfare. Jeremias quotes the *Mekhilta* and *Tractate Sanhedrin* to show that his flight was undertaken for Israel's sake: he did not want the Ninevites' repentance to throw into relief the impenitence of Israel.[55] Seidelin quotes R. Jonathan (c. A.D. 140) to the effect that Jonah offered to be thrown into the sea as a propitiation for Israel. It is very remarkable that a modern Christian literalist, who takes the story of Jonah to be completely authentic history, comes quite independently to exactly the same conclusion: 'Though he was guilty, what a shadowing-forth he provides of the Willing Victim and Divine Substitute [capitals in the original] who upheld the majesty of God's broken law!'[56] Ancient rabbinic exegesis and modern literalistic exegesis have much in common. Bickermann quotes Jerome, who, following Jewish tradition, said that Jonah knew the repentance of the Gentiles meant the fall of the Jews.[57]

The earliest post-canonical reference we have to Jonah's activity appears to occur in 3 Maccabees 6.8.[58] Already legend has got busy on the original story, for the verse runs: 'Thou didst look upon Jonah, wasting away in the belly of the fish, denizen of the deep, and showed him openly to all his household unharmed.' The showing to the household is legendary embroidery, and it is remarkable that Jonah is quoted not as a prophet of doom, but as an example of God's wonderful deliverance, just as Matthew uses him. C. Emmet, in his commentary on 3 Maccabees in Charles, vol. i, dates the book 'somewhere about 100 B.C.'. It is curious that the deliverance of Jonah should here be recorded *after* the deliverance of the three children in the furnace and the deliverance of Daniel from the den of lions. Were it not for the reference to the twelve in *Ben Sira* 49.10, one would be tempted to conjecture that in 100 B.C. Jonah belonged to the Hagiographa and not to the prophets.

In the Talmud we find that Jonah is certainly regarded as having visited the place of the dead.[59] R. Jeremiah ben Eleazar is quoted as saying: 'Gehenna has three gates, one in the wilderness, one in the sea, and one in Jerusalem.' Evidence for the gate in the sea is Jonah 2.3: 'Out of the belly of the nether world cried I, and thou heardest my voice.' Later on we are told that two of the seven names for Gehenna are *She'ol* and *Bōr*. The *Midrash on the Psalms* tells us that Jonah was the son of the widow of Zarephath whom Elijah restored to life.[60] He was a completely righteous man: 'He was tried when the fish swallowed him and was tried again in the depths of the sea but he did not die . . . so that Jonah, while still alive, entered into his glory, into the garden of Eden!' Strack-Billerbeck on Matthew 12.40 cite examples of extensive Haggada on Jonah: he was very comfortably accommodated inside the fish. R. Meir has an account of a regular dialogue between Jonah and the fish: the fish is afraid of being swallowed by Leviathan, but Jonah says: 'Bring me to him.' When they encounter Leviathan, Jonah shows him the seal of Abraham (circumcision), and Leviathan immediately swims two days' journey away from the fish. The fish then takes Jonah on a tour of the nether world; they visit the pillars of the earth, Gehinnom, and the lowest *She'ol*. In Jonah's subsequent prayer to God he says: 'Thou art called He who slays and brings to life; see my soul is near to death, so make me live.' Lundberg (op. cit., p. 68) quotes from the *Midrash to Jonah* where Jonah is described as visiting the plug-stone, the foundation stone whose removal would bring the nether waters flooding upon the earth.

Not all of this material is as early as the first century A.D., but it is quite plain from the evidence we have examined that by the time the First Gospel was written, Jonah was regarded as an example of a miraculous deliverance from death, as one who had made the *descensus ad inferos*, and possibly as one who had exhibited God's power during his sojourn in the place of the dead. Incidentally we may note that Jonah 2.6 runs in the LXX κατέβην εἰς γῆν and that this was certainly taken as meaning that Jonah made the *descensus*. Equally significant is Theodotion's rendering of Jonah 2.3: 'Thou hast cast me into the abyss (*abusson*).' It is therefore all the more likely that κατέβη εἰς τὰ κατώτερα τῆς γῆς in Ephesians 4.9 refers to the *descensus* also. We may thus confidently claim that the Book of Jonah as a whole is a major scriptural source for the doctrine of the *descensus* in the NT.

4

We finally consider an almost isolated reference to the *descensus* in Acts. We begin with an examination of a strange phrase in Acts 2.24. Peter in his speech on the day of Pentecost, describing Christ's resurrection, says:

But God raised him up, having loosed the pangs of death, because it was not possible for him to be held by it.

ὃν ὁ θεὸς ἀνέστησεν, λύσας τὰς ὠδῖνας τοῦ θανάτου.

The strange phrase is λύσας τὰς ὠδῖνας τοῦ θανάτου. The phrase ὠδῖνες τοῦ θανάτου is the LXX translation of *ḥlby mwt* or *ḥlby š"wl* which is found in 2 Samuel 22.6; Psalms 18.4; 116.3 (with *š"wl* in the first case, *mwt* in the other two). In all three cases the phrase is used with a verb meaning 'to encircle, surround'. There can be no doubt but that in all these three places the meaning is 'the snares, or cords, of death surrounded me'. However, the LXX translation has confused two Hebrew words, *ḥebel*, 'a cord or rope', and *ḥēbel*, 'labour-pains, travail', and in all three places (LXX 2 Kingdoms 22.6; Psalms 17.5; 115.3) it offers ὠδῖνες θανάτου, which means literally 'the labour-pains of death', strictly speaking a meaningless phrase. The phrase occurs in the *Hodayoth*: 1 QH iii.28 runs: *wḥbly mwt 'ppw l'yn plṭ*. Mansoor translates thus: 'And deadly pangs

Scriptural Background to the Doctrine of the 'Descensus ad Inferos'

have surrounded (me) with no escape.' But in fact there is no reason to translate *ḥbly* here with 'pangs'; quite the contrary, because birth-pangs do not surround. Both Delcor and Vermes translate 'les liens de la mort' and Vermes 'the bonds of death'. Incidentally Vermes and Mansoor assume that the object of the surrounding (not specified in the text) is the author of the hymn. Delcor takes it to be the damned. On the whole the context would seem to favour Delcor's translation. Strack-Billerbeck in their comment on Acts 2.24 make it plain that the rabbis were aware of the possibility that *ḥblym* could mean 'pangs' as well as 'cords'; but there seems to be no reason at all why we should read the meaning 'pangs' into the *Hodayoth* verse when the true meaning fits the context so much better.

Here then we have the problem: why does Luke use a verb λύσας, which is so much more appropriate to *ḥblym* in its sense of 'cords', if he wants to convey the sense 'having ended the birth-pangs of death'? Does it not suggest that somewhere in his sources is a Semitic text which read 'having loosed the cords of death'?[61] One group of scholars has attempted to solve the problem by taking the meaning of 'having loosed the birth-pangs of death' quite literally. To quote Rackham, who adopts this view: 'We are to conceive of Hades as travailing with the millions of dead souls in her womb. When Jesus – the first begotten of the dead – was brought forth from the tomb, the travail-pangs were loosed, and now the way is open for others to follow.' To this group belong also Holtzmann, Bertram, and Cox.[62] Haenchen, followed by Conzelmann, rightly dismisses this solution of the problem: the author of the pangs of death, says Haenchen, is Satan; the author of the resurrection is God.[63] We may add that if 'having loosed the birth-pangs of death' is to be taken literally, it ought to mean that God allowed Christ to die: the process which the pangs were bringing to a climax was death, just as the climax of a birth-process is the birth of the baby. This is borne out by the parallel from Plato cited by Bertram: ὠδῖνος ἀπολύω. The god frees the woman from labour by allowing the child to be born. This is also what the phrase in Job 39.3 means, if it means anything at all (we discuss it in note 68 on page 153).

We return then to our problem. Torrey has a short way with it. He is convinced that an Aramaic document lies behind this part of Acts. λύσας is a mistranslation: 'No writer composing his own Greek would ever have chosen this unsuitable word, and there is nothing in the Old Testament that could have led him to employ it.'[64] He boldly restores the Aramaic which he believes Luke had before him, šr' ḥbly' dy mwt'. Foakes-Jackson and Kirsopp Lake do not accept this:[65] 'The occurrence of ὠδῖνες θανάτου in the LXX had made it a fixed phrase capable of new combinations with verbs of holding, loosing, etc.' This is rather begging the question: the only passage where the 'pangs of death' are loosed, or where they hold their victim, is this one. The problem is why Luke used two verbs, λύσας and κρατεῖν, which are much more appropriate when applied to cords than to birth-pangs. Wilcox tries to help out the meaning by emphasizing the eschatological context: Luke means in a general sense that God in the resurrection of Jesus has overcome death. He would translate with 'having put an end to the pangs of death'.[66] This encounters the objections we have outlined above. He does not help his case by referring to 1 QH iii.28 (discussed on page 150 above) and translating the phrase there as 'the pangs of death will compass (people) about'. Pangs cannot 'compass about', cords can. There is no justification for not translating ḥbly as 'cords' in 1 QH iii.28. Bieder, who apparently assumes that the phrase has been imported by Luke himself and does not come from a source, believes that the meaning is simply 'death could not keep Jesus in its power' (op. cit., p. 66). Haenchen has made up his mind that Luke did not know Aramaic (on the basis of his translating 'Barnabas' as υἱὸς παρακλήσεως), and therefore cannot allow that an Aramaic (or any other) source lies behind this passage. He can only explain the phrase as having entered Acts through liturgical usage. I cannot see that this advances us one inch towards a solution of the problem. It is by no means certain that Luke's false etymology of 'Barnabas' necessarily implies ignorance of Aramaic. See an article by S. Brock, in which he argues that Luke may have accepted a popular and mistaken etymology of the name but one based on Aramaic. He adds: 'It is also possible that the etymology was taken over by [Luke] second-hand, conceivably from Barnabas himself.' This implies a source. (See S. Brock, '*ΒΑΡΝΑΒΑΣ ΥΙΟΣ ΠΑΡΑΚΛΗΣΕΩΣ*", in *JTS*, new series 25 (1974), 91-8).

Scriptural Background to the Doctrine of the 'Descensus ad Inferos'

R. P. C. Hanson can only suggest that 'it is much more likely that Luke used [the phrase] here to impart a suitably scriptural colour to the diction of the apostle's speech'.[67] But λύσας τὰς ὠδῖνας τοῦ θανάτου does not occur anywhere in Scripture, and ὠδῖνας δὲ αὐτῶν ἔλυσας only in a very obscure passage in Job.[68]

We conclude therefore that Luke did not arbitrarily write λύσας τὰς ὠδῖνας τοῦ θανάτου in order to give the sense 'overcoming the pangs of death'. The verb λύσας is appropriate for loosing cords, not for overcoming pangs, least of all birth-pangs. Somewhere behind this verse lies an Aramaic or Hebrew source, not necessarily directly used by Luke, in which the phrase means that God loosed the cords of death. Hence the concept is of Christ lying in the realm of death and being delivered from it by God. We are prepared for a reference to the *descensus*, and we find it in verses 25-8.[69]

Luke quotes Psalm 16.8-11, following the LXX exactly, including the LXX's curious rendering of *kbwdy* in verse 9a as ἡ γλῶσσά μου. Haenchen comments that the element of corruption has been imported by the Greek, which translated the Hebrew *šaḥat*, 'destruction', as if it had been *šiḥēt*, 'corruption'. But, as we shall be seeing, the sense of 'corruption' was well known to the rabbis. Both R. P. C. Hanson and Conzelmann maintain that Luke knows nothing of a doctrine of *descensus*, and the latter denies that Luke can be using a source here (see also p. 138 above, where Caird denies that Luke knew anything of a *descensus*). Lundberg, on the other hand, stoutly affirms that there is a doctrine of a *descensus ad inferos* implied here (op. cit., p. 205). Conzelmann thinks David himself is regarded as speaking. It is impossible to accept this conclusion. The whole point of the citation is to show that the Messiah and not David was to be rescued from corruption. It is the Messiah who says: 'My flesh also shall rest in hope.' We shall be drawing the necessary conclusions from this presently.

The rabbis were by no means unanimously agreed that this psalm implies that David's flesh was to be preserved from corruption. Some rabbis suggested that verse 9a might be a prayer: 'May my flesh rest in hope!'[70] Bonsirven quotes an extract from *Sanhedrin* 4.7 in which R. José said: 'Ezra would have merited that the Torah should have been given by him, if Moses had not lived before him; to both of them the Torah had been spoken on high.'[71] Then he quotes Psalm 16.8: 'I set the Lord before me continually.' This might suggest a period in heaven as well as a period in Hades, in which case one might find a pattern of *descensus-ascensio*. But this is very vague. In the *Midrash on the Psalms*, Psalm 16.11 is understood as a description of the state of the righteous in the age to come, so that the psalm is interpreted in terms of resurrection, even though it is still in the *eschaton*.[72] In this midrash also a more hopeful view is taken of David's resurrection. R. Isaac said that neither corruption nor worms had power over David's flesh.[73]

From these scanty and unsatisfactory references we can draw some definite conclusions: in the first place, there *is* a reference to the *descensus* here. The Messiah speaks as if he was already in Hades. The very fact that God will not leave him there implies that he is there already. His flesh resting in hope must apply to the *triduum*. Admittedly there is no suggestion of any activity in Hades, but that does not make a *descensus* impossible. Next, we should observe that we seem to have a more primitive conception of the state of the Messiah in Hades than that which we encounter in 1 Peter. In this passage there is no suggestion that Christ, being spirit, could not be destroyed by death. On the contrary, all that prevents his being destroyed is God's power. There is no suggestion of θανατωθεὶς μὲν σαρκὶ ζωοποιηθεὶς δὲ πνεύματι. Both flesh and spirit await God's quickening act. In any case the Messiah rests in hope; he has faith that God will raise him up. This would be quite pointless if he were thought of as immortal God whom physical death cannot destroy. Hence the reason why 'it was not possible for him to be held' by death (verse 24) is not that he was immortal God, as Lundberg hints,[74] but because it had been prophesied by the mouth of David long ago that the Messiah would be raised from the dead.[75]

We have therefore in this passage a more primitive Christology than we have in 1 Peter. It seems to me that 1 Peter's account of the *descensus* suggests rather more theological reflection about the *descensus* than the account we have here. The passage in Acts seems to spring from a somewhat unreflective application of an obvious proof-text to the fact of Christ's resurrection. When we add the conclusion we reached about λύσας τὰς ὠδῖνας τοῦ θανάτου, and the consideration that this

Scriptural Background to the Doctrine of the 'Descensus ad Inferos'

passage seems to be unconnected with any other *descensus* passages in the New Testament, we seem to be moving towards the conviction that Luke did not simply invent this speech nor simply discover this psalm-citation for himself.[76] Behind Peter's speech in Acts 2 there must be a source or sources.[77] The passage we have been examining has a genuinely primitive ring about it.

Perhaps we may be allowed some brief comments on the significance of the material which we have collected. Cranfield remarks at the end of his article that the doctrine of the *descensus* is 'an inference drawn by the faith of the early Church'.[78] This is of course true; there can be no empirical evidence for such a doctrine. But we would wish to add that it is an inference drawn by the faith of the early Church which was partly suggested to them by their reading of Scripture. The doctrine is based not merely on the fact that it was on the third day that Christ rose from the dead, nor merely on a desire to extend the benefits of his redemption to those who had lived before this day, but also on a messianic interpretation of Psalms 88 and 89, of Psalm 68, and of Psalm 16; and also on a typological interpretation of the Book of Jonah, especially chapters 1 and 2. It seems to me very likely indeed that a tradition of interpreting the psalms messianically already existed in Judaism before the advent of Christianity.

The doctrine of the *descensus* is, strictly speaking, a myth. Mythical elements are necessarily implied in it: the land of the dead, the waters of chaos, the spirits in prison, the triumph over the infernal powers. These elements existed already both inside Judaism and outside it. The NT writers, being heirs of first-century Judaism, inherited these mythical elements and made use of them in order to formulate their doctrine. This does not mean that they were unrestrained myth-makers, letting their imagination run riot for the sake of building up an imposing story. In one sense they had to use myths because of the nature of the subject. But the element of Scripture in their myth acted as a restraining and formulating influence on their doctrine. It gave backbone to their account of the *descensus*, restricted it to what was possible within the (admittedly very wide) limits of first-century Judaism. When we read in a book such as Lundberg's what happened to the myth in the subsequent history of Christian doctrine, we may well come to respect the relative restraint of the writers of the NT in dealing with this theme. That restraint was due, I believe, primarily to the scriptural background of the doctrine.

6

John's Technique in Using Scripture

Recently two books relevant to this study have appeared, both of which have already been referred to (see pages 114 and 115).[1] G. Reim's valuable study is more concerned with Old Testament background than with technique, and that of E. D. Freed is severely limited by being restricted to explicit citations. So there seems to be room for a study of John's technique in using Scripture.

One can distinguish five distinct ways in which the author of the Fourth Gospel uses Scripture. I propose to set out each, citing examples from the Gospel, and inquiring whether a similar technique can be found among other New Testament writers. The five ways are as follows:

1 *He uses Scripture because it has come to him in his source.* The citation of Isaiah 40.3 in 1.23 is a clear example of this. In common with the three other evangelists, John applies this citation to John the Baptist. There is no reason to suppose that our author is being original here. The other examples of this class are 12.13, where he quotes Psalm 118.25-6, and 12.15, where he quotes Zechariah 9.9, both applying to Jesus's entry into Jerusalem. Since Psalm 18.25-6 is quoted by all three Synoptic writers at this point, and Zechariah 9.9 by Matthew at this point, it is plain that these citations are simply part of the tradition which John had received. I do not think that John's addition of *mē phobou* in 12.15 is significant. In saying that these citations came to John in his source, I do not mean to suggest that no other citations came to him thus. As we shall be seeing immediately, all but two of the citations in class 2 came to John in his source. But those in class 1 seem to me simply to have been carried over because they were embedded in the source. John does not particularly underline them. They are part of the traditional description of John the Baptist and of Jesus as Messiah respectively.

Some scholars have attempted to use John's citations of Scripture in the interest of a more subtle source criticism than the very obvious conclusions reached above. Thus Reim tries to accommodate various types of interpretation to something like Bultmann's schema of the composition of the Gospel.[2] Windisch believes he can distinguish a separate source in the Bethel reference in 1.51.[3] B. Lindars thinks that the interpretation of Psalm 69.9 in John 2.17 was in John's source before he incorporated it into his Gospel.[4] I confess that I do not see that there is very much force in such reasoning. At least I cannot think of any example of Scripture interpretation in the Fourth Gospel, apart from the very traditional ones in classes 1 and 2, of which one could say with confidence: 'This is not like John's normal way of using Scripture. This must come from a source.' I have tried to show that Windisch's diagnosis of 1.51 does not really fit the case since the Bethel episode is referred to several verses before the point where Windisch believes the logion to begin.[5] I believe that, apart from the traditional citations in classes 1 and 2, all John's interpretations of Scripture are original and his own. This does not mean that a similar use of Scripture cannot be found elsewhere in the NT.

2 *He cites Scripture with the formal indication hina plērōthē/i hē graphē, or (once) hina teleiōthē/i hē graphē (19.28).* There are seven examples of this usage, as follows: 12.38-40; 13.18; 15.25; 17.12; 19.24; 19.28-9; and 19.36-7. In 12.38-40 two discrete passages from Isaiah are quoted, Isaiah 53.1 and Isaiah 6.10, in that order; in 17.12 no Scripture is actually cited; and in 19.36-7 we have two quite separate passages quoted, Exodus 12.46 (also in Numbers 9.12) and Zechariah 12.10. Thus we cannot confidently claim that the selection of *seven* places in which formally to point out that these things happened in order to fulfil Scripture is deliberate. What is interesting about these passages, however, is that they are all without exception concerned with the rejection, betrayal, passion, and death of Jesus. In addition, with two exceptions they are all passages that are either quoted or echoed in the Synoptists,[6] or elsewhere in the NT. The two exceptions are 15.25, where John quotes Psalm 69.4: 'They hated me without a cause',[7] and 19.36, where John quotes 'Not a bone of him

shall be broken' from Exodus 12.46 (or Numbers 9.12). It looks very much as if John regarded these eight passages (the six cited elsewhere in the NT plus Psalm 69.4 and Exodus 12.46) as in some sense the official, standard framework for the essential part of the Messiah's career, that is his betrayal, sufferings, and death. In this respect he is more restrained and careful than the author of the First Gospel, whose desire seems to be simply to find as many scriptural prophecies about Jesus's career as he can. The two citations not found elsewhere in the NT are probably John's own discovery. The citation of Psalm 69.4 is, however, hardly surprising: a psalm quoted so often of Jesus as the suffering servant in the NT could easily yield just one more prophecy. The citation from Exodus 12.46 is more peculiar. It is no doubt John's way of indicating that Jesus's death was foreshadowed by the slaughter of the lambs on the Day of Preparation.[8] As we know, in his chronology of the passion the crucifixion occurs on that day. The thought of Christ as the Passover offering is of course found in 1 Corinthians 5.7. In my opinion, John's placing the crucifixion on the Day of Preparation and then confirming it with this citation from Exodus implies that he believed that the crucifixion really did take place on that day. If he had, so to speak, 'fixed' the event so as to agree with the prophecy, the prophecy could have had no significance for him. But in all the other 'public' citations in class 2 it is obvious that John believes that the prophecy really was fulfilled.[9] We have now looked at all John's citations which he consciously shared with the tradition of the early Church, and we turn to the other three classes of citations, all of which, I believe, can be shown to be John's own discovery and application.

3 *Scripture is explicitly quoted and discussed, but without the formal introductory formula*: I find six clear instances here, 2.17 (Psalm 69.9); 3.14-15 (Numbers 21.9); 6.31 (Psalm 78.24); 6.45 (Isaiah 54.13); 7.35 (the source is not clear and must be discussed below); and 10.34 (Psalm 82.6). I have already discussed 2.17 in Chapter 4. The reference to the incident of the brazen serpent in Numbers 21.9 (John 3.14-15) needs little comment. John sees here a type of Jesus's crucifixion. It is not one of John's 'public' or 'traditional' proof-texts, but is his own

The New Testament Interpretation of Scripture

invention, worked into this discourse. In 6.31 the citation of Psalm 78.24 is formally made by Jesus's adversaries, but there can be little doubt but that John means to bring it in as part of his argument. It is to contrast with the living bread which the Son actually is. The great majority of editors assume that the point of 6.32 lies in the fact that God of old (not Moses) gave Israel the manna, and the same God now gives them the Son as spiritual bread. I suspect myself that there is a more subtle point here: if only Israel realized it, Christ has already given them bread from heaven, for it was he who was the source of manna in the wilderness. We must conclude that John is here using his own material. Even though we find a similar theme in 1 Corinthians 10.1-11, John is not in any way dependent on Paul. This discourse on the bread from heaven is his work, and the quotation from Psalm 78.24 must be his work also. This is not to suggest that the discourse has got no historical connection with Jesus; but we are certainly not justified in attributing the introduction of the scriptural citation here to anyone but John himself.

Freed's treatment of the citation of Isaiah 54.13 in 6.45 is illuminating. He thinks that John has left out from the Greek the words *tous huious sou* because he does not want to restrict the prophecy to the Jews. The context, he says, is eschatological. He concludes that John is here showing a thorough knowledge of Scripture and is using the citation in order to help his argument.[10] There can be no doubt that John has here the accession of the Gentiles in mind. The LXX in Isaiah 54.14 has understood the Hebrew *gwr ygwr* to refer to *ger*, a proselyte, and has rendered it to mean 'proselytes shall come to you through me'. This would undoubtedly appeal to John; indeed, in view of John 6.44, he probably understood it as a promise of the Father to the Son. Kittel in his *Biblia Hebraica* suggests we ought to read *bōnayk* for *bānayk*, and translate with 'your builders'. This rendering is heartily endorsed by the rabbis who tend to use this verse as a sort of tag to put at the end of their works. It occurs at the end of the *Tractates Berakoth, Yebamoth, Nazir, Kerithoth*, and *Tamid* in the Babylonian Talmud. In all cases 'your builders' is read and referred to teachers of the Torah. But we have no reason at all to think that John would have been attracted by any such idea. On the other hand there is plenty of evidence from the rabbis that Isaiah 54.13 was understood in an eschatological sense: in *Pesikta Rabbati* the time when all will be instructed by God is explicitly identified with the time of King Messiah;[11] and in the *Pesikta de Rab Kahana* this time is described as belonging to 'the world to come'.[12] Thus we have here a very clear example of John introducing a Scripture citation on his own initiative in order to underline and support his argument.

John 7.37-9 is a famous *crux interpretum*. We have no space here to deal with all the problems which it raises. Freed concludes that 'John was motivated by a combination of passages and then from memory wrote down a quotation to support his theology'.[13] Reim, on the other hand, very firmly opts for Isaiah 28.16 as the primary source; Jesus is identified with the sure stone of that passage. But he believes that there is also an identification of Jesus with the smitten rock in the wilderness.[14] I fear I can only dogmatically state my own conclusions: I am sure that we cannot possibly avoid a reference to the smitten water-giving rock in the wilderness. As many editors have pointed out, John has already in 6.31 associated Christ with the giving of the manna. But I do not think we can ignore the Zechariah reference either. In the LXX Zechariah 14.8 runs: 'And in that day living water shall go out from Jerusalem.' John has already in 2.17f identified Jesus with the true Temple. The language of the LXX of Zechariah 14.8, though not very close to John 7.38, is nevertheless closer than any other Scripture quotation yet suggested. Thirdly, I would make a suggestion of my own: one of the problems of this passage is the use of *ek tēs koilias*, 'out of the belly', in verse 38. May this not be an echo of Psalm 40(39).8? The MT runs: *wtwrtk btwk m'y*, which the LXX renders with: *kai ton nomon sou en mesō/i tēs koilias mou*. The context is of obedience to God's will:

> I delight to do thy will, O my God;
> thy law is within my heart.[15]

John probably has Psalm 40 in mind in an earlier passage in this chapter, 7.17-24, where there is much talk about doing God's will.[16] Instead of the Torah in his heart, Jesus has God's will; and the Spirit is the motive of his action rather than the Torah. This is why he can give the Spirit to believers. At any

161

rate, it must be clear that 7.37-9 is a passage where John has introduced a complicated set of references to Scripture in order to confirm and expound his own Christology.

I have given my own exposition of John 10.34-6 in two articles in *NTS*. But this passage must be mentioned here, since it falls clearly into class 3, no matter what interpretation is given it.[17] In fact I expounded it as being, in John's view, an address by the pre-existent Word to the Jews, admitting their privileges but deploring their unbelief. The last verse is an address by God to his Word, prophesying the resurrection and the accession of the Gentiles. This *must* be John's own invention: so elaborate a midrash could hardly be part of traditional material. In any case it fits in very well with John's theology.

We may therefore identify a third distinct use of Scripture in the Fourth Gospel: John uses it in order to confirm and expound some theological point he is making. We may be sure that when he uses it this way he is giving us his own Scripture material, not borrowing it from a source. The fact that sometimes in passages such as these he treats Scripture in ways which have parallels in some other NT writer, such as Paul or the author of Hebrews, does not mean that he is in any way dependent on them. It does suggest a common context and scope for the use of Scripture in the New Testament. It is hardly necessary to point out that there are plenty of parallels for this use of Scripture in the rest of the NT. The pages of Paul and the Epistle to the Hebrews are full of them.

4 *Scripture can be detected as the basis of his Christology*: in these instances, though Scripture is not formally quoted, it can be seen to lie behind his language, and may be presumed to be the means by which he reached his theological conclusions. I can detect four such passages, 1.18; 1.51; 5.35; 8.49 and 58. There may well be more which closer study of John's text may bring to light.

I have examined 1.18 in Chapter 3, and I believe I have shown that behind John's presentation of Jesus Christ as the divine Logos lies the conviction that it was the pre-existent Logos who appeared to Moses on the rock at Sinai. This conviction must have been arrived at by means of a study of Scripture, rather than Scripture being brought in later either

John's Technique in Using Scripture

as a confirmation or an adornment. Thus we may claim in some sense to have discovered the very springs of John's Christology. Whether we can say that John deliberately quotes Scripture in 1.14 is a nice question. I have indeed claimed that the phrase used here, *plērēs charitos kai alētheias*, is a direct translation of *rab ḥesed we'ᵉmeth* in Exodus 34.6, but this is probably more an incorporation of a significant phrase from Scripture into his Christology than a deliberate citation. It is unlikely that John expected his readers to recognize the quotation; if he did, he was certainly over-optimistic; for there is still considerable debate among scholars as to whether he is quoting Exodus 34.6 or not. I would conjecture that this use of Scripture, though certainly not unconscious, is hidden. John's subtle mind would naturally express itself in this implicit rather than explicit technique. I think this is true of all the examples of this class. In this respect these last two classes are at the opposite pole from the 'public' use of Scripture in class 2.

A second example of this class is 1.51, which we examined in Chapter 4. If my exposition is correct, then John sees in the vision of Jacob at Bethel narrated in Genesis 28 an instance of the pre-existent Logos appearing in Israel's history. This incident would be on very much the same footing as the last one. It is surely plain by now that John at least (whatever may be the case with Paul) did believe in the activity of the pre-existent Christ or Logos in Israel's history. For him the Logos was both the visibility and the audibility of God (see 1.18; 5.37), and he regards all those occasions on which God is described in Scripture as having been either seen or heard as manifestations of the pre-existing Logos. He incidentally betrays this belief in an instance of Scripture quotation which we have examined already, John 12.41, since he describes Isaiah as having seen Christ in the Temple. But since he uses Scripture there primarily and explicitly in order to show its fulfilment in the historical Jesus, we cannot list it in class 4. The same question arises concerning 1.51 as arose in the case of 1.14: does John deliberately cite Genesis 28.12? On the whole, I think we must give the same answer as we did about the scriptural phrase lying behind 1.14: it is not an explicit citation. John does not expect his readers necessarily to recognize it. It is a hidden reference.

The third example of this class is more complicated, 5.35. I believe I have demonstrated that behind this verse lie two passages in Scripture, Exodus 27.20-21 and Psalm 132.16-17.[18] The language of the LXX in these two passages explains the rather unusual language used of the Baptist in 5.35, both *luchnos kaiomenos* and *agalliathēnai* are accounted for, and the whole purpose of the Baptist's ministry in the Fourth Gospel is neatly summed up in the words of Psalm 132.17:

'I have prepared a lantern for my anointed.'

This may not at first sight seem to be a christological use of Scripture, but a moment's reflection will show that it must be so, granted John's christocentric approach to Scripture. For him the Baptist is primarily the one who points to Christ: he is the representative of believing Israel all through the ages, the last of the prophets who sums up in himself the message of the prophets. The author of the Fourth Gospel therefore finds these two passages in widely separated parts of Scripture and in them discovers a way of expressing the significance of the Baptist in relation to Christ. This is why we can justifiably describe this as a christological use of Scripture: for our author, the Baptist only has significance in as far as he is related to Christ. It therefore strengthens and completes his theology to be able to find in Scripture an image for the relation of the Baptist to Christ witnessed to in two such different passages in Scripture. There can be no doubt whatever here at least that John has found these passages and applied them for himself. Here is no suggestion at all of a traditional proof-text. In fact we are here probably closer to later patristic use of scriptural types and images than we are anywhere else in the Fourth Gospel. Whereas the last instance (1.51) could fairly be described as typology (Jacob is in a similar situation to Nathanael), in 5.35 we are dealing with allegory and nothing else. The Baptist is arbitrarily identified with the lamp, there is no intrinsic connection at all. I do not suggest that John was aware of this; he was no doubt carried away by the striking appropriateness of Psalm 132 (131).17:

hētoimasa luchnon tō/i christō/i mou,

and the passage from Exodus 27.20-21 fell into place. Again, we can hardly say that John expected his readers to recognize the

John's Technique in Using Scripture

allusion: perhaps very well-learned and subtle readers might do so, but he did not write 5.35 in order to draw his readers' attention to the allusion. He wrote it because he believed he had found the right image for the Baptist, an image provided by inspired Scripture. His task was to record it, not to draw attention to it.

The fourth and last example of this class of which I know occurs in 8.39-40, 56-8. I have expounded it in two works published some years ago.[19] This is another instance of the pre-existent Logos appearing in Israel's history. In 8.56 Jesus claims that Abraham has seen his day and rejoiced, and two verses later that he himself existed before Abraham did. I claim that this is a reference to the three angels whose visit to Abraham is narrated in Genesis 18.1-15. If we look back to John 8.40-41, we see that there the 'works of Abraham' are in effect defined as 'believing a man who spoke to him the truth which he had heard from God'. This exactly describes what Abraham did in Genesis 18.1-15; we can also parallel Abraham's 'rejoicing' from Genesis 18.13 (rabbinic tradition held that the angels at this point told Abraham the whole future history of his race). John identifies the pre-existent Logos with one of the angels at the oaks of Mamre, the one before whom Abraham prostrated himself and whom he addressed as 'My Lord' (Genesis 18.2-3). We have here then another 'hidden' reference, another of those manifestations of the pre-existent Logos which John believed he could detect in Scripture. Once again, it does not seem likely that John expected his readers to recognize the scriptural allusion immediately (though the Jews understand his meaning: 'Have you seen Abraham?' 8.57). We may conjecture that John regarded this allusion as one that would only be disclosed to those who, like himself, searched Scripture expecting to find in it references to Christ.

We can find parallels to this 'hidden' use of Scripture in other books in the NT. We have already explored a very similar use in Paul's writings in 1 Corinthians 2.16 and Romans 11.34-5. (See Chapter 2.) Paul regards the pre-existent Christ as the 'mind' of God and God's 'counsellor' very much as John sees him as the centre of the theophany on the rock, as the one who stood at the head of the heavenly ladder, and as the angel at the oaks of Mamre. Paul also found Scripture indispensable as an aid to building up his Christology. We can trace a similar process in the Epistle to the Hebrews. I have tried to show that there too we can find a doctrine of the activity of the pre-existent Christ in Israel's history.[20] The same technique was employed by all three writers: they went to Scripture in order to understand, integrate, and complete their Christology. They did not do so arbitrarily: once grant that God had been finally and uniquely revealed in the historical Jesus, and the question must arise: how is it that there was no hint of this during the centuries of his recorded activity before the birth of Jesus? The doctrine of the activity of the pre-existent Christ was their answer to this question.

5 *Scripture can be shown to have influenced his narrative.* I have detected five examples of this in the Fourth Gospel, though it may well be that a further study of the text would reveal more. None of them occurs in the passion narrative proper, which may confirm C. H. Dodd's observation that when John comes to narrate the passion he is less full of allusion and double meaning than in the rest of his Gospel. The first example is the story of Nathanael, or rather the story of the Baptist and Nathanael in 1.30-31, 43-51, which I have examined in Chapter 4. I have argued there that the references to the Bethel episode are not confined to 1.51, but are to be found in 1.30-31, where the Baptist's statement that Christ was among them but they did not recognize him is a verbal echo of Genesis 28.16. Then follows the association of Nathanael with Jacob in 1.47 and Nathanael's acknowledgement of Jesus as Son of God and King of Israel in 1.49. The narrative has been influenced by the story in Genesis 28. This might seem at first sight to be an example of the same scriptural allusion falling into two classes, but I do not think this is necessarily so. *Qua* narrative, this passage in the Fourth Gospel falls clearly into class 5. The fact that behind the allusion in 1.51 lies the belief that the pre-existent Logos it was who appeared at Bethel does not prejudice this. Of course John did not consciously classify his scriptural allusions in the way that we are doing, but there does not seem to be any reason why we should not keep the two usages found together in this passage separate for our purpose, which is to try to understand how John used Scripture.

John's Technique in Using Scripture

The second example is perhaps spread over three chapters of the Gospel, certainly over two. It is the use of Psalm 118 in 10.24, 11.41, and perhaps 12.13. I have worked this out in an article published some time ago.[21] In 10.24 the Jews are described as 'encircling' Jesus (*ekuklōsan*) in order to put hostile questions to him. In 11.41 Jesus, in his prayer at Lazarus's grave, says: 'Father, I thank thee that thou hast heard me', and in 12.13 the crowd exclaims 'Hosanna! Blessed is he who comes in the name of the Lord.' These words are all echoes of Psalm 118. In 118.10 the psalmist complains: 'All nations surrounded me (LXX *ekuklōsan*) . . . in the name of the Lord I cut them off.' In 10.25, where the Jews surround Jesus, he replies to them: 'The works which I do *in the name of my Father*, these witness concerning me.' The prayer in 11.41 is taken from Psalm 118.21: 'I thank thee that thou hast answered me', and of course the crowd's cry in 12.13 is taken from Psalm 118.25-6. I suggested in the article referred to that John regarded Psalm 118 as providing a sort of prophetic timetable for Jesus's actions as he approached his passion: first enmity repelled in the name of the Lord; then a prayer for salvation from death (the raising of Lazarus is seen as an anticipation of Jesus's own resurrection); then the acclamation of the crowd which hails him as what he really is, the chosen one who comes in the name of the Lord. The fact that I have already placed the allusion in 12.13 in class 1 does not, I think, prejudice my case that we have in these three chapters an instance of narrative influenced by Scripture. It may have been the traditional use of Psalm 118 in the early Church that originally alerted John to the possibility of finding an extended significance for it.

A third example occurs in 11.11-13. The narrative is influenced by the LXX text of Job 14.12-15.[22] John has understood the LXX text to imply that there is hope for a man if he dies, and has in some sense applied it to Lazarus, who was kept some time in Hades before Jesus awakened him. This example poses a nice question: have the details of John's narrative actually been adapted to fit in with the prophecy in Job? I suggested in my article that the mysterious event of two days narrated in 11.6 may have been influenced by Job 14.13:

Oh that thou wouldest hide me in Sheol,
that thou wouldest conceal me until thy wrath be past!

The New Testament Interpretation of Scripture

But I would prefer to leave the discussion of the question of the historicity of the narrative influenced by these scriptural allusions until we can pass all the instances under review.

A fourth example is the story of Jesus's anointing in Bethany by Mary, narrated in 12.1-8. We have examined it in Chapter 4, and have suggested that it is Haggai 2.6-9 in the LXX that is in the background here. Moreover we have traced the influence of this passage beyond the story of the anointing, finding a possible echo of the shaking of the heavens and earth in the heavenly voice of 12.28-9, and also of the coming of the Gentiles foretold in Haggai in the visit of the Greeks mentioned in 12.20. The reference to silver and gold in Haggai 2 was seen as echoed in Judas's concern about money related in 12.4-6. And of course the fragrant odour of the ointment was to be paralleled in Haggai's reference to filling the house of the Lord with glory. The link here between Haggai 2 and John 12 is the temple imagery which we discussed in Chapter 4. The Haggai passage is very unobtrusive, but nevertheless can, I believe, be detected in the background.

Our last example in this class is a new one which I have not published before. It must therefore be set out in some detail. I suggest that 12.19,32 are influenced by Job 21.32-3. In 12.19 we have the remark of the Pharisees: 'Behold, the world has gone after him': *ide ho kosmos opisō autou apēlthen*. There is a variant reading, *holos ho kosmos*, which Lagrange prefers. Then in 19.32 Jesus says that if he be lifted up from the earth he will draw all men to him, *pantas helkusō pros emauton* (the v.l. *panta* does not alter the sense as far as we are concerned). The passage which I claim has influenced these two verses, Job 21.32-3, is in fact a description of the pomp with which the rich man is buried:

32a When he is borne to the grave,
 b watch is kept over his tomb.
33a The clods of the valley are sweet to him;
 b all men follow after him,
 c and those who go before him are innumerable.

But, as in the case of Job 14.12-15, the LXX gives a very misleading rendering. We will quote the Greek of 32ab, 33bc, then we will translate it:

kai autos eis taphous apēnechthē
kai epi sorō/i ēgrupnēsen
kai opisō autou pas anthrōpos apeleusetai
kai emprosthen autō/i anarithmētoi

and he was borne away to the tombs
and he watched (lay awake) on the bier . . .
and every man shall go after him
and innumerable were before him.[23]

It will be seen at once that the LXX translation has altered the meaning so that it could be taken as a prophecy of the death of Jesus and the subsequent accession of the Gentiles. Verse 33b, 'and every man shall go after him', is very close indeed to John 12.19b. C. H. Dodd reminds us that the raising of Lazarus is mentioned in connection with this incident,[24] and that raising is regarded by John as an anticipation of Jesus's resurrection, so the resurrection is very much in mind here. In the very next verse, we have the incident of the Greeks coming to seek Jesus, so the accession of the Gentiles also forms part of the thought-background here. The relevance of 12.32 is that there Jesus says that after his cross (and subsequent triumph in the resurrection) he will draw all men to him. Schlatter, in commenting that *hupsoun* in 12.32 bears both a spatial and a spiritual sense, reminds us that the resurrection must be in mind here.[25] The LXX has in fact mistranslated the MT in Job 21.33b, giving *apeleusetai* for *yimšwk*, which properly means 'he will draw'. The Vulgate has rendered this correctly:

et post se omnem hominem trahet

It uses the same word in John 12.32: 'omnia traham ad me ipsum'. However, we cannot make any capital out of this, since it is the LXX mistranslation that gives us the remarkable parallel to 12.19b. Several editors (Strack-Billerbeck, Schlatter) equate *ho kosmos* or *holos ho kosmos* with the rabbinic phrase *kol-ʿwlām* and Bultmann actually says that 'die ganze Welt' means 'jedermann', which would make it exactly correspond to the *pas anthrōpos* of the LXX.[26] Lagrange and Bultmann suggest that this utterance of the Pharisees is intended as an unconscious prophecy, like Caiaphas's dictum in 11.50. The

The New Testament Interpretation of Scripture

rabbis do not find any reference to the resurrection in this Job passage, as far as I know. The only comment I can find identifies the person spoken of in Job 21.32-3 with the victim of the oppression of the violent man; he is actually brought to the grave by it.[27] But it would be quite unreasonable to expect a similar interpretation in rabbinic literature.[28] John is finding in Job a prophecy of Christ's resurrection and the accession of the Gentiles. One might conjecture that in his historical tradition he knew of a remark that the Pharisees had made to the effect that everyone was following Jesus, and John has expressed it in the language of 12.19b and 12.32 because he believed that this precisely had been predicted by the two verses in Job 21.32-3.

In some ways this is the most interesting class of scriptural allusions in the Fourth Gospel, because it is the most unobtrusive and also seems, in this exact form, to be peculiar to John. We might well ask, why does John use Scripture in this way? What does he think is the link between Scripture and his narrative in these passages? We must reject two mistaken answers to these questions: the first is to say that John did not believe there was any real link. He is simply using scriptural language because he thought it appropriate for a gospel, or because it was familiar to him and came naturally to his pen. Nothing that we have learned about John's technique would justify us in coming to such a conclusion, as if John were like some conventional clergyman writing his parish magazine, who likes to say 'as it were' and 'dearly beloved' because these are scriptural-sounding phrases! In any case the actual parts of Scripture which John uses in this way are not always the best known. One would hardly expect the obscurer parts of the Book of Job to come naturally to John's pen. The other mistaken solution is to say that John had studied various passages in Scripture which he thought must have a bearing on the life of Christ, and when he wrote his narrative he deliberately adapted it and altered his tradition so as to make it fall in with what was written in Scripture. The objection to this is that it would be a quite pointless action on John's part. He does not explicitly quote Scripture in these passages; indeed he keeps it very much in the background. Unless, therefore, he thought there was a real link between these Scripture passages and his narrative (not one invented by him) his technique here remains without explanation.

It must be that in John's mind the actual incidents related of Jesus had been predicted by the Scripture passages which he echoes. From this it follows that in his narrative he believes himself to be retailing actual events. The events have not been altered so as to agree with Scripture. It is likely that he uses this technique in order to point up or underline certain details, as a subtle way of saying 'Look, this is significant; it was predicted in Scripture.' The Baptist having failed at first to recognize Jesus; the sequence of events that led from the feast of the dedication to the triumphal entry; the two days' wait before Jesus proceeded to Lazarus's grave; the fragrance of the ointment filling the house; the almost random remark of the Pharisees – all these were small details if taken by themselves, but, because John understands them as having been predicted in Scripture, he reads a great deal more into them, and he subtly underlines and points them up so as to make them all contribute in one way or another to his picture of Jesus as the destined Son.

I have said that this last class of scriptural allusions is peculiar to John. Certainly nothing could be greater than the contrast between this very unobtrusive mode of introducing scriptural allusions and Matthew's extremely crude technique of finding scriptural fulfilments at every stage of Jesus's career. But we can point to one partial parallel. It occurs in Paul: I have pointed out elsewhere that in Romans 8.19-21 Paul is in fact offering a sort of midrash on Psalm 89.46-8.[29] He is not deliberately quoting the psalm; he is echoing it, as if this passage in Romans were the fruit of his meditation on this passage in Scripture. This parallel may well throw light on John's technique: he had certainly meditated on Scripture. He had searched the Scriptures in true Qumran style, not for allusions to the Qumran sect, but for allusions to Jesus Christ; and these subtle references in his narrative are the fruits of his meditations.

We have denied that John ever uses Scripture simply to adorn his narrative. But it may be that he can use other literature in this way. A. Feuillet has pointed out that Paul has used the language of the Book of Wisdom in several places in

The New Testament Interpretation of Scripture

order to provide himself with an adequate vocabulary, without there being any suggestion that Paul regarded Wisdom as sacred Scripture, or that he intended explicitly to quote it as an authority.[30] It is possible that John uses the same technique with the Book of Wisdom. John 8.28-9 runs as follows:

> When you have lifted up the Son of man, then you will know that I am he, and that I do nothing on my own authority but speak thus as the Father taught me. And he who sent me is with me; he has not left me alone, for I always do what is pleasing to him.

With this compare Wisdom 9.9-10:

> With thee is wisdom, who knows thy works and was present when thou didst make the world, and who understands what is pleasing in thy sight and what is right according to thy commandments.
> Send her forth from the holy heavens,
> and from the throne of thy glory send her,
> that she may be with me and toil,
> and that I may learn what is pleasing to thee.

What is common between these two passages is the sending of Wisdom or the Son into the world, and the fact that this results in that being done which is pleasing in God's sight, because the person sent knows from experience in heaven what the will of God is. The word *areston* ('pleasing') occurs significantly in both passages. It may even be that the difficult phrase in John 8.25, *tēn archēn ho ti kai lalō humin*, may be capable of being explained in the light of this passage in Wisdom. One interpretation of this phrase is that it should be rendered: 'At the beginning I am what I even now tell you.'[31] John is hinting ambiguously at the agency of the Son in creation perhaps inspired by this passage in Wisdom. I do not suggest that John regarded the Book of Wisdom as Scripture, but he may have been influenced by it and may even have allowed this passage to mould his writing in 8.25-9. But the very vagueness and elusiveness of the reference shows a contrast with the way in which he uses those books that he regards as inspired Scripture.

John's Technique in Using Scripture

Now that we have reviewed John's five distinguishable techniques of using Scripture, we should be in a good position to answer a question that has been put by a number of scholars: is there a scheme or pattern of Scripture lying behind the Gospel as a whole? I have in mind such theories as that put forward by Aileen Guilding.[32] She believes that some of the material in the Gospel is based on a Jewish synagogue lectionary. Similar schemes have been suggested for Mark's Gospel by Carrington, and for 1 Peter by Preisker, F. L. Cross, and others (in this latter case they detect a baptismal liturgy). Certainly, when one studies the Fourth Gospel in depth, one is constantly finding fresh scriptural allusions. One cannot help speculating whether there may not be some all-embracing scriptural pattern in the background, some basis of Scripture into which most of the events and discourses of the Gospel can be fitted. Just as Matthew's Gospel has often been described as conforming to a Pentateuchal pattern, and as some scholars have seen a Deuteronomic pattern behind parts of Luke's Gospel, may we not hope to find a similar scriptural scheme behind John's?

Of course further research may bring something of the sort to light, but it seems unlikely. No scheme hitherto put forward has produced very much conviction among scholars. Aileen Guilding's pattern, though expounded and defended with great learning, seems to require us to accept too many unproved – not to say improbable – assumptions. In order to function smoothly it asks us to believe that John was working on two different lectionaries – not in itself a very likely conjecture. Again it would seem to assume that all John's scriptural sources have been uncovered. But this is plainly not the case, and when a new one turns up (we have claimed to discover several new ones in this work alone), it does not fit into her scheme. But this puts a question mark against the entire pattern.[33]

In any case, to attempt to discover an overall scriptural pattern behind the Fourth Gospel is surely to mistake the nature of the Gospel itself. We may reasonably assume that by the time John wrote, the Gospel as a literary form had been established. John was writing a Gospel, not something like Philo's diffuse commentary on the first twenty-two chapters of Genesis. No matter how much John may have elaborated his historical tradition and worked up the dominical speeches, he was intending to write a Gospel, an account of the life, death, and resurrection of Jesus Christ in its full significance. He was not writing a *Poimandres*, not even a *Gospel of Truth*. Both these works were written after his, probably to some degree in imitation of his work; but just because they were written later, in a different environment, they do not fall into the same category. In the last resort, what determined the nature and order of the main events and speeches recorded in John's Gospel was historical tradition, not a scriptural schema imposed on the material. True, John was fully conscious of the influence of Scripture on the events as he recorded them, but this does not mean that he made the main events and discourses conform to some scriptural pattern which already existed in his mind. If we try to fasten some over-arching pattern of scriptural interpretation onto John's Gospel, we are in danger of turning him into a christianized Philo. John's various interpretations of Scripture are the precipitate of his historical tradition and his theological tradition. The one never gains complete control over the other.

In the course of this review of John's technique in using Scripture, we have pointed out from time to time what John has in common with other NT writers in this respect. Perhaps we should give some attention to what is different. Are there any techniques of scriptural usage in the NT which do not occur in the Fourth Gospel? Plainly there are: we can suggest two such varieties straight away, Scripture used in a purely illustrative way, and Scripture used directly as a basis for moral exhortation. The comparatively brief Epistle of James provides us with several examples of the first variety; it seems indeed to be a mode of handling Scripture which had a strong appeal to the author of James. In James 1.8,11; 4.6; 5.10-11,17 Scripture is simply used as illustration, not to show that anything is proved or foreshadowed. We also find Scripture used as a basis for straightforward moral exhortation in James 4.6, and also very extensively in 1 Peter 3.10-12; 5.5 (this latter is the same text as is quoted in James 4.6). These two usages are occasionally found in Paul and the deutero-Pauline epistles, though much more infrequently compared with the other usages. For simple illustration, see 1 Corinthians 15.32; 1 Thessalonians 5.8; Ephesians 6.14-17; and for Scripture used for moral exhortation, see Romans 7.7; 12.19-20;[34] 1 Corinthians 5.13; 2 Corinthians 13.1; Ephesians 4.25-6. These two relatively simple ways of using Scripture evidently had no appeal to John's austere, profound, and subtle mind.

Finally, we may indulge in one theological question about John's technique in using Scripture: can we find anything whatever in common between our understanding of Scripture and his? On the face of it, it certainly does not seem very likely. John, like all the NT writers, began from the Jewish tradition of scriptural interpretation, which we have long outgrown. His assumptions about the inerrancy and inspiration of Scripture cannot be ours. On several occasions he seems to have based his interpretation on a Greek translation of the Hebrew which we know to have been mistaken. How can an approach to Scripture based on presuppositions so very different from ours have anything in common with our modern interpretation of Scripture?

There is, however, one way in which we may find common ground with John on some occasions at least. One could reasonably say that in certain passages where Scripture underlies his teaching or his narrative, John by his use of Scripture is presenting Jesus Christ as the answer to Israel's questions. If we think of such passages as 1.18, 1.51, 11.11-13, 12.19, may we not say that behind the scriptural allusions lies a desire to wrestle with the great ultimate questions which Israel's master spirits threw up in the course of Israel's history, questions which we can trace in the Scriptures of the old dispensation? In 1.18 perhaps he is presenting Christ as an answer to the question: how can I see God? In 1.51 he faces the question: is there a mediator between God and man? In 11.11-13; 12.19 he is presenting Christ as an answer to the question: can man survive death? We might even suggest that in 8.40, 56-8, by means of his use of Scripture John is wrestling with the question which came to be posed among Christians with more and more urgency as the first Christian century came to a close: are there distinctions within the godhead? These were urgent, existential questions in John's day; we can sense behind the scriptural debates which the Fourth Gospel certainly implies the various competing groups, the devotees of wisdom, the Pharisees, the remnant of the conservative, rationalist Sadducees, the survivors of Qumran, the students of *Merkabah* mysticism. They were putting these questions. John, by means of his scriptural technique, tries to answer them in terms of Jesus Christ. The questions are very much the same today, though our way of using Scripture as an aid to answering them is very different. But those of us who are Christians can at least agree with John in seeing the solution to lie ultimately in terms of Jesus Christ.[35]

(The gist of this chapter was given as a paper at the annual conference of the Society for the Study of the New Testament, at Châtenay-Malabry, near Paris in July 1978.)

Notes

CHAPTER 1
The Significance of the Subject

1. To mention only two notable works, H. Vollmer's *Die Alttestamentlichen Citate bei Paulus*, Freiburg and Leipzig 1899, and O. Michel's *Paulus und seine Bibel*, Gütersloh 1929.
2. A good example of a distinguished Protestant scholar who felt himself bound by this attitude is C. Hodge, the American Presbyterian theologian and exegete; S. Amsler in *L'Ancien Testament dans l'Eglise*, Neuchâtel 1960, is an example of a modern Roman Catholic scholar who would still, by and large, defend the NT method of interpreting Scripture.
3. I have in mind J. Bright, *The Authority of the Old Testament* (London 1967), pp. 79, 92, where he uses the word 'charismatic' for the NT interpretation of Scripture, and goes on to suggest that it 'scarcely represents a systematic exegesis at all', a statement which tells us more about the author's ignorance of NT exegesis than anything else. That the desire to explain away scriptural proofs cited in the NT was not confined to Protestant scholars is shown by the remark of M.-J. Lagrange in his comment on John's citation of Ps. 69.9 in John 2.17: 'le psaume qui leur [sc. to the disciples] fournissait un meilleur exemple de zèle' (*Evangile selon Saint Jean*, Paris 1947, 3rd edn, in loc.). The zeal of the psalmist, he would have us understand, is only an example comparable to Christ's zeal, not a prophecy of it, still less a recorded utterance of the pre-existent Christ. If we want examples of ignoring NT exegesis of Scripture, we can read what commentators have said during the past 100 years on John's outright statement in 12.41 that Isaiah in the Temple *saw* Jesus's glory. Embarrassed silence or equally embarrassed apology is what we usually find.
4. Obvious examples of this are Rom. 10.6-7; 1 Cor. 10.4; Gal. 4.29. But instances could be multiplied.
5. I argue in Chapter 2, p. 68 that in fact Paul does just this in his scriptural quotation in 1 Cor. 2.9.
6. The school that regarded the NT from the standpoint of the comparative study of religion.

7. *Judaism and Hellenism*, referred to more than once in subsequent chapters.
8. A good analogy occurs in John's citation of Ps. 22.15 in John 19.28. If in fact Jesus was not thirsty, but only said 'I thirst' in order to fulfil Scripture (as some commentators understand John to be saying), then Scripture was not fulfilled. It is, in John's view, events and not merely words that fulfil Scripture.
9. Excellent examples of this can be found in 2 Cor. 4.13 as regards Paul (see *Jesus Christ in the Old Testament*, pp. 145-7). An example in the Fourth Gospel can be found in his treatment of Ps. 82 in John 10.34-6; he only quotes verse 6, but certainly has the whole psalm in mind.
10. For example, in Ps. 106.16 Aaron is described as 'the saint of the Lord' (*q'dōš YHWH*), a very different picture of Aaron to that presented in the earlier strata of the Pentateuch.
11. Quite apart from the fascinating account of the divine Wisdom's part in salvation history related in Wisd. chapters 10-11, consider the significance of the midrash on Isa. 40.13 which we meet in Wisd. 9.14-18 (see Chapter 2, pp. 82-3).
12. *De Somniis*, Bk. I, 61 (in L. Cohn and P. Wendland, eds., *Philonis Alexandri Opera Quae Supersunt*, vol. III (Berlin 1898), pp. 218 ff.
13. W. G. Braude, *Midrash on the Psalms*, vol. II, p. 93, on Isa. 90.6.
14. See Chapter 2, pp. 87-9.
15. As a matter of fact it is very doubtful whether this could ever have been said about Job 41, in view of the mythological connotation of Leviathan. Perhaps the very conception of anyone composing nothing but an interesting poem is an anachronism.
16. As a matter of fact I understand that a tiny fragment of a Targum on Leviticus has now been discovered among the Qumran finds. But this does not affect the argument.
17. J. Neusner, ed., *The Formation of the Babylonian Talmud*, Leiden 1970, and ed., *The Modern Study of the Mishna*, Leiden 1973.
18. At any rate A. Loisy and F. von Hügel seem to have held this view.
19. I assume that all four groups would pay little attention to the first question, the meaning in the original context; though on the whole it might be truer to say that of the four groups the Pharisees and the Christians would give this question more attention and the other two groups less.
20. I admit that Hebrews 13.11-13 finds a christological significance in certain features of the ritual of the Day of Atonement, and I think we must admit an exception here. Christian exegetes

did tend to identify important ritual sacrifices with Christ's one great sacrifice. But this can hardly be described as fantastic or far-fetched.
21. See *The Modern Study of the Mishna*, p. 75.
22. Christianity itself is in some sense a 'back to the Bible' movement originating within Judaism; but we have dealt with this already.
23. See the article 'Karaites' by A. De Harkavy, in the *Jewish Encyclopedia*, ed. I. Singer, New York and London 1904, vol. III; also the article 'Karaites' by Samuel Poznanski, in *Encyclopedia of Religion and Ethics*, ed. J. Hastings, Edinburgh 1914, vol. VII.
24. See an article by me, '*Claude Montefiore, a Modern Philo*', in *The Modern Churchman*, vol. XX, no. 3 (Spring 1977), pp. 109-14, where these issues are more fully discussed.
25. If the reader asks at this point: 'Is there one New Testament interpretation of Scripture or several?', I must refer him to Chapter 6. To some extent it depends on what you mean by 'interpretation'.
26. See *Studies in Paul's Technique and Theology*, ch. 11, pp. 225ff; *Grace and Truth*, pp. 74-6.
27. I do not think I am unjust in attributing something like this conclusion to D. H. Kelsey in his interesting and able book *The Uses of Scripture in Recent Theology*, London 1975.

CHAPTER 2

A Quasi-Gnostic Pauline Midrash: 1 Corinthians 2.6-16

SECTION I

1. The phrase is quoted from J. Weiss, *Der Erste Korinther Brief*, Göttingen 1910, though he does not adopt this opinion himself.
2. R. Bultmann, *Theology of the New Testament*, Eng. trans. London 1952, vol. I, p. 153.
3. See A. Ehrhardt, *The Beginning*, Manchester 1968; note especially ch. 7.
4. See A. W. Carr, 'The Rulers of This Age – 1 Corinthians 2.6-8', in *NTS* (October 1976), pp. 20-35. For other examples of those who reject this view, see T. Ling, 'A Note on 1 Corinthians ii.8' in *ET* 68 (1956-7), p. 26; and G. Miller, 'ΑΡΧΟΝΤΩΝ ΤΟΥ ΑΙΩΝΟΣ ΤΟΥΤΟΥ – a new look at 1 Corinthians 2.6-8', in *JBL* 91 (1972), pp. 522-8.
5. A. Feuillet, 'L'Enigme de 1 Cor. ii.9', in *RB* 70 (1963), pp. 52-74; see especially pp. 52ff, 68, 74.

6. U. Wilckens, *Weisheit und Torheit* (Tübingen 1959), p. 220. See also H. Conzelmann, *Der Erste Brief an die Korinther*, Göttingen 1969, in loc., where he emphasizes that wisdom is not identified with the Lord of glory.
7. Wilckens, op. cit., pp. 68, 70; see also his article *Sophia*, in *TWNT*, vol. VII (Stuttgart 1964), p. 519.
8. Bultmann, op. cit., vol. I, p. 327.
9. E. B. Allo, *Première Epître de Paul aux Corinthiens*, Paris 1956, in loc.
10. G. Bornkamm, 'μυστήριον', in *TWNT*, vol. IV, Stuttgart 1962.
11. R. Scroggs, 'Paul: ΣΟΦΟΣ and ΠΝΕΥΜΑΤΙΚΟΣ', in *NTS*, 14 (1967-8), pp. 33-58.
12. Art. cit., p. 53n.
13. I have set this out in greater detail in my work already referred to: *Jesus Christ in the Old Testament*. See pp. 65ff.
14. H. Conzelmann, 'Paulus und die Weisheit', in *NTS*, 12 (1965-6), pp. 231-44.
15. J. S. Ackermann, 'The Rabbinic Interpretation of Psalm 82 and the Gospel of John', in *Harvard Theological Review*, 59 (1966), pp. 186-91.
16. A. van Roon, 'The Relation between Christ and the Wisdom of God according to Paul', in *Nov. Test.*, 16 (1974), pp. 207-39.
17. W. L. Knox, op. cit., pp. 114-15, and p. 228 (see note 30 below).
18. This is not to suggest that *raz* in the Qumran documents had exactly the same meaning as *mustērion* has in Paul. Indeed the Qumran use of *raz* is more akin to the use of 'mystery' in Gnostic writings, that is, a piece of secret information only disclosed to the elect, usually connected with wholly celestial affairs. Thus in the *Gospel of Truth* the Son is described as hidden, but revealed to the aeons by the Spirit (see J.-E. Ménard, *L'Evangile de Vérité*, Leiden 1972, 24.8-10, p. 51); in 18.15 the Son is himself described as 'a hidden mystery'. But in 38.18-21 the Father is described as 'the mystery of the invisible'. Irenaeus, quoting a certain Gnostic Marcus and his disciples, says that they speak of 'the mystery of the passion of the defect' (see W. Foerster, *Gnosis*, vol. I (Oxford 1972), p. 215). The Naassenes seem to have made an effort to assimilate the pagan mysteries to the Christian faith, if Hippolytus is correct (Foerster, op. cit., pp. 267, 272, 277, 280). In *The Gospel of Philip*, 68 we read: 'And the Lord has [done] everything in a mystery, a baptism, and an anointing, and a eucharist, and a redemption' (Foerster, p. 89). The truth is that the Gnostics were mystagogues, and therefore used the word 'mystery' with great freedom, not really like the com-

paratively restricted way in which Paul uses it. See also A. Böhlig. *Mysterion und Wahrheit*, Leiden 1968, where he says that Gnosticism tended to relate everything to the All, and call that the *mustērion*; but the collection of intermediate beings could also be called mysteries (op. cit., pp. 34-5); Böhlig agrees that for Paul the career of Christ *was* the mystery: 'Dieses Mysterium ist der gekreuzigte Christus' (p. 25).

19. E. Evans, *The First Epistle of Paul the Apostle to the Corinthians*, Oxford 1930, in loc.
20. Bultmann, op. cit., vol. I, p. 175.
21. Wilckens, op. cit., pp. 79 and 215 respectively.
22. G. Delling, 'ἄρχων', in *TWNT*, vol. I, Stuttgart 1949.
23. C. K. Barrett, *The First Epistle to the Corinthians*, London 1969, in loc.
24. J. Héring, *La Première Epître de Saint Paul aux Corinthiens*, Neuchâtel-Paris 1949.
25. W. Bousset, 'Zur Hadesfahrt Christi', in *ZNTW*, 19 (1919-20), pp. 50-66. A useful summary of what the scholars of the *Religionsgeschichte* school believed to be the content of the 'myth of the descending redeemer' can be found in C. Colpe, *Die Religionsgeschichtliche Schule* (Göttingen 1961), p. 172.
26. Bultmann, op. cit., vol. I, p. 175. Colpe (op. cit., p. 199) rightly warns against the danger of assuming that the redeemer always had the same functions in every version of the myth.
27. See W. Schmithals, *Die Gnosis in Korinth* (Göttingen 1956), pp. 109, 120-22. On p. 109 he particularly emphasizes the phrase in Colossians 3.5: *ta melē ta epi tēs gēs*.
28. Wilckens, art. cit., σοφία, p. 519.
29. I have discussed this at greater length in my book *Studies in Paul's Technique and Theology* (London 1974), pp. 152-3. The reference to Jonah in Matthew 12.39-40 of course confirms this interpretation. As a matter of fact the midrash was known before the discovery of the Neofiti ms., since it is quoted in Etheridge's edition of the Targums on the Pentateuch. This evidence is ignored by both Bultmann and Wilckens. The whole topic is fully discussed in Chapter 5.
30. W. L. Knox, *St Paul and the Church of the Gentiles* (Cambridge 1961, reprint of edn of 1939), pp. 220-21.
31. All editors translate this phrase 'three mysteries worthy of proclamation' (or some such phrase). But I cannot discover that *kraugē* ever means 'proclamation' in any other context. It can mean 'acclamation', e.g. Matt. 25.6. Moulton and Milligan quote a passage in which Ptolemy III describes his triumphal reception *meta krotou kai kraugēs* 'with applause and acclamation' (see J. H. Moulton and G. Milligan, *The*

Vocabulary of the Greek Testament, London reprint of 1952, sub κραυγή). David Daube has realized that *kraugē* cannot mean *kērugma*. See his article 'τρία μυστήρια κραυγῆς Ignatius, Ephesians XIX.1', in *JTS*, 16, new series (1965), pp. 128-9. He suggests that Ignatius is simply stating that all three mysteries were in fact greeted with a cry: the virginal conception by Elizabeth's *kraugē megalē* in Luke 1.42; the birth by the *kraugē* of the midwife mentioned in the *Protevangelium of James*; and the death by Jesus's *kraugē* on the cross. I would prefer to translate *kraugē* here with 'acclamation'. Ignatius is contrasting the silence of God with the acclamation which these great events should receive from men.

32. Text of Ignatius in J. B. Lightfoot, *The Apostolic Fathers*, London reprint of 1898; my own translation.
33. J. Daniélou, *Theology of Jewish Christianity*, Eng. trans. London 1964, a new edn of the French original of 1958. It is vol. I of a work called *The Development of Christian Doctrine before the Council of Nicaea*; see p. 42.
34. T. Camelot, *Ignace d'Antioch*, Paris 1951, *Sources Chrétiennes*, 2nd edn.
35. R. H. Charles, *The Ascension of Isaiah*, London 1900. J. Flemming and H. Duensing in *New Testament Apocrypha*, vol. II, ed. W. Schneemelcher (London 1965), p. 643 think the *Vision* 'may have originated in the second century A.D.'.
36. Charles, op. cit., p. 77, n. 16.
37. Daniélou, op. cit., p. 207.
38. B. Altaner, *Patrologie* (Freiburg 1951), p. 47. A. K. Helmbold in his article, 'Gnostic Elements in "The Ascension of Isaiah"', in *NTS*, 18 (Jan. 1972), pp. 222-7, suggests that the work comes not from orthodox Christian circles but from a 'Christian-Gnostic' milieu. He would date it not earlier than the middle of the second century A.D. This seems a reasonable conclusion and rules out Charles's theory that it lies behind Ignatius's Ephesians.
39. It is impossible to agree with Daniélou (op. cit., p. 14) that the *Vision of Isaiah* is perfectly orthodox, unless indeed Daniélou's own Christology had a Docetic element in it.
40. Wilckens (op. cit., pp. 58-9) refers to an interesting parallel to the myth of the disguised descent in *Poimandres*: the soul has to pass through seven zones on its way to God, which are controlled by demonic powers. But the redeemer has already blazed the trail through them. Here is certainly full-blown Gnosticism.
41. See Charles, op. cit., p. 137.
42. Charles, op. cit., p. xxvii.

43. Feuillet, op. cit., p. 60. Flemming and Duensing also conclude that xi.2-22 'forms an extraneous unit' (op. cit., p. 643).
44. See my *Jesus Christ in the Old Testament* (London 1965), pp. 141-3.
45. See J. C. T. Otto, ed., *Dialogue cum Tryphone* (Jena 1843), vol. 2, 36, pp. 118-22 (my translation).
46. It is, however, quite possible that Justin was acquainted with the MT as well, for he claims that Christ is called 'Jacob' in the Scriptures. But only the MT has *mbqšy pnyk y'qb* in verse 6; the LXX has ζητούντων τὸ πρόσωπον τοῦ θεοῦ Ἰακώβ, and this is how Justin quotes it in Greek. But it is only fair to point out that he might have had the MT rendering available in Greek, since all the other non-LXX versions, Aquila, Theodotion, Symmachus, Quinta, and Sexta, offer τὸ πρόσωπόν σου, Ἰακώβ.
47. There is another reference to this psalm in *Apology* I, 51 (vol. 1, p. 238). Justin uses a freer translation and quotes verse 8 rather than verse 9 since he is only concerned here to prove that Christ was destined to ascend into heaven. See also *Dialogue* 127 (vol. 2, p. 424).
48. See *Tractate Shabbath*, ed. H. Freedman, 30a, p. 133.
49. W. G. Braude, *The Midrash on the Psalms*, vol. 1 (New Haven 1959), pp. 338-46.
50. In *Dialogue* 85 (vol. 2, p. 288) Justin mentions another Jewish tradition that would refer the psalm to King Hezekiah.
51. For the text and Charles's comment, see op. cit., pp. 135-6. The translation is mine. The phrase 'who was not according to their appearance' follows the Slavonic version, which has the equivalent of 'eorum' after 'formam'.
52. See Daniélou, op. cit., p. 207. For the attribution to Epiphanius see Altaner, op. cit., p. 273. Ursula Treu in an article, 'Zum Datierung der Physiologus', in *ZNTW* 57 (1966), pp. 101-4 inclines to put it in the second century A.D. just because of its resemblance to *The Ascension of Isaiah*. But she carefully refrains from labelling the work as 'Gnostic' or 'heretical', wisely remarking that 'it only indicates an early stage in which the fronts had not hardened, the concepts had not yet been labelled'.

    Hippolytus (ref. vv. 8, 18) says that the Naassenes use 'Lift up your heads, O ye gates' to describe the regeneration or ascent of the carnal man as he becomes spiritual (Foerster, vol. 1, p. 273).
53. We may appropriately quote here M. Hengel, *The Son of God* (Eng. trans., London 1976 of the German original, Tübingen 1975), p. 33: 'In reality there is no Gnostic redeemer myth in

Notes to page 43

the sources which can be demonstrated chronologically to be pre-Christian.' He emphatically rejects the notion that Paul was influenced by Gnosticism and claims that 'the Gnostic fever' is already dying down (see n. 66 on p. 33). It is very remarkable that Talbert, in a learned article on 'The Myth of a Descending-Ascending Redeemer in Mediterranean Antiquity', nowhere mentions 1 Cor. 2.6-16, or *The Ascension of Isaiah*, or Ignatius for that matter. See C. H. Talbert, art. cit., in *NTS* 22 (July 1976), pp. 418-40. Talbert points out that on the whole in Paul the ascent of the redeemer is implicit rather than explicit, as contrasted with the descent, or sending of the redeemer (art. cit., p. 435). But this does not really conflict with our suggestion on p. 38 that Paul has the ascent rather than the descent in mind in 1 Cor. 2.6-8. One must here also refer to Colpe's important work *Die Religionsgeschichtliche Schule* (see p. 30, n. 25); he denies, among other things, that the Wisdom myth was identical with the Gnostic redeemer myth (pp. 151, 193). He provides throughout his work a valuable critique of the arbitrary and unscientific way in which the scholars of the *Religionsgeschichtliche* school, up to and including Bultmann, dealt with their material. It is plain that Bultmann's sweeping application of the terms 'Gnostic' and 'Gnosticism' to Pauline and Johannine theological concepts and language can no longer be maintained.

SECTION 2

1. See J. P. Migne, ed., *Patrologiae Cursus Completus; Origenis Opera Omnia*, vol. 3 (Paris 1862), 916, section 117, p. 1769, my translation. Strack-Billerbeck say, not quite accurately, that according to Origen the citation was taken from a (Jewish) *Apocalypse of Elijah*. Origen is not as specific as this. (See S-B in loc., vol. II.) Some fragments of Origen's Commentary on 1 Corinthians survive. These have been edited by C. Jenkins in *JTS*, vol. IX (1908), pp. 236-9. Origen clearly identifies *tōn archontōn* in 1 Cor. 2.6,8 with *dunameōn aoratōn*; he also suggests that the 'wisdom of the world' of 1.20 is *poiētikē kai rhetorikē*. Of verse 7 he says that the rulers inspire (*energousin*), the wisdom of the world. He has no comment on the origin of the citation in verse 9. This would seem to indicate that when he wrote this commentary he had not heard of the suggestion that the citation came from an apocryphal work. R. P. C. Hanson in *Origen's Doctrine of Tradition* (London 1954), p. 26 puts Origen's Commentary on 1 Corinthians in the years A.D. 232-3 but his commentary on Matthew some twelve years later in 246. Presumably Origen came to hear of the suggestion

about the apocryphal work sometime in between these dates.
2. P. W. Schmiedel, *Die Briefe an die Thessalonicher und die Korinther*, Freiburg 1891, in loc.
3. H. Lietzmann, *An die Korinther I/II*, Tübingen 1969, in loc.
4. O. Michel, *Paulus und seine Bibel* (Gütersloh 1927), pp. 33-4. Michel rejects Isaiah 64.3 as a source for the citation on the grounds that Paul uses it to refer to the eschatological glory that lies before the faithful, whereas in the context of Isaiah it speaks of the grace of God which the believer can perceive. I argue below that this is a mistaken view.
5. J. Héring, *La Première Epître de Saint Paul aux Corinthiens* Neuchâtel-Paris 1949, in loc.
6. H. Conzelmann, *Der Erste Brief an die Korinther*, Göttingen 1969, in loc.
7. See Wilckens, op. cit., p. 66.
8. A. Oepke, 'κρύπτω', in *TWNT*, vol. III (Stuttgart 1938), p. 989.
9. G. Schrenk, 'γράφω', in *TWNT*, vol. I, Stuttgart, reprint of 1949. Harnack meets this difficulty by the ingenious suggestion that Paul wrote *kathōs gegraptai* in 1 Cor. 2.9 'through a momentary error' (see H. Vollmer, *Die Alttestamentlichen Citate bei Paulus* (Freiburg and Leipzig 1895), p. 46.) E. Stauffer, in his edition of P. Bachmann's Commentary, *Der Erste Brief des Paulus an die Korinther*, 4th edn, Leipzig 1936, says that the wide distribution of the citation in the Fathers, etc. argues against its having originated in an apocryphal work.
10. E. von Nordheim, 'Das Zitat des Paulus in 1 Kor. 2.9 und seine Beziehung zum koptischen Testament Jakobs', in *ZNTW* 65, 1/2 (1974), pp. 112-20. We can safely ignore the earlier claim by D. John to have found the source of the quotation in Empedocles. See his article, 'St Paul and Empedocles', in *ET* 39 (1927-8), pp. 237-8.
11. Von Otfried Hofius, 'Das Zitat 1 Kor. 2.9 und das koptisches Testament des Jakobs', in *ZNTW* 66, 1/2 (1975), pp. 140-42. H. F. D. Sparks, in an article, '1 Cor. 2.9, a Quotation from the Coptic Testament of Jacob?', in *ZNTW* 67 (1976), pp. 3-4, 269-79, takes up the question again. He points out that the apocryphal *Epistle of Titus*, composed (according to Harnack) by a fifth-century Priscillianist writer, has our citation in a modified version. Sparks suggests that the source of this author's citation might be an apocryphon of Elijah. But he does not think that this was the original source of the citation. He also rejects the notion of an original Jewish kernel in the *Testament of Jacob*, regarding it as an originally Christian work. He thinks the most likely conclusion is that Paul is loosely quoting Isa. 64.4. Unfortunately Professor Sparks did

not notice Von Otfried Hofius' article, though it appeared before his. Even more unfortunate is the fact that he seems to be unaware of the very significant occurrence of the citation in the *Liber Antiquitatum*.

12. A. Guillamont *et al.*, eds., *The Gospel according to Thomas* (Leiden and London 1959), p. 13.
13. I assume that Charles has decisively exploded the notion that this quotation occurs independently of Paul in *The Ascension of Isaiah*, even if that work were to be dated at the end of the first century A.D. We may quote here Prof. R. McL. Wilson's opinion on this point: 'It is not of course impossible that Paul is quoting a saying of Jesus, but in that case we should have expected him to indicate the fact ... On the whole, therefore, we should probably see in Logion 17 [sc. of *The Gospel of Thomas*] a Pauline saying growing into a word of Jesus' (see his *Studies in the Gospel of Thomas* (London 1960), pp. 102-3). K. H. Kuhn, in reviewing *Nag Hammadi Codices III, 2 and IV, 2*, edited by A. Böhlig and F. Wisse, Leiden 1975, in *JTS* (April 1976), p. 214, suggested that 'there is a possible verbal reminiscence of 1 Cor. ii.9 on p. 162, lines 7-9'. The lines in question run as follows (we reproduce III, 68, 1-9 on p. 162, op. cit.):
'This is the book ... which the great Seth wrote and placed in high mountains on which the sun has not risen, nor is it possible. And since the days of the prophets (*prophetēs*), and the apostles (*apostolos*), and the preachers (*kērux*), the name has not at all risen upon their hearts, nor is it possible. And their ear has not heard it.'
There may be here a remote echo of 1 Cor. 2.9; all the two passages have in common is the phrase 'risen upon their hearts' and 'their ear has not heard it'. The phrases are not apparently used in the same sense in which either Paul or the early Fathers understand the citation. It is true that there are references to *archons* in this document, but they seem to have no particular connection with this passage. The editors date the document thus (p. 38): 'This would indicate a composition date in the second or third century.' But they add that some parts may go back to 'a Gnosticism which preceeds [sic] the development of Christian Gnosticism'. The most that can be claimed therefore is that this is a remote echo of our citation coming from a much later period. The language of the citation would naturally appeal to Gnostics.
14. G. A. J. Skeel, H. J. White, and J. P. Witney, eds., *The Epistle of St Clement of Rome* in Texts for Students, London 1919. They reproduce J. B. Lightfoot's text, my translation.
15. D. A. Hagner, *The Use of the Old and New Testaments in Clement of Rome* (Leiden 1973), pp. 204-8. E. Werner in an article,

'Post-Biblical Hebraisms in the Prima Clementis', in *Harry Austryn Wolfson Jubilee Vol. II* (Jerusalem 1965), pp. 799-802, claims that Clement is quoting from an apocryphal source and is not echoing Paul. I cannot see, however, that he has produced any fresh evidence.

16. J. B. Lightfoot, ed., 'An Ancient Homily by an Unknown Author', in *The Apostolic Fathers*, my translation. In each of the last two quotations I have translated a larger amount than I have quoted in Greek, in order to give the context.
17. See K. P. Donfried, *The Setting of Second Clement in Early Christianity*, Leiden 1974.
18. For all this, see Donfried, op. cit., p. 86.
19. T. L. Camelot, ed., *Ignace d'Antioche; Polycarpe de Smyrne, Lettres* (Sources Chrétiennes, Paris 1950), II, 1. Camelot dates the account of the martyrdom at A.D. 177. My translation.
20. Vollmer, op. cit., p. 47.

SECTION 3

1. R. Kittel, ed., *Biblia Hebraica*, 6th edn, Stuttgart 1949.
2. The Isaiah Manuscript of the Dead Sea Scrolls offers only the most minute divergence from this text, in that it reads *l' h'zynw w'yn l' r'th*. It could be said to support the LXX reading οὐδὲ οἱ ὀφθαλμοὶ εἶδον, but the difference has no significance for the meaning (see M. Burrows, ed., *The Dead Sea Scrolls of St Mark's Monastery*, vol. I, New Haven 1950).
3. F. Field, ed., *Origenis Hexaplorum Quae Supersunt*, 2 vols., Oxford 1875. This last reading is witnessed to by Jerome, though he also knows the LXX reading.
4. J. F. Stenning, *The Targum of Isaiah*, Oxford 1949.
5. E. E. Ellis, *Paul's Use of the Old Testament* (Edinburgh 1959), pp. 35 and 151.
6. J. B. Bauer, '... τοῖς ἀγαπῶσιν τὸν θεόν – Rom. 8. 28 (1 Cor. 2.9; 1 Cor. 8.3)', in *ZNTW* 50 (1959), pp. 106-12.
7. G. H. Box, *The Book of Isaiah*, London 1916, actually reads *t'śh* here.
8. E. J. Kissane, in *The Book of Isaiah*, vol. II, Dublin 1943, actually suggests that 'the word "mercy" (*ḥesed*) may have been omitted after "works"'.
9. I am grateful to Dr Margaret Thrall, of the Department of Biblical Studies in the University College of North Wales, Bangor, for having drawn my attention to this passage.
10. C. C. Torrey, *The Second Isaiah: a new interpretation*, Edinburgh and New York 1928, in loc.

Notes to pages 53-59

11. L. Koehler and W. Baumgartner, *Lexicon in Veteris Testamenti Libros*, Leiden 1953, sub '*śh*.
12. But Kittel conjectures *ya'ăzōr*.
13. Kittel suggests *waya'ś*: 'and Pharaoh got to work'.
14. Some editors, on the basis of the Syriac, have suggested that this represents an original reading, καιρὸς κρᾶξαι τῷ κυρίῳ 'It is time to cry to the Lord.'
15. E. Delitzsch, *Biblical Commentary on the Prophecies of Isaiah*, Eng. trans., Edinburgh 1890, of the 4th German edn.
16. C. Westermann, *Das Buch Jesaja Kapitel 40-66*, Göttingen 1966.
17. I am indebted to my colleague, Dr R. N. Whybray, Professor of Old Testament in the University of Hull, for drawing my attenion to Duhm's conjecture. See B. Duhm, *Das Buch Jesaja*, Göttingen, edn of 1922.
18. S-B, op. cit., in loc.
19. This point is well made by P. Bachmann, op. cit., in loc.
20. Feuillet (art. cit., pp. 60, 67) considers these two passages as possible sources and decides in favour of Isaiah 65.16. M. Wilcox in *The Semitisms of Acts*, Oxford 1965, considers the origin of this phrase à propos Acts 7.23 where the phrase *anebē epi tēn kardian* occurs, and conjectures that it entered Luke's vocabulary through the early Church's use of Isaiah 65.16-17. He does not consider the claim of Jeremiah 3.16, though he mentions it in a series of references to the LXX usage (see p. 63 of his work).
21. Field, op. cit., in loc.
22. P. Prigent, 'Ce que l'œil n'a pas vu, 1 Cor. 2.9', in *Theologische Zeitschrift* 14 (1958), pp. 416-29.
23. H. St J. Thackeray, *The Relation of St Paul to Contemporary Jewish Thought* (London 1900), p. 244.
24. M. Philonenko, 'Quod oculus non vidit, 1 Cor. 2.9', in *Theologische Zeitschrift* 15 (1959), pp. 51-2.
25. M. R. James, *The Biblical Antiquities of Philo* (republished with a Prolegomenon by L. H. Feldman, New York 1971).
26. Ellis, op. cit., p. 35.
27. The text is quoted from Philonenko, art. cit.; the reference in James's edn is xxvi. 13.
28. D. J. Harrington (see below, note 30) discusses the possibility that the original language might have been Aramaic, but finally dismisses it.
29. G. Delling, 'Die Weise, von der Zeit zu reden, im Liber Antiquitatum Biblicarum', in *Nov. Test.* 13 (1971), pp. 305-21, points out that the citations do not invariably follow the

Vulgate; he concludes we cannot assume that the Latin trans. (made perhaps in the fourth century A.D.) was translated from Greek (p. 314n).

30. D. J. Harrington, 'The Original Language of Pseudo-Philo's *Liber Antiquitatum Biblicarum*', in *Harvard Theological Review* 63 (1970), pp. 503-14.
31. Thackeray, op. cit., pp. 185-6.
32. Feuillet, art. cit., p. 62.
33. The Vulgate offers: 'nec auris audivit nec in cor hominis ascendit', whereas the *Bibl. Ant.* version runs 'nec auris audivit et in cor hominis non ascendit' (*Biblia Sacra juxta Vulgatae*, ed. A.-C. Fillion, Paris 1887, vol. III).
34. James Moffatt, who edits 2 Maccabees in R. H. Charles's *Apocrypha and Pseudepigrapha of the Old Testament*, vol. I, Oxford 1913, remarks *à propos* 2.1-8: 'Legend has no scruple in transforming a prophet who was radically indifferent, if not hostile to the ritual of the Temple, into a pious conservative.' On the other hand it must be said that the Targum on Jeremiah 3.16 shows no tendency at all to qualify Jeremiah's forthright statement. See A. Sperber, *The Bible in Aramaic*, vol. III, in loc., Leiden 1962. We can trace the history of this legend a stage further back than 2 Maccabees: the Jewish historian Eupolemos, whom Hengel describes as a contemporary of the Maccabaean revolt (see M. Hengel, *Judaism and Hellenism*, Eng. trans., London 1974, of edn of 1973: Tübingen, vol. I, p. 93), as reported by Eusebius, recounts that when the Babylonians took the gold and silver and bronze from the Temple, 'Jeremiah returned the ark of the covenant and the tables' (see E. H. Gifford, ed., *Eusebii Pamphili Evangelicae Praeparationis Libri XV* (Oxford 1903), IX, 39, p. 454c). In the fifty (?) years between Eupolemos and the author of 2 Maccabees the legend has grown; the reference in 2 Maccabees does not form part of the epitome of Jason of Cyrene's work.
35. H. St J. Thackeray, *The Septuagint and Jewish Worship*, London 1923, 2nd edn.
36. G. F. Moore, *Judaism*, vol. I (Cambridge, Mass. 1944), p. 295.
37. He writes: 'It is likely that the Alexandrian Jews followed [the] pattern of having certain items in the vernacular.' I am most grateful to Professor Weingreen (my former teacher in Hebrew in Trinity College, Dublin) for so kindly replying to my inquiries.
38. In the reference in *The Gospel of Thomas* there is no suggestion whatever of a liturgical context.

SECTION 4

1. M. Simon, ed., *Tractate Berakoth* (London 1948), p. 215.

Notes to pages 63-68

2. *Tractate Abodah Zarah*, ed. A. Mishcon (London 1935), p. 316.
3. K. G. Kuhn, *Der Tannaitische Midrash Sifre zu Numeri* (Stuttgart 1959), p. 558. The comment is *à propos* Deut. 3.26, *rab l'kā*.
4. *Tractate Sanhedrin*, ed. H. Freedman (1935), pp. 670-71.
5. *Tractate Shabbath*, ed. H. Freedman (1938), p. 295.
6. W. G. Braude, ed., *Pesikta Rabbati* (New Haven and Yale 1968), vol. II, pp. 687-8. Braude does not write with any conviction about the date of *Piska* 37, the passage in which the quotation occurs. The *Piskas*, homilies delivered by rabbis on festival occasions, are generally attributed to 'teachers of the third, fourth, or fifth generation of the Palestinian Amoraim (the third and fourth centuries of the Common Era)' (p. 3). But we read, 'On the other hand, *Piskas* 34-7, which Freedman asserts to be of Tannaitic origin and therefore even earlier than the other *Piskas*, are very likely of post-Amoraic compilation, possibly in the seventh century' (p. 22). His final conclusion is that the compilation of *Pesikta Rabbati* took place in Palestine in the seventh century and that the teachers represented in it are all Palestinian Amoraim of the third and fourth centuries (p. 26). The material which they use is therefore not irrelevant to our purpose.
7. Indeed the perspective of God's design probably extends further than this, for it includes the activity of the pre-existent Christ in creation and in the history of Israel.
8. Cf. E. Schweizer, 'πνεῦμα', in *TWNT*, vol. VI (Stuttgart 1959), p. 424: 'εἶναι ἐν πνεύματι is synonymous with εἶναι ἐν Χριστῷ.'
9. See Hagner, op. cit., p. 206.
10. See Prigent, art. cit., pp. 416-17, 419.
11. A. Robertson and A. Plummer, *A Critical and Exegetical Commentary on the First Epistle of St Paul to the Corinthians*, Edinburgh 1911, in loc.
12. W. D. Davies, *Paul and Rabbinic Judaism* (London 1948), p. 307.
13. Wilckens, op. cit., p. 66.
14. 'M.D.', 'Twenty Misused Texts: 1, 1 Cor. 2.9', in *ET* 6 (1894-5), p. 201.
15. H. L. Goudge, *The First Epistle to the Corinthians*, London 1903, in loc.
16. Feuillet, art. cit., pp. 54, 57.
17. Hagner, op. cit., p. 208.
18. The phrase is Bultmann's; see R. Bultmann, *Das Evangelium des Johannes*, 10th edn (Göttingen 1941), p. 41, my translation.

SECTION 5

1. The only exception to this is *eis doxan hēmōn* in verse 7.
2. See Allo, op. cit., *Excursus on pneuma*, p. 106. In commenting on verse 11, however, he does admit that *pneuma* is used as the equivalent of *nous*.
3. See Comm. in loc., vv. 14-18.
4. Conzelmann, op. cit., in loc., vv. 11, 16.
5. See J. Weiss, op. cit., in loc., v. 11.
6. See E. Evans, op. cit., in loc., v. 10.
7. F. F. Bruce, *I and II Corinthians*, London 1971, in loc., v. 10. In Job 11.7 the LXX has quite a different rendering of the Hebrew which leaves out 'the deep things of God' altogether. But there is some reason to believe that the Greek text of Job which Paul used was not akin to that which we have in the LXX. See Ellis, op. cit., p. 144. See also Vollmer's discussion of this question (op. cit., pp. 22-3), even though it is somewhat outdated by the discovery of alternative Greek translations among the Qumran documents.
8. H. Lietzmann, op. cit., in loc., v. 11.
9. I note with interest that Talbert uses exactly this adjective 'proto-Gnostic' to describe the views of Paul's Corinthian opponents (art. cit., pp. 418-19). In fact the term 'proto-Gnostic' is one agreed on at a conference on Gnosticism held at Messina in 1966. It is meant to indicate 'early or incipient forms of Gnosticism'. See E. M. Yamauchi, *Pre-Christian Gnosticism* (London 1973), p. 18.
10. C. Hodge, *An Exposition of the First Epistle to the Corinthians*, reprint of 1959, London, in loc.
11. C. K. Barrett, op. cit., in loc.
12. Héring, op. cit., in loc., v. 13.
13. P. W. Schmiedel, *Die Briefe an die Thessalonicher und an die Korinther*, in loc.
14. But he has omitted to notice the usage in Philo; see p. 76.
15. See Allo, op. cit., pp. 89, 110, 111. In profane Greek from Aristotle onwards *pneumatikos* meant 'consisting of, or connected with, air'. Apart from Paul's Epistles, the first instance which Liddell and Scott give in which *pneumatikos* means 'spiritual' is from an interpolation in Plutarch's *Moralia* (H. G. Liddell and R. Scott, *A Greek-English Lexicon*, Oxford 1961, reprint of 1940 edn; the reference they give is *Plu.* 2.129c). The earliest instance of this usage that Moulton and Milligan can offer is in Vettius Valens in the second century A.D. But

in fact Philo used *pneumatikos* to mean 'spiritual' before Paul did, as I indicate below. All the references below are from L. Cohn and P. Wendland, eds., *Philonis Alexandri Opera quae Supersunt*, Berlin 1896.

16. For a similar view about the identity of the *pneumatikoi* to that expressed here, see W. L. Knox, op. cit., pp. 116, 118. He thinks *pneumatikos* means 'all Christians who like [Paul] himself are spiritual'; and he later defines the *pneumatikos* as 'the normal Christian who was "in Christ" and therefore possessed his "spirit" or "mind" '. Compare also E. Schweizer's article, 'πνεῦμα', pp. 423-4, where he points to the significant phrase *pneuma tēs pisteōs* in 2 Cor. 4.13.

17. Hodge commits himself to the far-reaching statement: 'The same person who is revealed in the New Testament as the Son of God was revealed of old as Jehovah.' Admittedly this view has a respectable ancestry; compare Charles Wesley's hymn:
    Jehovah in thy person show,
    Jehovah crucified;
    And then the pardoning God I know
    And feel the blood applied.
    But Paul is very far from identifying every reference to the ineffable Tetragrammaton in Scripture with the pre-existent Christ. John comes much closer to this view.

18. See Bultmann, *Theology of the NT*, vol. I, p. 124, where he casually includes this passage 'in a list of places where Paul uses *kurios* in the OT, to refer to Christ'. Michel (*Paulus und seine Bibel*, p. 151) thinks it is not possible to say whether *nous kuriou* here refers to God or Christ. But, astonishingly, he does not refer to the citation in Rom. 11.34. Equally astonishing is the fact that Michel's learned and valuable work should have been published in 1927 without any index whatever.

19. Why the LXX rendered it this way is another question, one which we consider on pp. 89-90.

20. Bultmann, op. cit., vol. I, p. 207. He says that Paul 'wants to confirm his statement about the Spirit of God with the quotation from Isaiah 40.13'. But if that was Paul's only motive, why could he not have translated the Hebrew for himself and used *pneuma*?

21. O. Michel, *Der Brief an die Römer*, 12th edn, Göttingen 1963, in loc.

22. F. J. Leenhardt, *L'Epître de Saint Paul aux Romains*, Neuchâtel and Paris 1957, in loc.

23. W. Eltester, 'Schöpfungsoffenbarungen und natürliche Theologie im frühen Christentum', in *NTS* III (1956-7), pp. 93-114. This remark occurs on p. 99.

Notes to pages 79-83

24. van Roon, art. cit., p. 216.
25. R. A. Lipsius, *Die Briefe an die Galater, Römer, Philipper*, Freiburg 1891, in loc.
26. Karl Barth, *The Epistle to the Romans*, Eng. trans. E. C. Hoskyns, London 1933, of 6th German edn, in loc.
27. Bultmann, op. cit., vol. 1, p. 211.
28. C. H. Dodd, *The Epistle of Paul to the Romans*, London 1932, reprint of 1947, in loc.
29. W. L. Knox, op. cit., pp. 117, 118.
30. E. Käsemann, *An die Römer*, Tübingen 1973, in loc., 11.33-6.
31. This is not to suggest that the modern theologian can take over Paul's concept of pre-existence intact. In this work we are mainly concerned with exploring Paul's thought, not with considering it in the light of systematic theology.
32. There is also an instance of the *Pi'el* of *tkn* in Sira 42.21a, but both Charles (*Apocrypha and Pseudepigrapha of the OT*, vol. 1, in loc.) and I. Lévi (*The Hebrew Text of the Book of Ecclesiasticus*, Leiden 1969 edn) here read *tikwn*, which is Niph'al fem. imperf. of *kwn*.
33. F. Delitzsch, *The Prophecies of Isaiah*, Eng. trans., Edinburgh 1890.
34. B. Duhm, *Das Buch Jesaja*, Göttingen edn of 1922.
35. C. Westermann, *Das Buch Jesaja, Kapitel 40-66*, Göttingen 1966.
36. See L. G. Rignell, *A Study of Isaiah*, Lund 1956, in loc.
37. K. Elliger, *Jesaja II*, Neukirchen-Vluyn 1970.
38. R. N. Whybray, *The Heavenly Counsellor in Isaiah XL.13-14*, Cambridge 1971.
39. Whybray, op. cit., pp. 16,18.
40. Op. cit., p. 84. M. Dahood, 'The Breakup of Two Composite Phrases in Isaiah 40.13', in *Biblica* 54 (1973), pp. 537-8, has challenged Whybray's interpretation. He wishes to get rid of the idea of 'a man of Yahweh's counsel', so he claims we should accept the meaning of the reading which Kittel suggests was actually in the original text, *my'yš*. He would render the verse thus chiastically:
    Who meted out the spirit of the Lord,
    and his counsel who taught him?
    I am not competent to decide a matter in a field which is not mine, but I doubt if Dr Whybray's elaborate thesis can be disposed of so simply.
41. Stenning, op. cit., in loc.
42. Talbert, art. cit., pp. 426-7.
43. C. Larcher, *Etudes sur le Livre de la Sagesse* (Paris 1969), p. 364.

44. Scroggs, art. cit., p. 49, goes so far as to say that Wisdom 9.13-18 lies behind 1 Cor. 2.6-16. I do not think this conclusion is necessary. It is enough to say that Paul knew the traditional interpretation of Isaiah 40.13.
45. A. T. S. Goodrick, *The Book of Wisdom*, London 1913.
46. W. O. E. Oesterley, *The Wisdom of Solomon*, London 1917.
47. E. Grafe, 'Das Verhältniss der paulischen Schriften zur Sapientia Salomonis', in *Theologische Abhandlungen*, ed. C. Weizsäcker (Freiburg 1892), pp. 251-86.
48. The verb was not apparently used in Hiph'il. Koehler-Baumgartner emend both the passages in which the Hiph'il occurs, this one and Amos 9.10.
49. Compare the reverse effect in 1 Cor. 2.9, where we suggested that *hētoimasen* might be a translation of *yĕ'ăśeh*.
50. Quoted in S-B, sub Rom. 11.35.
51. See W. L. Knox, op. cit., p. 118n.
52. E. Dhorme, *A Commentary on the Book of Job*, Eng. trans., London 1967, of French edn, Paris 1926.
53. G. Ewald, *Commentary on the Book of Job*, Eng. trans., London 1882.
54. M. H. Pope, *Job* (The Anchor Bible, New York 1965), pp. 277-8, 281.
55. S. R. Driver and G. B. Gray, *A Critical and Exegetical Commentary on the Book of Job*, Edinburgh 1921.
56. G. Hölscher, *Das Buch Hiob*, Tübingen 1952.
57. G. Fohrer, *Das Buch Hiob*, Gütersloh 1963.
58. A. Weiser, *Das Buch Hiob*, Göttingen 1963.
59. W. G. Braude, *Pesikta Rabbati*, Piska 25.2, p. 514.
60. W. G. Braude and I. Kapstein, *Pesikta de Rab Kahana* (London 1975), Piska 9.2, p. 173. This compilation was made sometime in the fifth century A.D. It is earlier than the *Pesikta Rabbati*. Most of the material cannot be dated earlier than the fourth century but some of it goes back much earlier.
61. R. Jeremiah reads *my pa'al 'ēl*, taking the sense 'who has worked together with God?' instead of the MT *māh pā'al 'ēl*.
62. As we have noted above, three of these four instances depend on a conjectural restoration of the Hebrew text; but it is a very probable conjecture. The peculiarity of the LXX's rendering is thrown into relief by the translations of both Aquila and Symmachus for verse 13a; Aquila offers τίς ἐσταθμήσατο πνεῦμα κυρίου; and Symmachus τίς ἡτοίμασε πνεῦμα κυρίου;

Notes to pages 91-95

63. We may surely dismiss the theoretical possibility that the texts were already coupled in Christian tradition when Paul used them. The same objections would apply to this hypothesis as apply to the suggestion that it was Paul who united them.
64. See Hengel, *The Son of God*, ch. 5, III and ch. 6.
65. Admittedly the LXX has translated *peleʾ ywʿēṣ* with the difficult phrase μεγάλης βουλῆς ἄγγελος, but Aquila offers θαυμαστὸς σύμβουλος. The verse is numbered 9.6 in the EVV.
66. It is a great pity that the recently discovered fragment of a *Targum on Job* does not cover this verse.
67. See my comment on this passage in my book already referred to: *Studies in Paul's Technique and Theology*, pp. 149-50; and see pp. 241ff.
68. It may be that Paul only envisages an 'economic' identity of Christ and the Spirit here, as is ably argued by Ingo Hermann *à propos* 2 Cor. 3.17-18. See his book *Kyrios und Pneuma*, Munich 1961.
69. See *Studies in Paul's Technique and Theology*, pp. 166-8.
70. This statement can be amply illustrated from the documents of Gnosticism. Thus in the *Gospel of Truth*, 16.36 the *Logos* is immanent in the *Nous* of the Father (see also 19.37). In 37.7 Ménard translates [speaking of the words of the Father]: 'Alors qu'elles étaient dans la Profondeur (*bathos*) de Sa Pensée, le Verbe (*Logos*) qui a procédé le premier les a manifesté, joint à l'Intelligence (*nous*) qui profère le Verbe (*Logos*) unique dans Sa Grâce (*charis*) silencieuse.' According to Irenaeus in Basilides' system *Nous* is the first emanation from the Father and *Logos* the next from *Nous* (Foerster, op. cit., vol. I, pp. 59-60). In the Ophite system, according to Irenaeus *Nous* is the product of Ialdaboth's desire. Ialdaboth himself is called 'a ruling *Logos* of pure *Nous*' (Foerster, op. cit., pp. 88-9, 97). Among the Barbelognostics, says Irenaeus, *Nous* is created to be a helper to Christ, and is subsequently united with *Prognosis* (ibid., p. 104). Cf. also *Apocryphon of John*, 31.10-2 (Foerster, p. 109). Clement of Alexandria in his *Excerpta ex Theodoto* gives an account of how the Valentinians expound John 1.1;1.18. They say that the *Logos* is in *Nous*, hence the *Logos* is 'in the Father', i.e. *Nous* is anterior to *Logos* (ibid., p. 223). Hippolytus, quoting the *Megale Apophasis* ascribed to Simon of Gitta, says that according to this work there are two offshoots of all the aeons. One of them is 'the mind of the universe'. He also quotes a Naassene hymn beginning with the words: 'First-born*Nous* was the law that engendered all' (ibid., pp. 259, 282). But it is the *Poimandres* that gives the greatest attention to *Nous*. Poimandres himself is described as 'the *Nous* of the Absolute'. He is '*Nous* your God', and from *Nous*

Notes to page 96

came forth the luminous *Logos*. *Nous* in fact is the Father-God. But *Nous* in time brought forth another *Nous*, the Demiurge. Man has *Nous* in himself and hence can recognize *Nous* (see Foerster, pp. 329, 330, 332). In the *Letter of Eugnostos* 73 the Father of All is identified with *Nous*. There also occurs in this work a being called *Archē*. The *Archē* reveals 'an immortal bisexual man', his masculine name is 'the perfect [*Nous*]' (ibid., vol. II, pp. 28, 30). Compare also Colpe, op. cit., pp. 12-13.

71. Very likely *pneumatikoi-psuchikoi* for instance.

After my ms. had been sent to the publisher, an article by K. Berger called 'Zur Discussion über die Herkunft von I Kor. ii.9' appeared in *NTS* (Jan. 1978), pp. 270ff. In this Dr Berger argues that the citation in 1 Cor. 2.9 originated in an apocryphal work, quoting extensively from Jewish and Christian literature. He only cites two allegedly purely Jewish works in which the citation is found, besides the reference in Pseudo-Philo which I have dealt with above. These are the *Ethiopian Ezra Apocalypse* and the *Syrian Daniel Apocalypse*. The latter I have not been able to identify, but I have examined the former. It is published in Ethiopic with a French translation by J. Halévy in *Te'azaza Sanbat* (Bibliothèque de l'Ecole des Hautes Etudes, Sources Historiques et Philosophiques, Fasc. 137, Paris 1902). Halévy found the ms. which contains it among the Falasha Jews in 1867; he makes no attempt to date it. He does, however, claim that it is to be divided in two parts (the division comes at the beginning of para. 3 on p. 183 of Halévy's translation). The first part he regards as wholly Jewish; the second part he describes thus: 'It is visibly of Christian origin, but expurgated to a large degree of dogmas contrary to Jewish belief' (p. xix, my translation). The citation occurs in the first half. It does not coincide exactly with Paul's version, and it ends thus: 'Voilà ce que Dieu a destiné à ses élus qui l'auront aimé' (p. 180). It seems to me that Halévy's division of the work into two parts is arbitrary. It appears to be quite uniform: both Jewish and Christian elements occur in both parts. Thus on p. 179, which belongs to the purely Jewish part in Halévy's reckoning, we have an echo of Matthew 25.32-3: 'On that day the angels of destruction will come, who will separate the sinners from the righteous as the shepherd separates the sheep from the goats, placing the sheep on his right and the goats on his left' (my translation of Halévy's French). Similarly there are several references to 'our Lord' in Halévy's 'second' part (see pp. 185, 186, 192). On p. 195 there is an echo of Revelation 11, the episode of the two witnesses. But this 'second' part contains plenty of Jewish material as well; see pp. 186-7, 194. I conclude therefore that the *Ethiopic Ezra Apocalypse* cannot be regarded as an independent Jewish witness to this citation. The form of the citation is influenced, I believe, both by 1 Cor. 2.9 and by the same citation as it occurs in II Clement 14, 5.

CHAPTER 3
John 14-18 and Exodus 34

1. B. F. Westcott, *The Gospel according to St John*, London 1908.
2. H. J. Holtzmann, *Evangelium, Briefe, und Offenbarung des Johannes*, Hand-Comm. z. NT, Tübingen 1908.
3. M.-J. Lagrange, *Evangile selon Saint Jean*, 7th edn, Paris 1948.
4. E. Hoskyns, *The Fourth Gospel*, 2nd edn, London 1947.
5. C. K. Barrett, *The Gospel according to St John*, London 1955.
6. M.-E. Boismard, *Le Prologue de Saint Jean* (Paris 1953), pp. 69ff. I have referred to this work in my book *Grace and Truth* (London 1975), p. 113.
7. L. J. Kuyper, 'Grace and Truth: an Old Testament description of God and its use in the Johannine Gospel', in *The Reformed Review* (September 1962), xvi, no. i.
8. R. Schnackenburg, *The Gospel according to St John*, Eng. trans. New York and London 1968 of German edn of 1965.
9. R. E. Brown, *The Gospel according to John*, Anchor Bible: New York 1966.
10. J. N. Sanders, *The Gospel according to St John*, London 1968.
11. B. Lindars, *The Gospel of John*, New Century Bible: London 1972.
12. S-B II.
13. J. H. Bernard, *A Critical and Exegetical Commentary on the Gospel according to Saint John*, 1, Edinburgh 1928.
14. C. H. Dodd, *The Interpretation of the Fourth Gospel* (Cambridge 1953), pp. 82, 175-6.
15. R. H. Lightfoot, *St John's Gospel, a commentary*, Oxford 1956.
16. A. Schlatter, *Der Evangelist Johannes*, 3rd edn (Stuttgart 1960), pp. 14 ff.
17. R. H. Strachan, *The Fourth Gospel: its significance and environment*, 3rd edn (London 1941), p. 14.
18. A. Loisy, *Le Quatrième Evangile* (Paris 1903), p. 188n, my translation.
19. R. Bultmann, *Das Evangelium des Johannes*, 10th edn (Göttingen 1962), p. 50n.
20. John Marsh, *Saint John*, London 1968.
21. E. E. Ellis and E. Grässer, eds., *Jesus und Paulus*, article '*Kharis* paulinienne et *kharis* johannique' (Göttingen 1975), pp. 256-82. Since the publication of this article I have been in correspondence with Prof. de la Potterie, and he has convinced me that I did him an injustice in accusing him of holding the 'correspondence' theory about the phrase *kharin anti kharitos*, as I did in the original article. For this I wish to apologize.

22. R. H. Charles, 'Ecclesiasticus', in R. H. Charles, ed., *The Apocrypha and Pseudepigrapha of the Old Testament*, 1, Oxford 1913.
23. F. Field, ed., *Origenis Hexaplorum Quae Supersunt*, 2 vols.; '*mwnh* is merely a variant of '*mt*.
24. This information is available in C. H. Dodd, op. cit., p. 175n; and also in Schnackenburg's commentary on John 1.14. De la Potterie seems to have missed both these references.
25. J. A. Montgomery, 'Hebrew *Hesed* and Greek *Charis*', in *HTR* xxxii (1939), pp. 97-107. He adds that *ḥsd* is the rendering of *kharis* in John 1.14, 17 in the Hebrew version of the NT translated by Franz Delitzsch.
26. M. Black, 'Does an Aramaic Tradition underlie John 1.16?', in *JTS* 42 (1941), pp. 69-70.
27. N. Glueck, *Hesed in the Bible* (Cincinnati, 1967; dissertation 1927), p. 72. As long ago as 1892 a correspondent writing to the *Expository Times* suggested that the phrase might mean 'the true grace or power'! (W. S. Curzon-Siggers, 'Grace and Truth', in *ET* iv (1892-3), p. 480.)
28. See Holtzmann, loc. cit.
29. E.g. A. E. Brooke, *The Johannine Epistles*, Edinburgh, 1912; R. R. Williams, *The Letters of John and James*, Cambridge 1965.
30. R. Bultmann, *The Johannine Epistles*, Eng. trans., Philadelphia, 1973, of the German edn of 1967. See also Robert W. Funk, 'The Form and Structure of II John and III John', in *JBL* lxxxv (1967), pp. 424-30, where he maintains that the author's address here corresponds to common literary form.
31. R. Bergmeier, 'Zum Verfasser-Problem des II und III Johannesbriefs', in *ZNTW* lvii-lviii (1966-7), pp. 93-100.
32. For a relative disparagement of the theological standard of the Johannine Epistles as a whole see also J. L. Houlden, *A Commentary on the Johannine Epistles*, London 1973.
33. Bultmann, op. cit., pp. 54-5. Schnackenburg seems to be adopting essentially the same view when he says that John is offering a criticism of contemporary trends in Jewish mysticism.
34. I have elaborated it myself in *Grace and Truth*, pp. 5-7. Compare also D. Eaglesham, *ET* xvi (1904-5), p. 428: 'It must follow therefore that, when the grace of God came to men in olden times "the only begotten Son, which is in the bosom of the Father, he declared him".'
35. This point is well made by S. Bartina in an article in *Biblica* (1968), xlix, fasc. 1, pp. 89-96, called 'La vida como historia en el prólogo al cuarto evangelio'. He relates the Prologue to the rest of the Gospel thus: "The historical life of Jesus (the rest of the Gospel) is an explanatory demonstration ... of the firmest

goodwill (*tēs kharitos kai tēs alētheias* i.14,17) towards men ... from the side of God the Father ... realized through Jesus Christ ... who is the Word incarnate ... and God only begotten' (my translation of the Spanish).

36. Because de la Potterie will not allow any reference to Exodus 34, he has to conclude that there was some sort of revelation in the Law, since χάριν ἀντὶ χάριτος must be understood in his view as referring to Christ in place of the Law (see op. cit., p. 277).
37. It can indeed be questioned whether χάριν ἀντὶ χάριτος can bear the meaning 'grace upon grace'. M. Bover in an article 'χάριν ἀντὶ χάριτος in *Biblica* vi (1925) pp. 454-60, has put the case against *anti* being the equivalent of *epi* very clearly and thoroughly. See also Adhémar d'Ales, 'χάριν ἀντὶ χάριτος (Joann. i.16)', in *Recherches de science religieuse* ix (1919) pp. 384-6, and Paul Jouon, 'Jean 1.16: 'χάριν ἀντὶ χάριτος, in *RSR* xxii (1932) p. 206 for further defence of this view. All these three adopt a 'correspondence' solution to the problem.
38. See I. Lévi, *The Hebrew Text of the Book of Ecclesiasticus* (Leiden 1969), p. 58. Also R. H. Charles, op. cit., 1, in loc.
39. For a good parallel see Rom. 11.34-5, where Paul quotes what was originally a rhetorical question from Isaiah, but obviously regards it as answered by the event of Christ.
40. Burton Lee Mack, *Logos und Sophia* (Göttingen 1975), pp. 22-32.
41. Op. cit., p. 26, my translation.
42. See W. G. Braude, ed. and trans., *Pesikta Rabbati*, 2 vols. (New Haven and London 1968), 1, pp. 113-14, *Piska* 5.11.
43. The last clause represents the rendering of the LXX. The MT means 'and let them not turn back to folly'.
44. W. Bacher, *Die Agada der Palestinischen Amoraer*, 3 vols. (Hildesheim 1965), iii, p. 194.
45. *Pesikta Rabbati*, i, pp. 343-4; see also pp. 703, 821.
46. A. Guilding, *The Fourth Gospel and Jewish Worship*, Oxford 1960. She devotes a whole chapter to the Hanukkah, but does not mention our passage.

CHAPTER 4

The Theme of Christ as the True Temple in the Fourth Gospel

1. As does Michaelis, for example, who says that the pericope begins at 1.45. See W. Michaelis, 'John 1.51, Gen. 28.12 und das Menschensohn Problem', in *Theologische Literaturzeitung* 85 (Aug. 1960), p. 566.

Notes to page 111

2. J. H. Bernard, who gives plenty of information about the rabbinic exaltation of the role of Jacob at Bethel, is nevertheless quite right when he insists that Jacob here is not a type of Christ. See J. H. Bernard, *A Critical and Exegetical Commentary on the Gospel according to St John*, Edinburgh 1928, in loc. See also S. Pancaro, 'The Relationship of the Church to Israel in the Gospel of John', in *NTS* 21 (1974-5) pp. 296-405, where he points out that in the Fourth Gospel 'Israel' and 'Israelite' are always used in a positive sense. Nathanael, he says, is a true Israelite because he recognizes Jesus and sees him as the one of whom Moses and the prophets wrote. R. Schnackenburg (*The Gospel according to St John*, Eng. trans. London 1968 of German original, Freiburg 1965, in loc.) agrees that Nathanael here takes the place of Jacob.

3. It may even be that the author of the Fourth Gospel saw something significant in the top of the ladder itself: in Gen. 28.12 'the top of it reached to heaven'; one Greek ms. translates *hē archē hēptato tou ouranou*, as compared with the LXX *hē kepalē aphikneito eis ton ouranon*. The MT for 'the top' is *rō'šw*. The Word was *en tē/i archē/i* and this phrase might have meant to John that the Word was in heaven at the time of Jacob's vision.

4. See H. Windisch, 'Angelophanien um den Menschensohn auf Erden: ein Kommentar zu Jon. 1.15', in *ZNTW* 30 (1931), pp. 215-33.

5. See J. C. T. Otto, ed., *Justini Opera Omnia Dialogue* 58.15; 86.17, Jena 1843.

6. The Hebrew is *niṣāb 'ālay*: the Vulgate seems to follow the LXX tradition here with 'et Dominum innixum scalae'.

7. See W. G. Braude, ed., *Midrash on the Psalms*, vol. II, pp. 104-5, in loc. Ps. 91.4-7. Hoskyns shows a strange predilection for this tradition. 'The place of the stone in the ancient story is now taken by Jesus the Son of Man' (see E. C. Hoskyns, *The Fourth Gospel*, London 1947, 2nd edn and compare Justin, *Dialogue* 58.5f).

8. See J. W. E. Etheridge, *The Targum of Onkelos*, etc. in loc., Gen. 28. See also *Tractate Hullin* 91b, pp. 512ff (E. Cashdan, ed., 1948).

9. See R. H. Lightfoot, *St John's Gospel, a Commentary*, Oxford 1956, and C. H. Dodd, *The Interpretation of the Fourth Gospel* (Cambridge 1960), pp. 254ff. Bultmann, who approves the 'double image' theory, sees here Gnostic influence (op. cit., p. 75n). C. K. Barrett thinks John accepts the rabbinic interpretation of *bw* (*The Gospel according to St John*, London 1955, in loc.). So also J. N. Lindars, *The Gospel according to St John*, London 1968, in loc.; R. H. Strachan in *The Fourth Gospel*, London 1944, 3rd edn, supports both theories.

10. See K. G. Kuhn, *Sifre zu Numeri* (Stuttgart 1959), p. 405.
11. See X. Léon-Dufour, 'Le Signe du Temple selon Saint Jean', in *RSR* 39 (1951-2), p. 171: T. Fawcett, *Hebrew Myth and Christian Gospel* (London 1973), p. 218.
12. See W. G. Braude and I. J. Kapstein, eds., *Pesikta de Rab Kahana* (London 1975), pp. 353ff at *Piska* 23.2.
13. See L. Cohn and P. Wendland, eds., *Philonis Alexandri Opera Quae Supersunt*, Berlin 1898; *De Somniis* I, 183f: *De Mig.* 165. See also F. H. Colson and G. H. Whitaker, *Philo, with English Translation*, London and New York 1932.
14. See W. G. Braude, ed., *Pesikta Rabbati* (New Haven and London 1968), vol. II, pp. 594-5, at *Piska* 30.3.
15. R. J. McKelvey, *The New Temple* (Oxford 1969), p. 77.
16. See G. Quispel, 'Nathanael und der Menschensohn (Jon. 1.51)', in *ZNTW* 47 (1956), pp. 281-3.
17. Michaelis, art. cit., pp. 568, 570-71.
18. A. Schlatter, *Der Evangelist Johannes*, Stuttgart 1960, 2nd edn, in loc.
19. G. Reim, *Studien zum Alttestamentlichen Hintergrund des Johannesevangeliums* (Cambridge 1974), pp. 154-5.
20. E. D. Freed, *Old Testament Quotations in the Gospel of John* (Leiden 1965), p. 9.
21. J. N. Sanders, *The Gospel according to St John*, London 1968, in loc.
22. X. Léon-Dufour, 'Le Signe du Temple selon Saint Jean', in *RSR* 39 (1951-2), p. 169. B. Lindars (*New Testament Apologetic*, London 1961, p. 104) is very definite on this point: 'The whole "plot" of the psalm is brought into play by the temple incident, not merely the line which is actually cited.'
23. C. K. Barrett, *The Gospel according to St John*, London 1955, in loc.
24. Midrash on Ps. 119.17 in Braude, vol. 2.
25. H.-J. Lagrange, *Evangile selon Saint Jean*, 3rd edn, Paris 1947.
26. Art. cit., p. 168.
27. Op. cit., p. 78.
28. B. Lindars, *New Testament Apologetic* (London 1961), p. 106.
29. B. Lindars, *The Gospel of John*, London 1972, in loc.
30. Op. cit., pp. 78-9.
31. Art. cit., p. 172.
32. A. M. Dubarle, 'Le Signe du Temple', in *RB* 48 (1939), pp. 21-44.
33. It is verse 8 in the Vulgate. The Targum shows no sign of messianic interpretation here. It renders the phrase with

Notes to pages 119-125

wyytwn ḥmdt kl 'mmy': 'and the desirable things of all the peoples will come' (see A. Sperber, *The Bible in Aramaic*, Leiden 1962, in loc.).

34. H. G. Mitchell, *A Critical and Exegetical Commentary on Haggai, Zechariah, Malachi, and Jonah*, Edinburgh 1912, renders the phrase back into Hebrew as follows: *wšlwm nphš lmhyh lkl ysd lqwmm 't hhykl hzh*. But he does not consider the clause formed part of the original text. Neither the Targum nor the Vulgate shows any sign of knowing the gloss.
35. H. Freedman, ed. (1935), pp. 659, 703-4.
36. A. Mishcon and A. Cohen, eds. (1935), p. 3.
37. R. Schnackenburg, *Das Johannesevangelium*, vol. 2, Freiburg 1971, in loc.
38. In his commentary on the Fourth Gospel referred to above, p. 117, in loc.
39. Op. cit., p. 317.
40. Op. cit., p. 284.

CHAPTER 5
Scriptural Background to the Doctrine of the 'Descensus ad Inferos'

1. See W. Diezinger, 'Unter Toten Freigeworden', in *Nov. Test.* 5 (1962), pp. 268-98.
2. See my *Studies in Paul's Technique and Theology* (London 1974), pp. 30-32.
3. My using the beginning of Psalm 89 in order to illuminate Psalm 88 may seem to need some defence. In fact the rabbis sometimes did this. See *Studies in Paul's Technique and Theology*, p. 37, where I have quoted an example of this in the rabbinic exposition of Psalms 44 and 45.
4. ἰατροί is the LXX's mistranslation of *r'phā'ym* as if it was *rōph 'ym*. The LXX was worried by this word with its overtones of the cult of the dead. Where it does not offer this mistranslation, it renders with γίγαντες (e.g. Gen. 14.5) or γηγενεῖς (e.g. Prov. 2.18); in one passage it offers τίτανες (2 Kingdoms 5.18, 22); occasionally it simply transliterates, e.g. Joshua 18.16.
5. I have included verse 16, because in my treatment of this psalm in my work already referred to (p. 122 and see p. 282, n. 27) I suggested that to an early Christian it would be seen as foreshadowing Christ's crucifixion. The theme of ὑψωθείς (itself probably a mistranslation) is explicitly applied to the crucifixion in the Fourth Gospel.

6. Thus D. R. Kittel (*Die Psalmen*, Leipzig and Erlangen 1922) suggested *hušabty*, Hoph'al of *yšb*, meaning 'I have been made to dwell'. This is followed by H. Schmidt (*Die Psalmen*, Tübingen 1934) and H.-J. Kraus (*Psalmen*, vol. II, Neukirchen 1960). A. Weiser (*The Psalms*, Eng. trans. London 1962 of German edn, Göttingen 1959) comments: 'The meaning is uncertain; perhaps it is better to read *naphshi*.' A. Maillot and A. Lelièvre (*Les Psaumes*, vol. II, Paris 1966) have *ḥophšy* unaltered, but translate it as 'ma couverture'.
7. W. O. E. Oesterley, *The Psalms*, London 1939.
8. H. Gunkel, *Die Psalmen*, Göttingen 1929.
9. The LXX has missed the reference, since it translates *ḥophšy* in Job 3.19 with δεδοικώς; but the Vulgate has grasped the right sense, since it offers 'et servus liber a domino suo'. Aquila also translates *ḥophšy* here with ἐλεύθερος.
10. W. G. Braude, *The Midrash on the Psalms*, vol. II (Yale 1959), p. 81.
11. Op. cit., p. 31.
12. M. Delcor, *Les Hymnes de Qumran* (Paris 1962), p. 210. I quote the Hebrew of III QH, viii, 28-9 from his edition.
13. M. Mansoor, *The Thanksgiving Hymns* (Leiden 1961), p. 156.
14. G. Vermes, *The Dead Sea Scrolls in English* (London, 2nd edn, 1965), p. 178.
15. P. Wernberg-Möller, ed., *The Manual of Discipline*, Leiden 1957; his translation is on p. 26 and his comment is note 49 on p. 41.
16. Vermes, op. cit., p. 77.
17. L. Fazekaš, 'Taufe als Tod in Röm. 6.3f', in *Theologische Zeitschrift* 22 (1966), pp. 305-18.
18. E. Klaar, 'Röm. 6.7 ὁ γὰρ ἀποθανὼν δεδικαίωται ἀπὸ τῆς ἁμαρτίας', in *ZNTW* 59-60 (1968-9), pp. 131-4.
19. I shall be referring to the following works: H. von Soden in *Hand-Commentar z. NT*, vol. III, Freiburg 1891; C. Bigg, *The Epistles of St Peter and St Jude*, Edinburgh 1901; J. A. MacCullagh, *The Harrowing of Hell*, Edinburgh 1930; P. Lundberg, *La Typologie baptismale dans l'Ancienne Eglise*, Leipzig and Uppsala 1942; B. Reicke, *The Disobedient Spirits and Christian Baptism*, Copenhagen 1946; W. Bieder, 'Die Vorstelling von der Höllenfahrt Jesu Christi', no. 19 in *Abhandlungen z. Theologie des A. und N. Testaments*, eds. W. Eichrodt and O. Cullmann, Zürich 1949; E. G. Selwyn, *The First Epistle of St Peter*, 2nd edn, London 1947; F. W. Beare, *The First Epistle of Peter*, Oxford 1947; H. Windisch and H. Preisker, *Die Katholischen Briefe*, 3rd edn, Tübingen 1951; E. Schweizer, '1 Petrus 4.6', in *Theologische Zeitschrift 8* (1952),

pp. 152-4; C. E. B. Cranfield, 'The Interpretation of 1 Peter iii.19 and iv. 6', in *ET* 69 (1957-8), pp. 369-72; K. H. Schelkle, *Die Petrusbriefe; Der Judasbrief*, Freiburg, Basel, Vienna 1961; B. Reicke, *The Epistles of James, Peter and Jude*, New York 1969; W. J. Dalton, *Christ's Proclamation to the Spirits*, Rome 1965; E. Best, *1 Peter*, London 1971; F. C. Synge, '1 Peter 3.18-21', in *ET* 82 (1970-71), p. 311; O. S. Brooks, '1 Peter 3.21 – The Clue to the Literary Structure of the Epistle', in *Nov. Test.* 16 (1974), pp. 290-305. Except in the case of Reicke's work of 1946 and Dalton's book, all references come from the commentary on the passage.

20. G. Friedrich, 'κηρύσσω', in *TWNT* III (Stuttgart 1938), pp. 705ff.

21. To the list of scholars already mentioned we may add the name J. Jeremias. In his article 'ᾅδης' in *TWNT* I (Stuttgart 1933), pp. 149-50, he writes: 'Christ has proclaimed the gospel to the souls in Hades (1 Peter 3.19f; 4.6).' See also G. Bertram, 'φυλακή', in *TWNT* IX (Stuttgart 1973), pp. 239-40, where he describes φυλακή in 3.19 as the 'place of waiting for the departed spirits'. Bieder (op. cit., pp. 106-7, 116-17, 119) suggests that we do not know where the author of 1 Peter thought the preaching took place.

22. For convenience I quote from J. W. Etheridge, *The Targums of Onkelos and Jonathan ben Uzziel* on the Pentateuch (new edn, New York 1968), p. 654. Even before the discovery of the Neofiti ms. this passage was available, but no scholar had used it to illuminate Rom. 10.6-8. Bieder (op. cit., pp. 71-5) denies that there is any reference to the *descensus* here, but he was not aware of the interpretation in the *Targum of Palestine*.

23. R. Le Déaut, *Liturgie juive et Nouveau Testament* (Rome 1965), p. 45, my translation.

24. M. McNamara, *The New Testament and the Palestinian Targum to the Pentateuch* (Rome 1966), pp. 75-7.

25. A. M. Goldberg, 'Torah aus der Unterwelt?', in *Biblische Zeitschrift* 14 (1970), pp. 127-31.

26. R. Rubinkiewicz, 'Ps. LXVIII 19 (=Eph. iv. 8). Another Textual Tradition or Targum?', in *Nov. Test.* 17 (1975), pp. 219-24. See also McNamara, op. cit., p. 80 and Le Déaut, op. cit., p. 46. Symmachus offers ἠγόρασας, which would certainly be susceptible of a Christian interpretation.

27. C. Hodge, *A Commentary on the Epistle to the Ephesians*, London 1964 edn of 1856 original. The LXX renders this phrase with τὰ θεμέλια τῆς γῆς, very unlike what we meet in Eph. 4.9. But Aquila has κατώτατα here.

28. H. von Soden, *Hand-Commentar z. NT*, vol. III, Freiburg 1891. Of course if the reading πρῶτον after κατέβη is correct, it greatly strengthens the case for a *descensus*. But it is probably

a gloss, though even as such it indicates how an early copyist understood the passage.

29. J. K. Abbott, *The Epistle to the Ephesians and the Colossians*, Edinburgh 1909.
30. G. B. Caird, 'The Descent of Christ in Ephesians 4.7-11', in *Studia Evangelica* II, ed. F. L. Cross (Berlin 1964), pp. 535-45.
31. E. Bröse, 'Der Descensus ad Inferos Eph. 4.8-10', in *Neue Kirchliche Zeitschrift* 9 (Erlangen 1898), pp. 447-55.
32. Op. cit., p. 321.
33. F. Büchsel, 'κάτω', in *TWNT* III (Stuttgart 1938), p. 641.
34. Op. cit., p. 81n.
35. See R. Bultmann, *Theology of the NT*, vol. 1 (Eng. trans., London 1952), p. 176. See also Bieder, op. cit., pp. 88-9; B. Lindars, *New Testament Apologetic* (London 1961), p. 53. Bultmann of course believes that the same Gnostic consideration influenced Paul. He has ignored Paul's reference to the *descensus* in Rom. 10.6-8. It is most unfortunate that the New English Bible has committed itself to the view that there is no reference to the *descensus* in 4.9 with its translation 'to the lowest level, down to the very earth'.
36. Dibelius-Greeven also take the view that verse 9 refers to the incarnation not to a *descensus*, but without producing any new arguments. See M. Dibelius, ed. H. Greeven, *An die Kolosser, Epheser, An Philemon*, Tübingen 1953.
37. S-B, in loc. Eph. 4.7-10.
38. *Tractate Shabbath*, ed. H. Freedman, p. 423; W. G. Braude, ed., *Pesikta Rabbati*, vol. 1 (New Haven and London 1968), pp. 405-9. See also *Shabbath* 88b.
39. *Tractate Hagiga*, ed. D. H. M. Lazarus, 12b (1938), p. 72.
40. Vol. I, p. 411.
41. B. Noack, 'Das Zitat in Ephes. 5.14', in *Studia Theologica* 5-6 (1951-2), pp. 52-64.
42. See R. P. C. Hanson, *Allegory and Event* (London 1959), p. 77n. I cannot, however, follow him in his suggestion that $yt'\check{s}t$ ('will give a thought to us') in Jonah 1.6 was misunderstood as coming from the verb '$\check{s}t$, 'to be smooth or shiny', and thus gave the sense 'perhaps thy God will shine upon us'. It is very doubtful whether there ever was a verb '$\check{s}t$ meaning 'to be shiny'. It only occurs once, in Jer. 5.28, where W. Rudolph in Kittel's *Biblica Hebraica* suggests emending it. Koehler-Baumgartner regard it as corrupt. The LXX simply omits the verb. It is extremely unlikely that anyone could mistake the verb in Jonah 1.6 for this.

43. LXX 87.6. It is remarkable that in two of the passages which we have quoted here, Jonah 1.5 and Ps. 88.5, we find exceptions to Noack's rule that generally the LXX translates škb with κοιμᾶσθαι and yšb with καθεύδειν (Noack, p. 59).
44. Commentators on Eph. 5.14 are not very helpful on the problem of the origin of the quotation. All are agreed that it is a liturgical formula or hymn, and most that it refers to baptism. Dibelius-Greeven deny that it is derived from Isa. 60.1, but they cite as a parallel Rom. 6.3-11, which certainly connects it with the pattern we are seeking to trace.
45. A. Oepke, 'λούω', in *TWNT* IV (Stuttgart 1942), p. 306. J. L. Houlden, *Paul's Letters from Prison*, London 1970.
46. C. Gore, *St Paul's Epistle to the Ephesians*, London 1902. F. Hauck, 'κάθαρος', in *TWNT* III (Stuttgart 1938), p. 429. R. Kittel, 'λέγω and Cognates', in *TWNT* IV, p. 117.
47. But the Greek here is λόγος, not ῥῆμα. J. Armitage Robinson actually makes a cross-reference to Rom. 10.6f.
48. Jeremias concludes that both the Lukan explanation which makes the sign consist in the preaching to the Ninevites and the Matthaean explanation in Matt. 12.40 are additions by the early Church; but believes that Jesus did refer to the sign of Jonah, meaning by this his own death and subsequent resurrection. This is not inconsistent with the Markan account, which makes Jesus simply refuse a sign altogether because 'God gives no sign that is not associated with the person of Jesus and with scandal' (see article "*Ιωνᾶς*', in *TWNT* III, pp. 410ff). Seidelin says that the logion could be authentic, but that we cannot go beyond a 'could be' (see P. Seidelin, 'Das Jonaszeichen', in *Studia Theologica* 5 (Lund 1951), pp. 118-131).
49. O. Linton, 'The Demand for a Sign from Heaven', in *Studia Theologica* 19-20 (1965-6), pp. 112-29.
50. F. D. Meyer, 'The Gentile mission in Q', in *JBL* 89 (1970), pp. 405-17. Compare also Bultmann's conclusion about Matt. 12.40: 'It seems clear to me that the interpretation of the sign of Jonah in terms of the death and resurrection of Jesus is a quite secondary formulation of the Church.' See R. Bultmann, *History of the Synoptic Tradition* (Eng. trans. Oxford 1968 of German 2nd edn of 1931), p. 118.
51. H. J. Holtzmann, *Die Synoptiker*, vol. I, Freiburg 1889; A. H. McNeill, *The Gospel according to St Matthew*, 2nd edn, London 1938; K. Stendahl, *The School of St Matthew*, 2nd edn, Lund 1967; L. Cope, 'Matthew 12.40 and the Synoptic Source Question', in *JBL* 92 (1973), p. 115. The Justin reference is *Dialogue* 107.2 (see J. C. T. Otto, ed., *S. Justini Opera* (Jena 1843), vol. II, p. 358).
52. H. B. Green, *The Gospel according to Matthew*, London 1975.

53. E. Klostermann, *Das Matthausevangelium*, Tübingen 1971. By contrast Bieder (op. cit., p. 42) denies a reference to the *descensus* here. But he has not taken the rabbinic evidence into account.
54. See *Tractate Sanhedrin* 89b, ed. H. Freedman (1935), p. 593.
55. Jeremias, op. cit., p. 411; Seidelin, op. cit., p. 124.
56. R. A. Rayner, 'The Story of Jonah, An Easter Story', in *Evangelical Quarterly* 22 (1950), pp. 123-5.
57. E. J. Bickerman, 'Les deux erreurs du prophète Jonas', in *Revue d'Histoire et de Philosophie religieuses* 45 (1965), p. 239. See also P. D. Meyer, art. cit., p. 408.
58. The earliest post-canonical indication that Jonah is regarded as one of the prophets occurs in *Sira* 49.10, where the author speaks of 'the twelve prophets', though he does not mention Jonah by name. Bewer is mistaken in citing Tobit 14.4 as a pre-Christian reference to Jonah's activity (J. A. Bewer, *The Book of Jonah*, Edinburgh 1912). D. C. Simpson in his commentary on Tobit (in R. H. Charles, *The Apocrypha and Pseudepigrapha of the OT*, London 1913) points out that Codex Sinaiticus at this point and at 14.8 has no reference to Jonah: in it Tobit 14.4 refers to Nahum as a prophet who foretold doom on Nineveh. The two codices Vaticanus and Alexandrinus were, he says, edited by Jews in the Antonine period, when Jonah was substituted for Nahum. No doubt they did it in order to emphasize Jonah as the prophet of doom upon the Gentiles rather than Jonah as the type of Christ risen from the dead.
59. *Tractate 'Erubin*, ed. W. Slotki (1938), 19a, pp. 130ff.
60. *Midrash on Ps. 26.9*, Braude, vol. I, p. 363. Seidelin refers to this tradition, p. 128.
61. C. S. C. Williams in *The Acts of the Apostles*, London 1957, points out that the Aramaic *ḥabalayya* bears exactly the same ambiguity as the Hebrew *ḥblym*.
62. See R. B. Rackham, *The Acts of the Apostles*, 4th edn, London 1909; H. J. Holtzmann, *Hand-Commentar z. NT*, vol. I, Freiburg 1889; G. Bertram, 'ὠδίν, etc.', in *TWNT*, vol. IX (1973), pp. 668ff; W. H. Cox, 'The Pains of Death (Acts ii. 24)', in *The Interpreter* 8 (1911-12), pp. 330-31.
63. E. Haechen, *Die Apostelgeschichte*, 13th edn, Göttingen 1961; H. Conzelmann, *Die Apostelgeschichte*, Tübingen 1963.
64. C. C. Torrey, *The Composition and Date of Acts* (Cambridge, Mass. 1916), pp. 28-9.
65. F. J. Foakes-Jackson and K. Lake, *The Beginnings of Christianity*, Part I, *The Acts of the Apostles*, vol. IV, London 1933.
66. M. Wilcox, *The Semitisms of Acts* (Oxford 1965), p. 48.

Notes to pages 153-154

67. R. P. C. Hanson, *The Acts*, Oxford 1967.
68. The MT of Job 39.3b runs *ḥēblēyhem t'šalaḥnāh*: literally, 'they send forth their birth-pangs'. The passage refers to the wild goats; if the phrase means anything, it means that the dams 'deliver themselves of their young'. The LXX (39.2b) translates this with ὠδῖνας δὲ αὐτῶν ἔλυσας, which gives the sense that God has put an end to their labour by delivering their young. Most editors agree that *ḥblym* here means 'embryos, foetuses', not 'birth-pangs', a meaning which it bears in Arabic. The newly discovered Targum on Job offers *wḥblyhn twšr*, which the editors translate with 'et fais-tu sortir leurs porteés?' (J. P. M. Van der Ploeg and A. S. Van der Woude, eds., *Le Targum de Job de la Grotte XI de Qumran* (Leiden 1971), pp. 74-5). All editors agree that *ḥblym* here is a poetical way of describing what is brought forth, and many are the parallels quoted from classical literature: sic E. J. Kissane, *The Book of Job*, Dublin 1939; E. S. C. Gibson, *The Book of Job*, London 1899; S. R. Driver and G. B. Gray, *A Critical and Exegetical Commentary on the Book of Job*, Edinburgh 1921; E. Dhorme, *A Commentary on the Book of Job*, Eng. trans. London 1967 of French edn, Paris 1926; G. Hölscher, *Das Buch Hiob*, Tübingen 1952; G. Fohrer, *Das Buch Hiob*, Gütersloh 1963; A. Weiser, *Das Buch Hiob*, Göttingen 1963; H. H. Rowley, *Job*, The Century Bible, London 1970. Dhorme points out that Theodotion rendered the phrase with ὠδῖνας δὲ αὐτῶν ἐξαποστελεῖς, which has actually been encapsulated in the LXX as 39.3b. M. H. Pope (The Anchor Bible, New York 1965) well remarks: 'Because this word in Hebrew usually designates the pains of childbirth, this line has been misunderstood as depicting painful delivery rather than the easy and rapid parturition normal for wild animals.' We may well agree with Torrey's comment: 'This grotesquely confused passage is as far removed as possible from the ideas with which the author of Acts is here dealing' (op. cit., p. 28).
69. The problem is neatly outlined in two articles in *The Bible Translator*: R. G. Bratcher ('Having loosed the pangs of death' 10 (1959), pp. 18-70) and J. L. Swellengrebel (no title, under 'Readers' Corner' 10 (1959), pp. 127-8). The former puts the problem very clearly and concludes that we must translate the phrase with 'unfastening the bonds of death'. The latter argues that 'St Peter has accepted the LXX text on its face value'. This does not explain why the blessed saint had to use λύσας!
70. See *Tractate Baba Bathra* 17a, eds. M. Simon and W. Slotki (1935), p. 86.
71. J. Bonsirven, *Textes rabbiniques des deux premiers siècles chrétiens* (Rome 1955), p. 520.

Notes to pages 154-159

72. *Midrash on Psalm 45*, verse 2, vol. I.
73. *Midrash on Psalm 16.10*, vol. I.
74. Op. cit., p. 206.
75. Holtzmann makes this point. Bieder (op. cit., pp. 67-8) says that this psalm quotation betrays the same emphasis on the glorified flesh of Christ as we find in Luke's narrative of the resurrection appearances, and is therefore Luke's own composition. But he agrees that the continuous element between the dying and risen Christ is his flesh.
76. Ps. 16.10 is cited again in Paul's speech in Pisidian Antioch in 13.35. It occurs in a row of other citations, all probably *testimonia* used by early Christian preachers.
77. I would therefore disagree with Caird's claim (see above, p.138) that this passage shows a later development of the doctrine found in Eph. 4.8-10.
78. Art. cit., p. 372.

CHAPTER 6
John's Technique in Using Scripture

1. See Chapter 4, nn. 19, 20.
2. See G. Reim, op. cit., pp. 206ff.
3. See H. Windisch, art. cit.
4. B. Lindars, *New Testament Apologetic*, p. 104.
5. See above Chapter 4, p. 110.
6. Isaiah 53.1, cited in 12.38, is quoted in Romans 10.16; Isaiah 6.10, cited in 12.40, is quoted in all the Synoptists and in Acts 28.26f.; Psalm 41.9, cited in 13.18, is echoed in Mark 14.18 (it is also cited in the *Hodayoth*; see 1 QH v. 23-4). There is no specific Scripture reference in 17.12, but it was generally held in the early Church that Judas's betrayal was foretold in Scripture; see Acts 1.20. Psalm 22.18, cited in 19.24, is referred to by all three Synoptists in this passion narrative; Psalm 69.21, cited in 19.28-9, is echoed in Matthew and Mark. Zechariah 12.10, cited in 19.37, is echoed in Matthew 24.30, and quoted in Revelation 1.7.
7. Psalm 69.4 is a more likely source than Psalm 35.19, because Psalm 69 is a favourite messianic psalm with NT writers, and John himself quotes from it also in 2.17 and 19.29. Freed agrees with this view (op. cit., p. 95). So also Reim, op. cit., p. 160.
8. Freed (op. cit., p. 114) with his usual caution describes this conclusion as 'enticing, if not convincing'.
9. Reim, who believes the citation in 19.30 comes from Numbers 9.12, concludes that John got this *testimonium* from his tradition (op. cit., p. 108).

Notes to pages 160-171

10. See Freed, op. cit., pp. 18-20. Reim, following his special theory, assigns this citation to John's 'Wisdom source' (op. cit., p. 164).
11. *Pesikta Rabbati*, ed. W. G. Braude, *Piska* 32, 3/4, p. 626.
12. Eds. W. G. Braude and I. J. Kapstein (London 1975), *Piska* 12.21, p. 243.
13. Freed, op. cit., p. 37.
14. Reim, op. cit., pp. 71-82. Freed agrees that both the manna story and the story of the stricken rock may be in the background here (p. 36).
15. Freed writes: 'No passage satisfies *ek tēs koilias*.' Later he quotes Ps. 40.11, but strangely ignores 40.10 (pp. 24-5).
16. Bernard sees an echo of Psalm 40 here.
17. See the article 'John's citation of Psalm LXXXII' in *NTS* 11 (1965), pp. 158-62; and 'John's citation of Psalm LXXXII Reconsidered', in *NTS* 13 (1966), pp. 363-7.
18. See my *Studies in the Pastoral Epistles* (London 1968), pp. 12-14.
19. See my *Jesus Christ in the OT* (London 1965), pp. 123-6 and *Grace and Truth* (London 1975), pp. 68-9.
20. See *Jesus Christ in the OT*, pp. 48-82.
21. See my article 'The OT Background to the Raising of Lazarus', in *Studia Evangelica* (Berlin 1973), pp. 252-5. I am glad to see that my friend Prof. Max Wilcox agrees that 11.41 is a citation of Ps. 118.21, though he does not agree with my interpretation of how John uses it; see his article 'The Prayer of Jesus in John XI, 416-42' in *NTS* (Oct. 1977), p. 130.
22. See above, art. cit.
23. The MT of these four lines is as follows:
    w'hw' l'qibārōt ywbāl
    w'ᶜal gādyš yšqwd
    wa'aḥrāyw kol-'ādām yimšwk
    wl' pānāyw 'ēyn mispar.
    Instead of the LXX *epi sorō/i* Aquila and Theodotion have *epi thēmōnias*, 'on heaps'.
24. C. H. Dodd, *The Interpretation of the Fourth Gospel* (Cambridge 1960), p. 361.
25. A. Schlatter, *Der Evangelist Johannes*, 3rd edn, Stuttgart 1970, in loc.
26. R. Bultmann, *Johannes Evangelium*, pp. 320-21.
27. See *Tractate Sanhedrin*, ed. H. Freedman (1935), 109a, p. 750.
28. Unfortunately Job 21.32-3 is not represented in the fragmentary *Targum on Job* found in Qumran.
29. See my *Studies in Paul's Technique and Theology* (London 1974), pp. 32ff.

30. See A. Feuillet, *Le Christ Sagesse de Dieu* (Paris 1966), pp. 150ff, 336-7, etc. We could also claim that the author of Hebrews does the same; cf. his use of *apaugasma* in Heb. 1.3, probably taken from Wisdom 7.26.
31. This is favoured by F. N. Davey editing E. Hoskyns's *The Fourth Gospel*, 2nd edn, London 1947, in loc.
32. See A. Guilding, *The Fourth Gospel and Jewish Worship*, Oxford 1960.
33. If I am right in pointing to several places where John has used the LXX text as his source, this would argue against a synagogue origin for any scriptural scheme.
34. But see my discussion of this and similar passages in *Studies in Paul's Technique and Theology*, pp. 126ff, 173.
35. I have not attempted a completely exhaustive examination of John's scriptural allusions in this chapter. For example, I have not thought it worth while to refer to 7.42, as I do not believe that John is engaged in interpreting Scripture there.

Bibliography

BOOKS REFERRED TO IN THE TEXT

Abbott, T. K. *The Epistle to the Ephesians and Colossians*. Edinburgh 1909.
Allo, E. B. *Première Epître de Paul aux Corinthiens*. Paris 1956.
Altaner, B. *Patrologie*. Freiburg 1951.
Amsler, S. *L'Ancien Testament dans l'Eglise*. Neuchâtel 1960.
Bacher, W. *Die Agada der Palestinischen Amoräer*. Hildesheim 1965.
Bachmann, P. *Der Erste Brief des Paulus an die Korinther*, ed. E. Stauffer, Leipzig 1947.
Barrett, C. K. *The Gospel according to St John*. London 1955.
—*The First Epistle to the Corinthians*. London 1969.
Barth, K. *The Epistle to the Romans*. Eng. tr. London 1933 of 6th German edn.
Baumgartner, W. see Koehler, L.
Beare, F. W. *The First Epistle of Peter*. Oxford 1947.
Bernard, J. H. *A Critical and Exegetical Commentary on the Gospel according to St John*. Edinburgh 1928.
Best, E. *1 Peter*. London 1971.
Bewer, J. A. *The Book of Jonah*. Edinburgh 1912.
Bieder, W. *Die Vorstellung von der Höllenfahrt Jesu Christi*. Zürich 1949.
Bigg, C. *The Epistles of St Peter and St Jude*. Edinburgh 1901.
Böhlig, A. *Mysterion und Wahreit*. Leiden 1968.
—ed., with Wisse, F., Nag Hammadi Codices III, 2 and IV, 2. Leiden 1975.
Boismard, M. E. *Le Prologue de Saint Jean*. Paris 1953.
Bonsirven, J. *Textes rabbiniques des deux premiers siècles chrétiens* (Rome 1955).
Box, G. H. *The Book of Isaiah*. London 1916.
Braude, W. G. ed., *Midrash on the Psalms*. New Haven 1959.
—ed., *Pesikta Rabbati*. New Haven and Yale 1968.
—ed., with Kapstein, A. *Pesikta de Rab Kahana*. London 1975.

Bibliography

Bright, J. *The Authority of the Old Testament*. London 1967.
Brooke, A. E. *The Johannine Epistles*. Edinburgh 1912.
Browne, R. E. *The Gospel according to John*. New York 1966.
Bruce, F. F. *The Epistle to the Ephesians*. London 1961.
—*I and II Corinthians*. London 1971.
Bultmann, R. *Das Evangelium des Johannes*. 10th edn, Göttingen 1941.
—*Theology of the New Testament*. Eng. tr. London 1952.
—*The Johannine Epistles*. Eng. tr. Philadelphia 1973 of German edn of 1967.
—*History of the Synoptic Tradition*. Eng. tr. Oxford 1968 of German edn of 1931.
Burrows, M. ed., *The Dead Sea Scrolls of St Mark's Monastery*. New Haven 1950.
Camelot, T. *Ignace d'Antioch et Polycarpe de Smyrne*. Paris 1951.
Cashdan, E. ed., *Tractate Hullin in BT*. London 1948.
Charles, R. H. ed., *The Ascension of Isaiah*. London 1900.
—ed., *Apocrypha and Pseudepigrapha of the Old Testament*. Oxford 1913.
—ed., *Ecclesiasticus in A. and Ps. of OT*.
Charlesworth, J. H. ed., *The Odes of Solomon*. Oxford 1973.
Cohen, A. see Mishcon, A.
Cohn, L. and Wendland, P. eds., *Philonis Alexandri Opera Quae Supersunt*. Berlin 1898.
Colpe, C. *Die Religionsgeschichtliche Schule*. Göttingen 1961.
Colson, F. H. and Whitaker, G. H. *Philo with English Translation*. London and New York 1932.
Conzelmann, H. *Die Apostelgeschichte*. Tübingen 1963.
—*Der Erste Brief an die Korinther*. Göttingen 1969.
Dalton, W. J. *Christ's Proclamation to the Spirits*. Rome 1965.
Daniélou, J. *Theology of Jewish Christianity*. Eng. tr. London 1964 of French edn of 1968.
Davies, W. D. *Paul and Rabbinic Judaism*. London 1948.
Delcor, M. *Les Hymnes de Qumran*. Paris 1962.
Delitzsch, F. *Biblical Commentary on the Prophecies of Isaiah*. Eng. tr. Edinburgh 1890 of 4th German edn.
Dhorme, E. *A Commentary on the Book of Job*. Eng. tr. London 1967 of French edn, Paris 1926.
Dibelius, M. *An die Kolosser, Epheser, An Philemon*, ed. H. Greeven, Tübingen 1953.

Bibliography

Die Griechischen Christlichen Schriftsteller der Ersten Drei Jahrhunderte. Leipzig 1941.
Dodd, C. H. *The Epistle to the Romans.* London 1932.
—*The Interpretation of the Fourth Gospel.* Cambridge 1953.
Donfried, K. P. *The Setting of Second Clement in Early Christianity.* Leiden 1974.
Driver, S. R. and Gray, G. B. *A Critical and Exegetical Commentary on the Book of Job.* Edinburgh 1921.
Ehrhardt, A. *The Beginning.* Manchester 1958.
Elliger, K. *Jesaja II.* Neukirchen-Vluyn 1970.
Ellis, E. E. *Paul's Use of the Old Testament.* Edinburgh 1959.
Emmet, C. ed., *3 Maccabees* in R. H. Charles's *A. and Ps. of OT.*
Etheridge, J. W. E. *The Targums of Onkelos and Jonathan ben Uzziel on the Pentateuch,* new edn New York 1968.
Evans, E. *The First Epistle of Paul the Apostle to the Corinthians.* Oxford 1930.
Ewald, G. *Commentary on the Book of Job.* Eng. tr. London 1882.
Fawcett, T. *Hebrew Myth and Christian Gospel.* London 1973.
Feuillet, A. *Le Christ Sagesse de Dieu.* Paris 1966.
Field, F. ed., *Origenis Hexaplorum Quae Supersunt.* Oxford 1875.
Fillion, A. C. ed., *Biblia Sacra juxta Vulgatae.* Paris 1887.
Foakes-Jackson, F. J. and Lake, K. *The Beginnings of Christianity.* London 1933.
Foerster, W. *Gnosis.* Oxford 1972.
Fohrer, G. *Das Buch Hiob.* Gütersloh 1963.
Freed, E. D. *Old Testament Quotations in the Gospel of John.* Leiden 1965.
Freedman, H. ed., *Tractate Sanhedrin* in BT. London 1935.
—ed., *Tractate Shabbath* in BT. London 1938.
Gibbon, E. S. C. *The Book of Job.* London 1899.
Gifford, E. H. ed., *Eusebii Pamphili Evangelicae Praeparationis Libri* xv. Oxford 1903.
Glueck, N. *Hesed in the Bible.* Cincinnati 1969.
Goodrick, A. T. S. *The Book of Wisdom.* London 1913.
Gore, C. *St Paul's Epistle to the Ephesians.* London 1902.
Goudge, H. L. *The First Epistle to the Corinthians.* London 1903.
Gray, G. B. see Driver, S. R.
Green, H. B. *The Gospel according to St Matthew.* London 1975.
Guilding, A. *The Fourth Gospel and Jewish Worship.* Oxford 1960.

Bibliography

Guillamont, A. *et al.* eds., *The Gospel according to Thomas*. Leiden and London 1959.
Gunkel, H. *Die Psalmen*. Göttingen 1929.
Haenchen, E. *Die Apostelgeschichte*. 13th edn, Göttingen 1961.
Hagner, D. A. *The Use of the Old and New Testaments in Clement of Rome*. Leiden 1973.
Halévy, J. ed., *Te'azaza Sanbat*. Paris 1902.
Hanson, A. T. *Jesus Christ in the Old Testament*. London 1965.
—*Studies in the Pastoral Epistles*. London 1968.
—*Studies in Paul's Technique and Theology*. London 1974.
—*Grace and Truth*. London 1975.
Hanson, R. P. C. *Origen's Doctrine of Tradition*. London 1954.
—*Allegory and Event*. London 1959.
—*The Acts*. Oxford 1967.
Hermann, I. *Kyrios und Pneuma*. Munich 1961.
Hodge, C. *A Commentary on the Epistle to the Ephesians*. London 1959 reprint.
—*An Exposition of the First Epistle to the Corinthians*. London 1964 edn of 1866 original.
Hölscher, G. *Das Buch Hiob*. Tübingen 1952.
Holtzmann, H. J. *Die Synoptiker*, vol. 1. Freidburg 1889.
—*Evangelium, Briefe, und Offenbarung des Johannes*. Tübingen 1908.
Hoskyns, E. C. *The Fourth Gospel*. 4th edn, London 1947.
Houlden, J. L. *Paul's Letters from Prison*. London 1970.
—*A Commentary on the Johannine Epistles*. London 1973.
James, M. R. *The Apocryphal New Testament*. Oxford 1924.
—ed., *The Biblical Antiquities of Philo*. Republished with a prolegomenon by J. H. Feldman. New York 1971.
Kapstein, I. see Braude, W. G.
Käsemann, E. *An die Römer*. Tübingen 1973.
Kelly, J. N. D. *A Commentary on the Epistles of Peter and Jude*. London 1969.
Kelsey, D. H. *The Uses of Scripture in Recent Theology*. London 1975.
Kent, J. R. C. and Painter, K. S. *The Wealth of the Roman World*. London 1977.
Kissane, E. J. *The Book of Job*. Dublin 1939.
—*The Book of Isaiah*. Dublin 1943.
Kittel, G. R. *Die Psalmen*. Leipzig and Erlangen 1922.
Kittel, R. ed., *Biblia Hebraica*. 6th edn, Stuttgart 1949.

Bibliography

Klostermann, E. *Das Matthäusevangelium*. Tübingen 1971.
Knox, W. L. *St Paul and the Church of the Gentiles*. Cambridge 1939.
Koehler, L. and Baumgartner, W. *Lexicon in Veteris Testamenti Libros*. Leiden 1953.
Kraus, H.-J. *Psalmen*. Neukirchen 1960.
Kuhn, K. G. *Der Tannaitische Midrash Sifre zu Numeri*. Stuttgart 1959.
Lagrange, M.-J. *L'Evangile selon Saint Jean*. 3rd edn, Paris 1947.
Lake, K. see Foakes-Jackson, F. J.
Larcher, C. *Etudes sur le Livre de la Sagesse*. Paris 1969.
Lazarus, D. H. M. ed., *Tractate Hagiga in BT*. London 1938.
Le Déaut, R. *Liturgie juive et Nouveau Testament*. Rome 1965.
Leenhardt, F. J. *L'Epître de Saint Paul aux Romains*. Neuchâtel and Paris 1957.
Lévi, I. *The Hebrew Text of the Book of Ecclesiasticus*. Leiden 1969.
Liddell, H. G. and Scott, R. *A Greek-English Lexicon*. Oxford 1940 edn.
Lietzmann, H. *An die Korinther I/II*. Tübingen 1969.
Lièvre, L. see Maillot, A.
Lightfoot, J. B. *The Apostolic Fathers*. London 1898.
Lightfoot, R. H. *St John's Gospel, a Commentary*. Oxford 1956.
Lindars, B. *New Testament Apologetic*. London 1961.
—*The Gospel of John*. London 1972.
Lipsius, R. A. *Die Briefe an die Galater, Römer, Philipper*. Freiburg 1891.
Loisy, A. *Le Quatrième Evangile*. Paris 1903.
Lundberg, P. *La Typologie baptismale dans l'Ancienne Eglise*. Leipzig and Uppsala 1942.
MacCullagh, J. A. *The Harrowing of Hell*. Edinburgh 1930.
Mack, B. L. *Logos und Sophia*. Göttingen 1975.
McKelvey, R. J. *The New Temple*. Oxford 1969.
McNamara, M. *The New Testament and the Palestinian Targum to the Pentateuch*. Rome 1966.
McNeill, A. H. *The Gospel according to St Matthew*. 2nd edn, London 1938.
Maillot, A. and Lièvre, A. *Les Psaumes*. Paris 1966.
Mansoor, M. *The Thanksgiving Hymns*. Leiden 1961.
Marsh, J. *Saint John*. London 1968.
Ménard, J.-E. *L'Evangile de Vérité*. Leiden 1972.

Bibliography

Michel, O. *Paulus und seine Bibel*. Gütersloh 1929.
—*Der Brief an die Römer*. 12th edn, Göttingen 1963.
Migne, J. P. ed., *Patrologiae Cursus Completus: Origen Opera Omnia*, vol. 3. Paris 1962.
Milligan, G. see Moulton, J. H.
Mishcon, A. ed., *Tractate Abodah Zarah* in BT. London 1935.
Mitchell, H. D. *A Critical and Exegetical Commentary on Haggai, Zechariah, Malachi, and Jonah*. Edinburgh 1912.
Mitton, C. L. *The Epistle to the Ephesians*. Oxford 1951.
Moffat, J. ed., *2 Maccabees* in R. H. Charles, *A. and Ps. of the OT*.
Moore, G. E. *Judaism*. Cambridge, Mass. 1944.
Moulton, J. H. and Milligan, G. *The Vocabulary of the Greek New Testament*. London 1952 reprint.
Neusner, J. ed., *The Formation of the Babylonian Talmud*. Leiden 1970.
—ed., *The Modern Study of the Mishna*. Leiden 1973.
Oesterley, W. O. E. *The Wisdom of Solomon*. London 1917.
—*The Psalms*. London 1933.
Otto, J. C. T. *Justini Martyris Opera Omnia*. Jena 1843.
Painter, K. S. see Kent, J. P. C.
Plummer, A. see Robertson, A.
Pope, M. H. *Job*. New York 1965.
Preisker, H. see Windisch, H.
Rackham, R. B. *The Acts of the Apostles*. 4th edn, London 1909.
Reicke, B. *The Disobedient Spirits and Christian Baptism*. Copenhagen 1946.
—*The Epistles of James, Peter, and Jude*. New York 1969.
Reim, G. *Studien zum Alttestamentlichen Hintergrund des Johannesevangelium*. Cambridge 1974.
Rignell, A. G. *A Study of Isaiah*. Lund 1956.
Robertson, A. and Plummer, A. *A Critical and Exegetical Commentary on the First Epistle of St Paul to the Corinthians*. Edinburgh 1911.
Robinson, J. A. *St Paul's Epistle to the Ephesians*. 2nd edn, London 1914.
Rowley, H. H. *Job*. London 1970.
Sanders, J. N. *The Gospel according to St John*. London 1968.
Schelkle, K. H. *Die Petrusbriefe; Der Judasbrief*. Freiburg, Basel, Vienna 1961.
Schlatter, A. *Der Evangelist Johannes*. 3rd edn, Stuttgart 1960.

Bibliography

Schlier, H. *Religionsgeschichtliche Untersuchungen zu den Ignatiusbriefen.* Giessen 1929.
—*Christus und die Kirche im Epheserbrief.* Tübingen 1930.
Schmidt, H. *Die Psalmen.* Tübingen 1934.
Schmiedel, P. W. *Die Briefe an die Thessalonicher und die Korinther.* Freiburg 1891.
Schmithals, W. *Die Gnosis in Korinth.* Göttingen 1956.
Schnackenburg, R. *The Gospel according to St John,* vol. I, Eng. tr. New York 1968 of German edn of 1965.
—*Das Johannesevangelium,* vol. II. Freiburg 1971.
Schneemelcher, W. *New Testament Apocrypha.* London 1952.
Scott, R. see Liddell, H. G.
Selwyn, E. G. *The First Epistle of St Peter.* 2nd edn, London 1947.
Simon, M. ed., with W. Slotki, *Tractate Baba Bathra* in BT. London 1935.
—ed., *Tractate Berakoth* in BT. London 1948.
Simpson, D. C. ed., *Tobit* in R. H. Charles, *A. and Ps. of the OT.*
Skeel, G. A. J. with White, A. J. and Witney, J. P. eds., *The Epistle of St Clement of Rome.* London 1919.
Slotki, I. ed., *Tractate Erubin* in BT. London 1938.
—and see Simon, M.
Sperber, A. *The Bible in Aramaic.* London 1962.
Stendahl, K. *The School of St Matthew.* 2nd edn, Lund 1967.
Stenning, J. F. *The Targum of Isaiah.* Oxford 1949.
Strachan, R. H. *The Fourth Gospel: its significance and environment.* 3rd edn, London 1941.
Thackeray, H. St. J. *The Relation of St Paul to Contemporary Jewish Thought.* London 1900.
—*The Septuagint and Jewish Worship.* 2nd edn, London 1923.
Torrey, C. C. *The Composition and Date of Acts.* Cambridge, Mass. 1916.
—*The Second Isaiah: a new interpretation.* Edinburgh and New York 1928.
van der Ploeg, J. P. M. and van der Woude, A. S. *Le Targum de Job de la Grotte XI de Qumran.* Leiden 1971.
Vermes, G. *The Dead Sea Scrolls in English.* 2nd edn, London 1965.
Vollmer, R. *Die Alttestamentlichen Citate bei Paulus.* Freiburg and Leipzig 1899.

Bibliography

von Soden, H. *Hand-Commentar zum Neuen Testament*, vol. III. Freiburg 1891.
Weiser, A. *The Psalms*. Eng. tr. London 1962 of German edn, Göttingen 1959.
—*Das Buch Hiob*. Göttingen 1963.
Weiss, J. *Der Erste Korintherbrief*. Göttingen 1910.
Wendland, P. see Cohn, L.
Wernberg-Møller, P. *The Manual of Discipline*. Leiden 1957.
Westcott, B. F. *The Gospel according to St John*. London 1908.
Westermann, C. *Das Buch Jesaja Kapitel 40-66*. Göttingen 1966.
Whitaker, G. H. see Colson, F. H.
White, H. J. see Skeel, G. A. J.
Whybray, N. J. *The Heavenly Counsellor in Isaiah XL, 13-14*. Cambridge 1971.
Wilckens, U. *Weisheit und Torheit*. Tübingen 1959.
Wilcox, M. *The Semitisms of Acts*. Oxford 1965.
Williams, C. S. C. *The Acts of the Apostles*. London 1957.
Williams, R. R. *The Letters of John and James*. Cambridge 1965.
Wilson, R. McL. *Studies in the Gospel of Thomas*. London 1960.
Windisch, H. and Preisker, K. *Die Katholischen Briefe*. 3rd edn, Tübingen 1951.
Yamauchi, E. M. *Pre-Christian Gnosticism*. London 1973.

ARTICLES REFERRED TO IN THE TEXT

Ackermann, J. A. 'The Rabbinic Interpretation of Psalm 82 and the Gospel of John', in *Harvard Theological Review* 59 (1966), 186-91.
Bartina, S. 'La vida como historia en el prólogo al cuarto evangelio' in *Biblica* xlix (1968), fasc. 4, 89-96.
Bauer, J. B. '... τοῖς ἀγαπῶσιν τὸν θεόν – Rom.8.22 (1 Cor. 2.9; 1 Cor. 8.3)' in *ZNTW* 50 (1959), 106-12.
Berger, K. 'Zur Discussion über die Herkunft von 1 Kor. ii.9' in *NTS* (Jan. 1978), 270ff.
Bergmeier, R. 'Zum Verfassers-Problem des II und III Johannes Briefs' in *ZNTW* (1966-7), 57-8, 93-100.
Bertram, G. 'φυλακή' in *TWNT* IX. Stuttgart 1973. 'ὠδίν' in *TWNT* IX. Stuttgart 1973.
Bickermann, E. J. 'Les deux erreurs du prophète Jonas' in *RHPR* 45 (1965), 239.

Bibliography

Black, M. 'Does an Aramaic Tradition underlie John 1.16?' in *JTS* 42, new ser., (1941), 69-70.

Bornkamm, G. 'μυστήριον' in *TWNT* iv. Stuttgart 1962. (1959) 18-70.

Bousset, W. 'Zur Hadesfahrt Christi' in *ZNTW* 19 (1919-20), 50-66.

Bover, M. 'χάριν ἀντὶ χάριτος' in *Biblica* vi (1925), 454-60.

Bratcher, R. G. 'Having loosed the pangs of death' in *The Bible Translator* 10.

Brock, S. 'ΒΑΡΝΑΒΑΣ ΥΙΟΣ ΠΑΡΑΚΛΗΣΕΩΣ' in *JTS* 25 new ser., (1947), 91-8.

Brooks, O. S. '1 Peter 3.21 – the Clue to the Literary Structure of the Epistle' in *Nov. Test.* 16 (1974), 290-305.

Bröse, E. 'Der Descensus ad Inferos Eph. 4.8-10' in *Neue Kirchliche Zeitschrift* 9 (1898), 447-55.

Büchsel, F. 'κάτω' in *TWNT* iii (Stuttgart 1938) p. 641.

Caird, G. B. 'The Descent of Christ in Ephesians 4.7-11' in *Studia Evangelica* ii, ed. F. L. Cross (Berlin 1964), 535-45.

Carr, A. W. 'The Rulers of This Age – 1 Corinthians 2.6-8' in *NTS* (Oct. 1976), 20-35.

Conzelmann, H. 'Paulus und die Weisheit' in *NTS* 12 (1975-6), 231-44.

Cope, L. 'Matthew 12.40 and the Synoptic Source Question' in *JBL* 92 (1973), 115.

Cox, W. H. 'The Pains of Death (Acts ii.24)' in *The Interpreter* 8 (1911-12), 330-31.

Cranfield, C. E. B. 'The Interpretation of 1 Peter iii.19 and iv.6' in *ET* 69 (1957-8), 369-72.

Curzon-Siggers, W. S. 'Grace and Truth' in *ET* 4 (1892-3), 480.

Dahood, M. 'The Breakup of Two Composite Phrases in Isaiah 40.13' in *Biblica* liv (1973), 537-8.

D'Ales, A. 'χάριν ἀντὶ χάριτος (Joann. i.16)' in *RSR* 9 (1919), 384-6.

Daube, D. 'τρία μυστήρια κραυγῆς Ignatius Ephesians xix.1' in *JTS* 16, new ser., (1965), 128-9.

de Harkavy, A. 'Karaites' in *The Jewish Encyclopedia*, ed. I. Singer. New York and London 1904.

de la Potterie, I. '*Kharis* paulinienne et *kharis* johannique' in *Jesus und Paulus*, eds. E. E. Ellis and F. Grässer. Göttingen 1975.

Bibliography

Delling, G. 'ἄρχων' in *TWNT* I. Stuttgart 1949.
—'Die Weise, von der Zeit zu reden, im Liber Antiquitatum Biblicarum' in *Nov. Test.* 13 (1971), 305-21.
Diezinger, W. 'Unter Toten Freigeworden' in *Nov. Test.* 5 (1962), 268-98.
Dubarle, A. M. 'Le Signe du Temple' in *RB* 48 (1939), 21-44.
Eaglesham, D. 'Note on John i.17' in *ET* 16 (1904-5), 428.
Eltester, W. 'Schöpfungsoffenbarungen und Natürliche Theologie im Frühen Christentum' in *NTS* 3 (1956-7), 93-114.
Fazekaš, L. 'Taufe als Tod in Röm. 6.3f' in *Theologische Zeitschrift* 22 (1966), 305-18.
Feuillet, A. 'L'Enigme de 1 Cor. ii.9' in *RB* 70 (1963), 52-74.
Friedrich, G. 'κηρύσσω' in *TWNT*. III. Stuttgart 1938.
Funk, R. W. 'The Form and Structure of II John and III John' in *JBL* 86 (1967), 424-30.
Goldberg, A. M. 'Torah aus der Unterwelt' in *Biblische Zeitschrift* 14 (1970), 127-31.
Grafe, E. 'Das Verhältnis der Paulischen Schriften zur Sapientia Salomonis' in *Theologische Abhandlungen*, ed. C. Weizsäcker, Freiburg 1892.
Hanson, A. T. 'John's Citation of Psalm lxxxii' in *NTS* 11 (1965), 158-62.
—'John's Citation of Psalm lxxxii Reconsidered' in *NTS* 13 (1966), 363-7.
—'The Old Testament Background to the Raising of Lazarus' in *Studia Evangelica* (Berlin 1973), 252-5.
—'Claude Montefiore, a Modern Philo' in *The Modern Churchman* (Spring 1977), 109-14.
Harmon, M. 'Aspects of Paul's Use of the Psalms' in *Westminster Theological Journal* 32 (1969), 1-23.
Harrington, D. J. 'The Original Language of Pseudo-Philo's Liber Antiquitatum Biblicarum' in *HTR* 63 (1970), 503-14.
Hauck, F. 'κάθαρος' in *TWNT* III. Stuttgart 1938.
Helmbold, A. K. 'Gnostic Elements in "The Ascension of Isaiah"' in *NTS* 18 (Jan. 1972), 222-7.
Hofius, O. von 'Das Zitat 1 Kor. 2.9 und das koptisches Testament des Jakobs' in *ZNTW* 66 1/2 (1975), 140-42.
Jenkins, C. 'Some Fragments of Origen's Commentary on 1 Corinthians' in *JTS* 9 (1908), 236-9.

Bibliography

Jeremias, J. 'ᾅδης' in *TWNT* I. Stuttgart 1933.
—'Ἰωνᾶς' in *TWNT* III. Stuttgart 1938.
John, D. 'St. Paul and Empedocles' in *ET* 39 (1927-8), 237-8
Jouon, P. 'Jean 1.16' in *RSR* 22 (1932), 206.
Kittel, R. 'λεγω and Cognates' in *TWNT* IV. Stuttgart 1942.
Klaar, E. 'Röm. 6.7 ὁ γὰρ ἀποθανὼν δεδικαίωται ἀπὸ τῆς ἁμαρτίας' in *ZNTW* 59-60 (1968-9), 131-4.
Kuhn, K. H. Review of 'Nag Hammadi Codices III, 2 and IV, 2' by A. Böhlig and F. Wisse in *JTS* 27 new ser. (Apr. 1976), 214.
Kuyper, L. J. 'Grace and Truth, an Old Testament Description of God and its use in the Johannine Gospel' in *The Reformed Review* (Sept. 1962), xvi, no. 1.
Léon-Dufour, F. X. 'Le Signe du Temple selon Saint Jean' in *RSR* 39 (1951-2), 171.
Ling, T. 'A Note on 1 Corinthians ii.1' in *ET* 68 (1956-7), 26.
Linton, O. 'The Demand for a Sign from Heaven' in *Studia Theologica* 19-20 (1965-6), 112-29.
'M.D.' 'Twenty Misused Texts, 1, 1 Cor. ii.9' in *ET* 6 (1894-5), 201.
Meyer, F. D. 'The Gentile Mission in Q' in *JBL* 89 (1970), 405-17.
Michaelis, W. 'Jon. 1.51, Gen. 28.12 und das Menschensohn Problem' in *Theologische Literaturzeitung* 85 (Aug. 1960), 566.
Miller, J. 'ΑΡΧΟΝΤΩΝ ΤΟΥ ΑΙΩΝΟΣ ΤΟΥΤΟΥ – a new look at 1 Corinthians 2.6-8' in *JBL* 91 (1972), 522-8.
Montgomery, J. A. 'Hebrew *Hesed* and Greek *Charis*' in *HTR* 32 (1939), 97-107.
Noack, B. 'Das Zitat in Ephes. 5.14' in *Studia Theologica* 5-6 (1951-2), 52-64.
Oepke, A. 'κρύπτω' in *TWNT* III. Stuttgart 1938.
—'λούω' in *TWNT* IV. Stuttgart 1942.
Pancaro, S. 'The Relationship of the Church to Israel in the Gospel of John' in *NTS* 21 (1974-5), 296-405.
Philonenko, M. 'Quod oculus non vidit, 1 Cor. 2.9' in *Theologische Zeitschrift* 15 (1959), 51-2.
Poznanski, S. 'Karaites' in *Encyclopedia of Religion and Ethics*, ed. J. Hastings, Edinburgh 1914.
Prigent, P. 'Ce que l'œil n'a pas vu, 1 Cor. 2.9' in *Theologische Zeitschrift* 14 (1958), 416-29.

Bibliography

Quispel, G. 'Nathanael und der Menschensohn (Jon. 1.51)' in *ZNTW* (1956), 281-3.
Rayner, R. A. 'The Story of Jonah. An Easter Story' in *Evangelical Quarterly* 22 (1950), 123-5.
Rubinkiewicz, R. 'Ps. lxviii.19 (= Eph. iv.8). Another Textual Tradition or Targum?' in *Nov. Test.* 17 (1975), 219-24.
Schmid, J. 'Der Epheserbrief des Apostel Paulus' in *Biblische Studien*, ed. G. Bardenhewer, Freiburg 1928.
Schrenk, G. 'γράφω' in *TWNT* I. Stuttgart 1933.
Schweizer, E. '1 Petrus 4.6' in *Theologische Zeitschrift* 8 (1952), 152-4.
—'πνεῦμα, πνευματικός', in *TWNT* VI. Stuttgart 1959 387f.
Scroggs, R. 'Paul: ΣΟΦΟΣ ΚΑΙ ΠΝΕΥΜΑΤΙΚΟΣ' in *NTS* 14 (1967-8), 33-58.
Seidelin, P. 'Das Jonaszeichen' in *Studia Theologica* 5 (1951), 118-31.
Sparks, H. F. D. '1 Cor. 2.9, a Quotation from the Coptic Testament of Jacob?' in *ZNTW* 67 (1976), 3-4, 269-79.
Swellengrebel, J. 'Readers' Corner' in *The Bible Translator* 10 (1959), 127-8.
Synge, F. C. '1 Peter 3.18-21' in *ET* 82 (1970-71), 311.
Talbert, C. H. 'The Myth of a Descending-Ascending Redeemer in Mediterranean Antiquity' in *NTS* 22 (July 1976), 418-40.
Treu, U. 'Zum Datierung der Physiologus' in *ZNTW* 57 (1966), 101-4.
van Roon, A. 'The Relation between Christ and the Wisdom of God according to Paul' in *Nov. Test.* 16 (1974), 207-39.
von Nordheim, E. 'Das Zitat des Paulus in 1 Kor. 2.9 und seine Beziehung zum koptischen Testament Jakobs' in *ZNTW* 65 1/2 (1974), 112-20.
Werner, E. 'Post-Biblical Hebraisms in the Prima Clementis' in *Harry Austryn Wolfson Jubilee Vol. II.* Jerusalem 1965, 799-802.
Wilckens, U. 'σοφία' in *TWNT* VII. Stuttgart 1974.
Williams, R. R. 'The Pauline Catechesis' in *Studies in Ephesians* ed. F. L. Cross. London 1956, 89-96.
Windisch, H. 'Angelophanien um den Menschensohn auf Erden: ein Kommentar zu Jon. 1.15' in *ZNTW* 30 (1931), 215-33.

Index of Names

Abbott, T. K. 137, 144
Ackermann, J. A. 28
Allo, E. B. 25, 29, 67, 72ff, 77
Altaner, B. 36
Amsler, B. 36
Amsler, S. 177n
Apocalypse of Elijah 44
Aquila 39, 125, 183n, 194n, 195n, 204n, 210n
Arians 111
Aristotle 23, 191n
Augustine 144

Bachmann, P. 185n, 188n
Barbelognostics 195n
Barrett, C. K. 29f, 51, 72, 73f, 97, 116, 120, 200n
Barth, K. 79
Bartina, S. 198-9n
Basilides 75, 195n
Bauer, W. 135
Baumgartner, W. 53, 194n, 205n
Beare, F. W. 128f
Berger, K. 196n
Bergmeier, R. 102
Bernard, J. H. 98, 106, 113, 116, 120, 200n, 210n
Bertram, G. 151, 204n
Best, E. 130
Bewer, J. A. 207n
Bickermann, E. J. 148
Bieder, W. 128f, 152, 204n, 205n, 207n, 209n
Bigg, C. 128f
Black, M. 100
Böhlig, A. 26, 181n
Boismard, M.-E. 97-8, 103
Bonsirven, l 153-4

Book of Elijah 44
Bornkamm, G. 25
Bousset, W. 30f
Bover, M. 199n
Bratcher, R. G. 208n
Braude, W. G. 178n
Bright, J. 177n
Brock, S. 152
Brooks, D. S. 130
Bröse, E. 139
Brown, R. E. 98
Bruce, F. F. 71, 73, 139-40, 143
Büchsel, F. 139
Bultmann, R. 5, 21, 23ff, 29, 31, 77, 98ff, 102ff, 112, 116, 120, 140, 158, 169-70, 181n, 190n, 200n, 206n
Burrows, M. 187

Caird, G. B. 138, 153, 209n
Carr, A. W. 23f
Cashdan, E. 200n
Charles, R. F. 35f, 38, 100, 105, 186n, 189n, 193n, 207n
Charlesworth, J. H. 134f
Cohen, A. 202n
Cohn, L. 192n
Colpe, C. 181n, 184n, 196n
Conzelmann, H. 27, 44, 70ff, 153
Cope, L. 147
Cox, W. H. 151
Cranfield, C. E. B. 128f, 155
Curzon-Siggers, W. S. 198n
Cyrus 81

Dahood, M. 193n
D'Ales, A. 199n
Dalton, W. J. 128f

Index of Names

Daniélou, J. 33f, 42
Daube, D. 182n
Davies, W. D. 5, 67
Davy, F. N. 211n
de Harkavy, A. 179n
de la Potterie, I. 99-104 passim, 198n
Delcor, M. 127, 151
Delitzch, F. 53, 81, 198n
Delling, G. 24, 29
Dhorme, E. 85f, 208n
Dibelius, M. 144, 205n, 206n
Diezinger, W. 122f
Docetism, 37
Dodd, C. H. 79, 98, 112, 166, 169, 198n
Donfried, K. P. 48f
Driver, S. R. 86, 208n
Dubarle, A. M. 117
Duhm, B. 53, 81

Eaglesham, D. 198n
Ehrhardt, A. 23
Elliger, K. 81f
Ellis, E. E. 21, 51, 58, 191n
Eltester, W. 79
Emmet, C. 149
Etheridge, J. W. E. 181n, 200n, 204n
Ethiopian Ezra Apocalypse 196n
Eupolemos 189n
Evans, E. 29, 71, 74
Ewald, G. 86

Fawcett, T. 113
Fazekaš, L. 128, 203n
Feldman, J. H. 59
Feuillet, A. 22, 25, 38, 62, 67f, 171-2, 188n, 211n
Field, F. 51, 52, 57
Fillion, A. C. 189n
Foakes-Jackson, F. J. 152
Foerster, W. 34, 37, 70, 75, 180n, 183n, 195-6n
Fohrer, G. 86, 208n
Freed, E. D. 115, 157, 160, 161, 209n, 210n
Freedman, H. 63, 190n, 202n

Friedrich, G. 130
Funk, R. W. 198n

Gerhardsson, B. 5
Gibson, E. S. C. 208n
Gifford, E. H. 189n
Glueck, N. 100-101
Gnosticism, 21, 23, 31, 34, 37, 42, 70, 71, 74, 95n, 134, 140, 183-4n, 186n, 195-6n
Goldberg, A. M. 136
Goodrick, A. T. S. 83
Gore, C. 144
Goudge, H. L. 67, 74
Grafe, E. 84
Gray, G. B. 86, 208n
Green, H. B. 147
Greeven, H. 144, 205n, 206n
Guilding, A. 108, 173
Guillamont, A. 46
Gunkel, H. 84f

Haenchen, E. 151f
Hagner, D. A. 47f, 58, 66
Halévy, J. 196n
Hanson, R. P. C. 142, 153, 184n
Harmon, M. 136
Harrington, D. J. 59
Hauck, F. 144
Hegel, G. 96
Helmbold, A. K. 182n
Hengel, M. 5, 6, 92, 183-4n, 189n
Heracleon 76
Héring, J. 44, 51, 73
Herman, I. 195n
Hodge, C. 72, 73, 77, 137, 144
Hofius, D. von 45, 186n
Hölscher, G. 86, 208n
Holtzmann, H. J. 97, 101, 103, 147f, 151, 209n
Hoskyns, E. 97, 103, 116, 120, 200n, 211n
Houlden, J. L. 144, 198n

James, M. R. 46, 58f
Jason of Cyrene 189n
Jenkins, C. 184n
Jeremias, J. 5, 112, 132, 146-7 148, 204n, 206n

226

Index of Names

Jerome 148, 187n
John, D. 185n
Jouon, P. 199n

Käsemann, E. 22, 80
Kelly, J. N. D. 127, 128f
Kelsey, D. H. 179n
Kent, J. P. C. 145
Kissane, E. J. 208n
Kittel, D. R. 203n
Kittel, R. 50, 80, 144, 160, 188n
Klaar, E. 128
Klausner, J. 5
Klostermann, E. 148
Knox, W. L. 22, 28, 32, 79, 192n
Kohler, L. 53, 194n, 205n
Kraus, H. J. 203n
Kuhn, K. J. 63, 112, 186n
Kuyper, L. J. 98

Lagrange, M-J. 97, 103, 116, 120 169-70, 177n
Lake, K. 152
Larcher, C. 83
Lazarus, D. H. M. 205n
Le Déaut, R. 135-6
Leenhardt, F. J. 78
Leivestadt, R. 5
Léon-Dufour, F. X. 113, 117
Lévy, I. 193n 199n
Liberal Judaism 17f
Liddell, H. G. 191n
Lietzmann, H. 44, 71, 73f, 77
Lièvre, A. 203n
Lightfoot, J. B. 35, 133, 145
Lightfoot, R. H. 98, 112, 116
Lindars, B. 21, 98, 100, 117, 120, 140, 158, 200n, 201n, 205n
Ling, T. 179n
Linton, D. 147
Lipsius, R. A. 79
Loisy, A. 98, 103, 178n
Lundberg, P. 128f, 153, 154, 156
Luther, M. 16

MacCullagh, J. A. 127, 128f
Mack, B. L. 105
McKelvey, R. J. 113, 116, 117
McNamara, M. 136, 139, 204n

McNeill, A. H. 147
Maillot, A. 203n
Mandaean Literature 9
Mansoor, M. 127, 151
Marcus 34, 180n
Marsh, J. 98
Martyrdom of Isaiah 35
'M.D.' 67
Ménard, J.-E. 70, 180n, 195n
Merkabah Mysticism 92, 113-14, 136, 175
Meyer, F. D. 206-7n
Michaelis, W. 114
Michel, O. 44, 78, 192n
Migne, J. P. 184n
Miller, G. 179n
Milligan, G. 181-2n, 191n
Mischcon, A. 190n, 202n
Mishna 9, 12, 13, 15
Mitchell, H. D. 202n
Mitton, C. L. 139
Modernist controversy 13
Moffatt, J. 189n
Montefiore, C. G. 17
Montgomery, J. A. 100
Moore, G. E. 62
Moulton, J. H. 181-2n, 191n

Naassenes 180n, 183n, 195n
Neofiti ms. 1, 9, 181n, 204n
Neusner, J. 12
Noack, B. 142, 206n

Oepke, A. 44, 144
Oesterley, W. O. E. 84, 125-6
Ophites 37, 195n

Painter, K. S. 145
Philonenko, M. 58f
Plato, 151
Plummer, A. 67, 72, 73f
Poimandres, 195-6n
Pope, M. H. 86, 208n
Poznanski, S. 179n
Preisker, H. 128
Prigent, P. 58, 59, 62, 66

Qaraites 16f
Quinta 100, 183f
Quispel, G. 113

Index of Names

Rackham, R. B. 151
Rayner, R. A. 207n
Reickie, B. 129f
Reim, G. 114, 157, 158, 161, 209n, 210n
Rignell, A. G. 81
Robertson, A. 67, 72, 73f
Robinson, J. A. 139, 144, 206n
Rowley, H. H. 208n
Rubinkiewicz, R. 137
Rudolph, W. 205n

Sanders, J. N. 98, 103-4, 116
Schelkle, K. H. 128f
Schlatter, A. 103, 114, 169
Schlier, H. 35, 130, 137f, 146
Schmid, J. 137
Schmidt, H. 203n
Schmiedel, P. W. 44, 74, 77
Schmithals, W. 31
Schnackenburg, R. 98, 120, 198n, 200n, 202n
Schneemelcher, W. 135
Schoeps, H. J. 5
Schrenk, G. 44
Schweizer, E. 71, 75, 128f, 192n
Scott, R. 191n
Scroggs, R. 25, 194n
Seidelin, P. 148, 206n, 207n
Selwyn, E. G. 139
Sexta 100, 183n
Simon, M. 189n, 208n
Simon of Gitta 195n
Simon Magus 37
Simpson, D. C. 207n
Skeel, G. A. J. 186n
Slotki, W. 207n, 208n
Sparks, H. F. D. 185-6n
Sperber, A. 189n, 202n
Stauffer, E. 61, 185
Stendahl, K. 147
Stenning, J. F. 187n
Strachan, R. H. 98, 120, 200n
Strack-Billerbeck 8, 54, 67, 98, 141, 149, 151, 169, 184n
Swellengrebel, J. 208n
Symmachus 39, 53, 82, 100, 125, 127, 183n, 194n, 204n

Synge, F. C. 131
Syrian Daniel Apocalypse 196n

Talbert, C. H. 83, 184n, 191n
Talmud 9, 12, 13, 15, 40
Te'azaza Sanbat 196n
Testament of Hezekiah 35
Testament of Jacob 44f, 58, 66, 185n
Thackeray, H. St. J. 58f, 62
Theodotion 24, 39, 80, 100, 183n, 208n, 210n
Torrey, C. C. 53, 151-2, 208n
Torrey, C. C. 53, 151-2, 208n
Treu, U. 183n

Valentinian system 34, 70, 76, 195n
Van der Ploeg, J. P. M. 208n
Van Roon, A. 28, 79
Van der Woude, A. S. 208n
Vatican Council II 19
Vermes, G. 5, 127, 151
Vollmer, R. 50, 185n, 191n
Von Hügel, F. 178n
Von Nordheim, E. 44f
Von Soden, H. 128f

Weingreen, J. 62
Weiser, A. 86, 203n, 208n
Weiss, J. 25, 67, 71, 72, 74, 77f
Wendland, P. 192n
Wernberg-Møller, P. 127
Werner, E. 186-7n
Wesley, C. 192n
Westcott, B. F. 97, 103, 116
Westermann, C. 53, 81
White, A. J. 186n
Whybray, R. N. 81f, 188n
Wilckens, U. 25, 29, 31, 38, 44, 67, 181n
Wilcox, M. 152f, 188n, 210n
Williams, C. S. C. 207n
Williams, R. R. 143
Wilson, R. McL. 186n
Windisch, H. 28, 113, 128, 158
Witney, J. P. 186n

Yamauchi, E. M. 191n

Index of Biblical References

GENESIS
14.5	202n
18.1-15	165
18.2-3	165
18.13	165
28	110-14 passim, 163
28.11	9
28.12	11, 163, 200n
28.13	112
28.16	9
28.17	117
40.15	126
41.34	53

EXODUS
12.29	126
12.46	158, 159
18.16	81
20.6	52
27.20-21	164
28.16	110
33.7-34.7	97
33.12-34.8	102, 108
33.20	104
34.6	97-109 passim, 163
34.1-8	107

NUMBERS
9.12	158, 159, 209n
21.9	159
23.23	88

DEUTERONOMY
3.26	180
4.9	81
30.11-14	31, 140, 141
30.13	135

JOSHUA
18.16	202n

1 SAMUEL
14.6	53

2 SAMUEL
2.6	100
5.18	202n
5.22	202n
10.2	100
22.6	150

2 KINGS
12.5	54, 56

1 CHRONICLES
16.30	81

ESTHER
2.9	100

JOB
3.19	125-6, 203n
11.7	71, 191n
14.12-15	157f, 168
21.32-3	168f, 210n
28.25	80
28.27	105
39.3	151, 208n
41.11	78f
41.12	87

PSALMS
16.8-11	153-6
16.10	116, 209n
18.4	150
18.16	128

Index of Biblical References

(Psalms)
22.15	178n
22.18	209n
24	24, 95
24.6	183n
24.7, 9	38f, 68
30.7	100
33.5	100
33.9	33
33.18	100
35.19	209n
40.8	161f
40.10	210n
40.11	210n
41.9	209n
63.9	139
68.9	141
68.18	136f
69.4	159, 209n
69.9	115f, 158, 159, 177n
69.21	209n
69.33	115
75.4	80
76.6	143
78.24	159f
82	210n
82.6	159f, 178n
85	106
85.5	107
85.7-10	106-7
85.8	108
88	122f, 125
88.4	126
88.5	125, 143, 206n
88.6	125f
88.7	126
88.11	126
88.13	126
88.17	145
89	124
89.1	145
89.2	131
89.9	132
89.24	100
89.46-8	171
93.1	81
96.10	81
102.25	2
106.16	178n
116.3	150
118.10	167
118.21	167, 210n
118.25-6	157, 167
119.126	53
132.16-7	164f
139.15	139

PROVERBS
2.18	202n
20.27	72
31.26	100

ISAIAH
6.10	158
14.15	126
24.22	127
26.19	142
28.16	161
29.19	142
40.3	157
40.12	80
40.13	22, 27, 69f, 78f, 178n, 192n
44.23	137
52.15	50
53.1	158, 209n
54.13	159f
54.14	160
60.1	141, 206n
60.2	142
60.19-20	60
64.3	47f, 49f, 61, 63f
65.16	51, 54, 56
65.16-17	56f, 60f, 188n

JEREMIAH
3.16	55, 56, 60f
5.28	205n
32.35	55
37.16	126
44.21	55
51.50	55

EZEKIEL
1.1	113
20.32	55

Index of Biblical References

HOSEA
11.1 — 1
13.14 — 126

AMOS
9.10 — 194n

JONAH
1.2 — 131
1.5 — 206n
1.6 — 205n
1.5-6 — 142-3
2.3 — 150
2.5 — 128
2.6 — 136, 150
3.4 — 131

HAGGAI
2.6-9 — 118-21 passim, 168

ZECHARIAH
9.9 — 157
12.10 — 158, 209n
14.8 — 161

TOBIT
14.4 — 207n

JUDITH
8.14 — 71

WISDOM
1.4-7 — 84
7.26 — 211n
9.9-10 — 172
9.13-17 — 82f, 178n
10.10 — 112

ECCLESIASTICUS
(Sirach)
1.9 — 105
7.33 — 100
10.17 — 100
17.11 — 105
17.22 — 100
24 — 106
24.8 — 106
42.21 — 92, 193n

43.31 — 105
49.10 — 149, 207n

2 MACCABEES
2.1-8 — 60

MATTHEW
2.15 — 1
12.38-41 — 146-50 passim, 181n
12.40 — 133, 206n
24.30 — 209n
25.5 — 143
25.6 — 181n
25.32-3 — 196n
26.13 — 120

MARK
10.38 — 144
14.9 — 120
14.18 — 209n

LUKE
1.42 — 182n

JOHN
1.11 — 106
1.14 — 97, 163, 198n
1.16 — 100
1.17 — 97, 99, 102f, 198n
1.14-18 — 97-109 passim
1.18 — 68, 162f, 175
1.23 — 157
1.30-31 — 110, 166f
1.33 — 110
1.43-51 — 166f
1.47 — 110
1.51 — 110-14 passim, 117, 158, 162f, 175
2.17-22 — 114-17 passim, 119, 147, 161
2.17 — 158, 159, 177n, 209n
3.14-15 — 159
4.24 — 76
5.35 — 162f
5.37 — 103, 163
6.31 — 159f, 161
6.45 — 159f

231

Index of Biblical References

(John)		2.24-8	138, 150-56 passim
7.17-24	161-2	2.25-8	135
7.35	159f	2.33	138
7.37-9	161-2	7.23	188n
7.42	211n	13.35	209n
8.25	172	28.26f	209n
8.29-8	172		
8.40	175	**ROMANS**	
8.44	16	1.11	75
8.49	162f	1.20	80
8.56-8	114, 175	1.30	45
8.58	162f	6.1-11	122f, 206n
10.22	108	6.3f	128
10.24	167	6.4	123
10.34	159f	6.7	122f
10.34-6	178n	7.7	174
11.6	167-8	7.14	75
11.11-13	167f, 175	8.19-21	171
11.41	167, 210n	8.25-7	71
11.50	24, 170	8.27-9	52
12.1-8	118-21 passim, 168	8.38	23, 39
12.4-6	119	8.39	139
12.13	157, 167	9.33	48
12.15	157	10.6-8	31, 48, 135-41 passim,
12.19	168f, 175		177n, 204n, 205n, 206n
12.20f	119, 168	10.7f	30
12.28-9	119, 168	10.16	209n
12.29-30	111	11.25	26
12.32	168f	11.33	71, 146
12.38	209n	11.34-5	22, 27, 165, 199n
12.38-40	158	11.34	77f, 192n
12.40	209n	11.35	78f
12.41	103, 108, 163, 177n	12.19-20	174
13.18	158, 209n	14.11	48
15.3	144	15.3	115
15.25	115, 158, 159		
17.12	158, 209n	**1 CORINTHIANS**	
19.24	158, 209n	1.10	80
19.28	158, 178n	1.20	23, 24
19.29	115k 209n	1.17-24	23
19.28-9	168, 209n	1.30	25
19.36-7	158-9	2.1	26
19.37	209n	2.5-6	30
20.9	116	2.6	42
		2.6-16	21-96
THE ACTS		2.6-8	23, 24f, 31f
1.20	209n	2.6-10	41
2.24	115	2.7	21, 68, 146

Index of Biblical References

(*1 Corinthians*)
2.8   29, 68, 70, 95
2.9   22, 38, 43f, 95, 186n, 194n, 196n
2.10   52, 69fn
2.12   65
2.16   22, 27, 77f, 165
3.1   74
3.3   75
4.1   27
5.7   159
5.13   174
10.1   136
10.1-11   160
10.3-4   75
10.4   114, 177n
14.37   75
15.3   116
15.4   123
15.24   23, 39
15.32   174
15.51   26-7
15.55   126

2 CORINTHIANS
4.13   178
10.1-4   35
13.1   174-5

GALATIANS
4.3   22
4.29   177n
6.1   75

EPHESIANS
1.10   138
1.21   23, 39
2.6   138
3.10   23, 42, 146
3.15   138
3.18   138
4.7-10   135-41 *passim*, 209n
4.8   139
4.9   31, 139, 204n, 205n
4.10   138
4.25-6   175
5.14   138-9, 142-3, 206n
5.25-7   138-9, 143-6

6.12   23
6.14-17   174

PHILIPPIANS
2.10   139

COLOSSIANS
1.16   23
2.10   23
2.15   23
3.5   181n

THESSALONIANS
5.8   174

1 TIMOTHY
1.2   102

2 TIMOTHY
1.2   102
3.8   44

TITUS
3.5   144

HEBREWS
1.1   146
1.3   211n
5.11   26-7
12.26-7   119
13.11-13   178-9n

JAMES
1.8   174
1.11   174
4.6   174
5.10-11   174
5.17   174

1 PETER
3.10-12   174
3.18-4.6   122-56 *passim*
3.18   134, 154
3.19   126f, 131, 204n
3.22   130
4.1   122f, 133
4.6   132f, 204n
5.5   174

233

Index of Biblical References

1 JOHN		REVELATION	
4.7-12	101	1.7	209n
4.19-20	101	2.24	70
2 JOHN		11	196n
1-3	99, 101-2	20.7	127
		21.8	45
3 JOHN	102	22.15	45

Index of References to Non-Canonical Jewish and Christian Books

PHILO
Philo	14
De Opif. Mundi	
1, 67	76
1, 134f	76
De post. Caini	
43	104
De Mig.	
165	113
De Prim. et Poen.	
v, 48	76
De Somniis	
1, 61	9
1, 83f	113
De Abrahamo	
IV, 113	76

PSEUDO PHILO
Biblical Antiquities	22, 51
xxvi.13	58f

TARGUMS
Onkelos	9
Pseudo Jonathan	9
Palestine	9, 11, 31, 112, 135, 140
Isaiah	51, 57, 82

MIDRASH
Midrash on the Psalms	9, 41, 112, 116, 126, 149, 154
Pesikta Rabbati	141
5.11	107, 108
25.2	86f
30.3	113
32.3-4	161
37.1	64

QUMRAN DOCUMENTS
1QS iv.13	127
1QH iii.28	150-51, 152
1QH v.23-4	209n
1QHviii.28-9	127, 129
Tj. J	11, 208n, 210n

3 MACCABEES
6.8	148-9

ENOCH
lx 1-10	86
lx 24	26
lx 25	86

RABBINIC SOURCES

Pesikta d'Rab Kahana
9.2	87
12.21	161
23.2	113

TALMUD
Yebamoth	160
Nazir	160
Baba Bathra	
17a	153
97b	119
Sanhedrin	
99a	63, 67
103b	118
Abodah Zarah	
2b	119
65a	3

Index of References

(*Talmud*)
Shabbath
- 30a — 40
- 63a — 64
- 89a — 141

Erubin
- 19a — 149

Berakoth
- 34b — 63

Hullin
- 91b — 200n

Kerithoth — 160
Tamid — 160

Berakoth — 160

PATRISTIC LITERATURE

1 CLEMENT
- 34.8 — 46f, 49
- 35.3-4 — 47
- 35.4 — 66

2 CLEMENT
- 11.7 — 48
- 12.1 — 48, 66
- 14.5 — 48f, 196n

IGNATIUS
Ephesians
- XV.1 — 33
- XVII — 120
- XVIII.2 — 145
- XIX — 24, 32f
- XIX.1 — 182n

Magnesians
- VIII — 33

Trallians
- V — 34

HERMAS
- 9.XVI, 5-6 — 132-3

ODES OF SOLOMON
- 22.4-8 — 134
- 28 — 134-5
- 42.11-17 — 134
- 42.17 — 188n

ASCENSION OF ISAIAH — 31, 33f, 66
Vision of Isaiah:
- VI.1-XI.40 — 35
- IX.13-15 — 35
- X.8 — 36
- X.17f — 36
- XI.16f — 36
- XI.23f — 36, 41f
- XI.34 — 38

JUSTIN — 7
Dialogue with Trypho:
- 2.36 — 39f
- 2.85 — 40
- 58.15 — 111-12
- 85 — 183n
- 86.17 — 111-21
- 107.2 — 147
- 127 — 183n

Apology
- I, 51 — 183n

MARTYRDOM OF POLYCARP — 49f

IRENAEUS — 34, 37, 180n, 195n

HIPPOLYTUS — 37, 70, 75, 180n, 183n, 195n

CLEMENT OF ALEXANDRIA — 70, 76, 195n

ORIGEN — 14, 76
Comm. in Matt.
- 12.40 — 147-8
- 27.9 — 43
Comm. in 1 Cor — 184n

EUSEBIUS
Evangelica Praeparatio
- IX, 39, 454c — 189n

EPIPHANIUS — 34, 42, 76

Index of References
GNOSTIC LITERATURE

LETTER OF
EUGNOSTOS   34, 196n

GOSPEL OF THOMAS
log.17   46, 66, 186n, 189nl

ACTS OF PETER
39   46

GOSPEL OF TRUTH
16.36   195n
18.15   180n
19.37   195n
23.25   70
24.8-10   180n

26.7   70
35.15f   70
37.7f   70, 195n
38.18-21   180n

ACTS OF THOMAS
10   140

GOSPEL OF PHILIP
68   180n

APOCRYPHON OF JOHN
31.10-12   195n

PHYSIOLOGUS   42

www.ingramcontent.com/pod-product-compliance
Lightning Source LLC
Chambersburg PA
CBHW051636230426
43669CB00013B/2318